# COLLABORATIVE METHODS

EDITED BY
KAYLAN C. SCHWARZ,
CLAUDIA MITCHELL,
AND REBEKAH HUTTEN

# COLLABORATIVE METHODS

PARTICIPATORY
DATA ANALYSIS
IN FEMINIST
RESEARCH

UNIVERSITY *of* **ALBERTA** PRESS

Published by
University of Alberta Press
1-16 Rutherford Library South
11204 89 Avenue NW
Edmonton, Alberta, Canada  T6G 2J4
amiskwaciwâskahikan | Treaty 6 | Métis
Territory
ualbertapress.ca | uapress@ualberta.ca

Copyright © 2025 University of Alberta Press

**Library and Archives Canada Cataloguing
in Publication**

Title: Collaborative methods : participatory
data analysis in feminist research / edited
by Kaylan C. Schwarz, Claudia Mitchell,
and Rebekah Hutten.
Names: Schwarz, Kaylan C., editor | Mitchell,
Claudia, editor | Hutten, Rebekah, editor.
Description: Includes bibliographical
references and index.
Identifiers: Canadiana (print) 20250157349 |
Canadiana (ebook) 20250157365 |
ISBN 9781772127980 (softcover) |
ISBN 9781772128338 (EPUB) |
ISBN 9781772128345 (PDF)
Subjects: LCSH: Feminism—Research—
Methodology. | LCSH: Feminist
theory—Research—Methodology. |
LCSH: Participant observation—
Methodology. | LCSH: Quantitative
research—Methodology.
Classification: LCC HQ1180 .C65 2025 |
DDC 305.42072/1—dc23

First edition, first printing, 2025.
First printed and bound in Canada by
Houghton Boston Printers, Saskatoon,
Saskatchewan.
Copyediting by Clorinde Peters.
Proofreading by Tania Therien.
Indexing by Tanvi Mohile.

GPSR: Easy Access System Europe |
Mustamäe tee 50, 10621 Tallinn, Estonia |
gpsr.requests@easproject.com

This book has been published with the
help of a grant from the Federation for the
Humanities and Social Sciences, through the
Awards to Scholarly Publications Program,
using funds provided by the Social Sciences
and Humanities Research Council of Canada.

University of Alberta Press gratefully
acknowledges the support received for its
publishing program from the Government
of Canada, the Canada Council for the Arts,
and the Government of Alberta through the
Alberta Media Fund.

# CONTENTS

# ACKNOWLEDGEMENTS

THIS COLLECTION was a collaborative labour of love. We would like to thank all the chapter contributors for thoughtfully and reflexively sharing their methodological engagements with participatory data analysis. It was a great pleasure to work with Mat Buntin and the staff at the University of Alberta Press, who consistently demonstrated enthusiasm for and commitment to our project. We also appreciate the two anonymous peer reviewers and our copyeditor Clorinde Peters for the care and attention to detail they each provided to the manuscript. We are grateful to the Social Sciences and Humanities Research Council, whose funding enabled the production of this book.

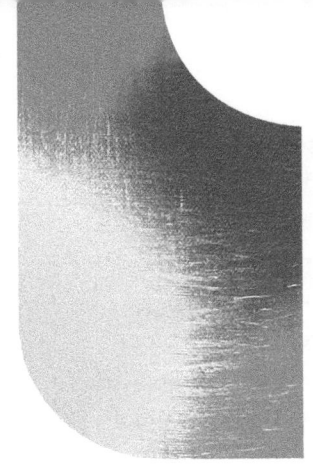

REBEKAH HUTTEN,
KAYLAN C. SCHWARZ,
AND CLAUDIA MITCHELL

# PARTICIPATORY, COLLABORATIVE, AND FEMINIST DATA ANALYSIS

THE IDEA FOR THIS COLLECTION grew out of our Insight Development Grant project "Constructing Feminist Identities through Visual and Participatory Methods," a shared endeavour of the three volume editors—Kaylan is the Principal Investigator, Claudia is the Co-Investigator, and Rebekah is the Research Assistant. In the study, we sought to understand the ways young self-identified feminists construct their identities (an empirical focus), and we aimed to do so through a set of visual and participatory methodologies that align with feminist research practices (a methodological focus). While some scholars publish their findings first, we wanted to establish our co-publication record by grounding ourselves in the recent literature (one demand of writing an introductory chapter) and by contributing to this literature in *a participatory way* (by bringing together scholars who are, like us, working at the intersection of participatory and feminist research).

In response to our call for papers, we received submissions from emerging and established scholars across Canada. While all the chapters fall under the broad umbrella of feminist research, they engage with different communities and address a wide spectrum of topics: racialized residents' use of public greenspaces; refugee girls' experiences of resettlement; young men's involvement in preventing gender-based violence; pregnant adolescents' and young mothers' agency in low-resource urban settings; young people's perceptions of gender roles and gender inequalities; young people's understandings of risk; teachers' and students' responses to the subject of Missing and Murdered Indigenous Women, Girls, and 2SLGBTQQIA people (MMIWG2S); and teachers' approaches to educating their students about the climate crisis. Furthermore, the chapters focus on two forms of participatory data analysis. In the first, rather than simply collecting data *from* participants, researchers *involve* participants in examining the datasets they helped to produce. In the second, teams comprised of multiple researchers work with datasets in non-hierarchical and collaborative ways.

Many scholarly sources highlight the findings of their studies without substantially describing their methodological designs, decision points, procedures, and processes. We share Rachelle Miele et al.'s (2024) position that writing about methodology in rich detail constitutes a feminist praxis: "As feminist researchers, we are committed to doing research that is not transactional (i.e., does not primarily benefit the researcher). Part of this commitment includes publishing our *processes* to elevate and transform feminist research practices" (129, emphasis in original). The goal of this collection is to be *descriptive* rather than *prescriptive* about the ways researchers might employ collaborative methods. We encouraged authors to make visible their use of participatory data analysis in feminist research and to be explicit and specific about how it played into and played out in their work.

In this introductory chapter, we provide an overview of feminist research, participatory research, and participatory data analysis, highlighting the complementary aspects of these methodological traditions and demonstrating the spectrum of approaches and practices within them.

## FEMINIST RESEARCH

Early feminist research traditions formed, in part, as a response to androcentrism in the academy, by "calling attention to the fact that women had been left out of much mainstream research" (Hesse-Biber 2012, 13). Feminist researchers—now sometimes referred to as feminist empiricists (Hundleby 2012)—pursued a corrective approach that resisted masculinist epistemologies and challenged the assumption that men's perspectives are neutral and universal (Hesse-Biber 2012). However, rather than establishing "a new feminist monological theory of knowledge to supplant the old masculinist ones" (Code 1995, 42), some feminist researchers saw an opportunity to promote a wider "nonauthoritative" agenda that "allow[ed] for 'others' to be heard and empowered" (Nast 1994, 58).

Feminist scholarship also developed as a response to positivist research. As Sharlene N. Hesse-Biber (2012) summarizes, positivism begins from the premise "that truth lies 'out there' in the social reality waiting to be discovered, if only the scientist is 'objective' and 'value free' in the pursuit of knowledge building" (8). While positivistic principles—such as "reducing phenomena to variables, specify-ing rigorous protocols for measuring those variables, and limiting researchers' influence on the research process"—are appropriate for answering *some* research questions, other research questions are best understood through particularized, subjective, and socially con-structed ways of knowing (Schwarz and Williams 2021, 4). Feminist constructivists and post-structuralists tend to demonstrate open-ness to one's lived experience, preferring multiple, contextual, and nuanced perspectives (and their embeddedness in questions of power) over singular or generalized principles.

Feminist scholars' embrace of subjectivity applies not just to research topics and participants, but to researchers themselves. Christina E. Gringeri et al. (2010) define reflexivity as "the process in which researchers and participants use themselves, their critical reflec-tions about themselves, their praxis, and their positionalities to create knowledge and collective action" (393). Feminist scholars do not aspire to "neutrality" because they recognize that they are present throughout the design and implementation of the investigation: the ways they respond to and interpret the dataset are necessarily situated (Haraway 1988). In this way, reflexivity is also part of researchers' analytical practice, in that they consider "the influence they have as researchers on the study and its results" (von Unger et al. 2022, 1).

Here, "reasserting the self in scholarly work" is not a limitation to be mitigated but rather a research cornerstone and "feminist intervention into the patriarchal ideal of disembodied and objective knowledge" (McGregor 2022, 43). Reflexivity, however, is not an agreed-upon practice, leading Brendan Gough (2003) to encourage researchers to adopt the pluralistic term *reflexivities*. While it is now somewhat commonplace for researchers to integrate their thoughts and reflections, the ways researchers express their positionality vary considerably. Reflexivity does not require researchers to present a "shopping list" of their identity characteristics and social locations (Folkes 2023). Instead, researchers' reflexivity is a recognition that interpretations come from somewhere, and explaining where that somewhere is may help the reader better understand the researcher's relationship with the research study.

Beyond reflexivity and positionality, much feminist research is also broadly characterized by "an analysis of gender, a heightened concern for research ethics and care for participants, an attempt to address the hierarchical nature of relationships between the researcher and the researched, and an awareness of the potential of research encounters to empower [participants]" (Walters 2020, 361). While these are noble aspirations, fully realizing feminist research goals can be challenging, and understandably, many projects "fall short of transforming the power relations of inequality" (Lykes and Hershberg 2012, 356). Feminist research encounters are not absent of ethical concerns; they do not necessarily resolve power disparities nor do they always or automatically empower participants. Yet striving toward feminist goals shows researchers' willingness to engage with difficult-to-overcome issues that are deeper and more structural than any one research study.

Developments in intersectional, Black, Indigenous, queer, and transnational feminisms have moved feminist scholarship well beyond the construct of gender and revealed the *plurality* of feminist epistemologies. Across a wide array of topics and disciplines, contemporary feminist scholars ask us to consistently (re)consider *what knowledge* and *whose knowledge* is marginalized and urge us to "strive for the voices of *all* to be heard and valued" (Guy and Arthur 2021, 104, emphasis in original). In this collection, chapter contributors adopt feminist perspectives within their research (be it topically, theoretically, conceptually, methodologically, or practically), but they do not share a unified feminist stance. We encouraged authors to articulate the specific feminist traditions and diverse entry points they use to frame their work.

Intersectionality has had a significant impact on feminist scholarship over the last three decades, and several chapters in our collection make use of this theoretical framework. Intersectionality gained traction with Kimberlé Crenshaw's (1989) seminal anti-discrimination work, building on early Black feminist thought that interrogated white, mainstream feminism's tendency to ignore overlapping and compounding systems of oppression. Intersectionality holds that "race, class, gender, and other axes of inequality are always intertwined, co-constructed, and simultaneous," and that these axes must be considered in research and policy settings to eschew injustices (Thornton Dill and Kohlman 2012, 162). Intersectionality and participatory methods have a similar ethos: both democratize knowledge by centring diverse voices and perspectives, foster agency and empowerment, critique positivistic research approaches, and make power structures explicit.

Participatory methods and feminist research are not automatically compatible in the sense that, as Barbara Risman (1993) argues, "one can take a feminist perspective and epistemological concerns and incorporate them into any methodological technique. And one can ignore feminist insights and agendas in any methodological tradition" (24). We are not the first to notice the intersections between and potentials of blending feminist and participatory research. Patricia Maguire's (1987) book *Doing Participatory Research* helped solidify a shift within participatory research to integrate feminist epistemologies, grounded in the argument that "surely feminist research has something to offer participatory research, and vice versa" (74). More recently, Martina A. Caretta and Yvonne Riaño (2016) devoted a special edition of *Qualitative Research* to examining feminist and participatory methodologies in the field of geography, while Kye Askins (2018) reviewed articles addressing the interwovenness between feminist and participatory methodologies published in *Gender, Place and Culture* since the journal's inception. We build upon this body of work and enhance it with a specific focus on participatory data analysis and its myriad operationalizations.

## PARTICIPATORY RESEARCH

Researchers are typically viewed as experts and often occupy "a position of power, owing to their ability to decide what questions to ask, how to interpret the data collected, and where and in what form the research results should be presented" (Caretta and Riaño 2016, 258). Participatory approaches attempt to flatten and interrogate these hierarchies by involving participants in the creation and dissemination of research—treating knowledge production as a *negotiation* (Gubrium and Harper 2013)—and by redefining expertise to include first-hand, localized experience, not just academic or subject-matter knowledge. This aspect of participatory research complements feminist standpoint theory and intersectional feminism, praxes that centre the role of individual identities and lived experiences as valuable forms of knowledge.

Participatory methods are part of a wider "turn" toward co-production in the social sciences, which both acknowledges "the harms of extractive research practices" and seeks to create "more egalitarian and ethicised methodological alternatives" (Mason 2023, 710). Through shared commitments to relationship-building and its grounding in specific local contexts, participatory research is compatible with many community-engaged frameworks, such as community-based participatory research (Amauchi et al. 2022) and critical community-engaged scholarship (Lin 2023). However, Caitlin

Cahill (2007a) cautions that simply labelling a study "participatory" can be problematic and tokenistic if it gives "the illusion of consultation" without meaningfully working toward emancipatory aims (299).

Heidi Gottfried (1996) argues that the *doing* of feminist research has mostly been ignored in favour of abstract conceptualizations; as a remedy, she advocates that researchers consider adopting methodological approaches chiefly concerned with *how* to make a difference. Scholars use a variety of terms to emphasize their commitments to pursuing social change as a project outcome, including participatory action research (Kindon et al. 2007), feminist participatory action research (Lykes et al. 2021), queer feminist participatory action research (Fields 2019), postcolonial feminist participatory action research (Hayhurst et al. 2015), Chicana feminist participatory action research (López et al. 2020), youth participatory action research (Liebenberg et al. 2020), Black feminist youth participatory action research (Payne 2023), critical participatory action research (Fine and Torre 2019), relational participatory action research (Datta et al. 2015), participatory action research counterspace (West 2024), and other approaches. Here, the addition of the word "action" indicates that the research project "is oriented toward problem-solving, and its aim is to produce practical knowledge that is useful to people in everyday life" (Snooks et al. 2021, 165). This is the *praxis* element of participatory research, which is grounded in theory but includes reflecting and acting (Stanley 2013).

Participatory research traditions exist along a spectrum—from "minimally participatory" to "fully egalitarian"—though the majority "are situated somewhere in between the two with the level of participation changing throughout the process" (Brown 2022, 200). For example, Caitlin Cahill (2007a, 2007b) wanted to understand the everyday lives of young women living in New York City and sought to incorporate participant feedback throughout the entire investigation, from co-developing research questions, to co-analyzing data, to co-presenting study findings. Cahill (2007a) explains that she was committed to following the participants' lead and "helping them to take ownership over the whole process" (299). Cahill (2007b) facilitated a participatory data analysis procedure (that one participant described as "torture" because they felt it too closely resembled schoolwork) wherein participants coded the dataset individually, conferred about their overlapping and contradictory interpretations, and recoded the dataset as a group.

Because of the accelerated timelines associated with completing a doctoral degree, the young women who participated in Rosie Walters's (2020) study about celebrity feminism did not help to shape the research design—rather, the author organized a participatory data analysis session, where she "discussed my findings with the groups, inviting their feedback, and presenting them with extracts of transcriptions that I felt demonstrated [relevant] findings" (365). Mary-Elizabeth Vaccaro (2023) hesitated to pursue a "fully egalitarian" study design in her research with women experiencing chronic homelessness because of the time, energy, and resources it would require from participants. The author adopted a "low barrier approach" because meeting with the same participants on several occasions was not feasible given their transient circumstances—only six of the forty women who participated in an initial interview could participate in a second study phase. While a fulsome participatory process may be possible and beneficial in some research settings, Vaccaro (2023) problematizes the idea of evaluating participatory research based on "the technical aspects of traditional 'participation', such as attending meetings, working collaboratively with a larger research team and contributing to the work of a project," since these metrics can reflect "gendered, colonial, ablest and classist expectations about what it means to make contributions to the work" (337; see also Rosen 2023). Indeed, in some cases, participants' *non-participation* can be as illuminating as participants' active and ongoing research contributions (Harding 2020; Switzer 2020; Weaver et al. 2022).

Even when researchers choose to pursue a participatory approach, participants are not always interested in being "more involved" than they would be in a "traditional" research study. For example, Erik Mey and Bettina van Hoven (2019) encountered difficulties recruiting participants because the individuals they approached had recently participated in another research project or "saw no benefit in becoming co-researchers" (327); Catherine Vanner (2015) observed that some participants "had little interest in contributing to the research design, which they perceived to be my job and responsibility" (9); and Anne Byrne et al. (2009) abandoned the idea of co-authoring a paper with participants because "motivation to be involved in the project went up and down, tapering away as [participants'] attention moved on to newer events" (75). Vanner (2015) aptly summarizes this quandary: "What if the participants do not want to be researchers? Just as a non-participatory process can be imposed on participants who desire to be involved, so too a participatory process can be imposed on participants who do not want to be" (9).

This section demonstrates that there are multiple versions of participatory research. Researchers should choose the approach that best aligns with their research questions, study context, and participant availability and interest.

## PARTICIPATORY DATA ANALYSIS

Qualitative inquiry is a process through which "researchers turn what can be voluminous data into understandable and insightful analysis" (Liamputtong 2009, 133). By asking participants to engage in data analysis, or by asking participants to share their views on researchers' initial analyses, participatory data analysis helps to ensure study findings "more accurately reflect the realities of participants' lives" (Liebenberg et al. 2020, 2).

Researchers can incorporate participatory data analysis into a wide range of methodological techniques, including interviews (Lykes et al. 2021), focus groups (Walters 2020), photovoice (Ingram 2014), cellphilming (MacEntee et al. 2022), carousel papers (Vanner et al. 2022), pamphlets (Caretta 2016), archives (Moore et al. 2023), collage (Burkholder et al. 2022), map making (Harding 2020), digital storytelling (Rouhani 2019), arts-based think tanks (Vaccaro 2023), and TikTok videos (Ryu 2022), among others. Within these techniques, some researchers provide "full access to the collected data-set" (Datta et al. 2015, 594), while others "[reduce] data into manageable forms" based on participants' level of interest, skill, and availability (Nind 2011, 352).

Participatory data analysis is emergent, meaning that researchers cannot control (and do not aim to predetermine) what participants might say in response to the dataset. For this reason, "participatory data engagement requires exceptional openness to change, to uncertainty and ambiguity, and to attending carefully to how different forms of knowledge emerge" (Ellingson and Sotirin 2020, 95). However, while participatory researchers tend to foreground participants' perspectives and interpretations, researchers are not absent from the data analysis process. Depending on the study context, researchers may play a variety of roles including "trainer, coach, 'scaffolder', mentor, partner in dialogue, co-learner, reciprocal learner and practical facilitator" (Nind 2011, 359). Typically, researchers who utilize participatory data analysis endeavour to "[balance] participants' interpretations of [data] with the researcher's ability to look across the data set and literature" (Switzer 2020, 175) and aim to describe how these different perspectives were "prioritised or diminished in the overall research account" (Drew and Guillemin 2014, 57).

We view participatory research as inherently collaborative. Collaboration can occur in the interactions between researchers and participants, as described above, but also within research teams themselves. Collaborative research stems from the premise that bringing together "a number of individuals, with potentially contrasting viewpoints, interpretive frameworks, personal characteristics, histories, and experience, that all contribute to knowledge production" can strengthen findings (Thomas et al. 2009, 313). However, the processes and procedures employed within collaborative research are typically not well understood because "research accounts provide little insight into *how* researchers go about doing research and constructing knowledge *in practice* and *as a team*" (Mauthner and Doucet 2008, 974, emphasis in original). There is often limited space in a thesis or article to fully articulate the "how"; it is also the case that the "how" is not seen as part of the findings. The chapters in our collection attend to this lacuna, both because we are addressing collaborative methods as a topic, and because the collection itself is a collaborative research effort. As an editor team, we are working across different institutions, in different provinces, in different disciplines, and at different career stages. Similarly, chapter contributors reveal the opportunities and complications of analyzing data within international, intergenerational, interdisciplinary, multilingual, and cross-sectoral research teams.

Participatory data analysis is time-consuming and "demands far more responsibilities and commitments than under conventional extractive forms of social science research" (Amauchi et al. 2022, 16). The structure of the academy—with its pressures to publish, attract competitive research funding, and meet hiring, tenure, and promotion criteria—is often at odds with the practical realities of carrying out collaborative feminist methods. May Lin (2023) recalls having to reject such institutional norms during her doctoral work with a youth-led racial and educational justice organization, because ultimately, building ethical research relationships with collaborators "required slowing down and moving at the speed of trust" (18).

Working in teams can be difficult and labour-intensive, so it is important for feminist researchers "to note the elements of joy in collaborations that exist alongside and in tandem with frustrations and disconnections" (Browne et al. 2017, 1377–1378). Collaborative researchers must negotiate team members' individual priorities and allow room for team members to develop their skills and voice their thoughts—challenges which necessitate ongoing reflexivity and care (Meer and Müller 2023). For these reasons, Tamsin Hinton-Smith et al. (2022) found that checking in with team members at the beginning of each meeting—a "welcoming of personal selves into academic lives"— foreclosed interpersonal tensions and served to "humanise the research process" (270).

Some collaborative research teams have reflexively documented the successes and struggles they encountered over the course of their projects and partnerships. For example, Jasmine R. Linabary et al. (2021) utilized "collaborative reflexive journaling," wherein team members individually replied to shared writing prompts in a communal online document; Ziyu Long et al. (2020) employed "retrospective sense-making," wherein team members responded to a list of reflection questions such as "What feminist praxis did we enact or not enact in our collaboration?" (491); and Hella von Unger et al. (2022) organized "reflection labs," wherein team members reviewed and discussed the various field notes, meeting minutes, and analytical memos they had collected. All of these approaches make team members' differential roles and contributions transparent, provide opportunities to address tensions, and archive the group's key decision-points. Linabary et al. (2021) aptly summarize the benefits of such exercises:

> Our reflexive practices highlighted the co-constructedness of the research process, encouraging us to make sense of and make explicit our epistemological, methodological, and ethical commitments. As a result, we were forced to confront implicit epistemological differences among team members as well as dwell in the messy inconsistencies in our positions and commitments. (725)

Beyond reflective strategies, some collaborative research teams detail their data analysis processes. For example, Thurayya Zreik et al. (2022) used a "collaborative coding" approach, wherein each team member conducted an individual analysis, then pairs of more and less experienced researchers met to compare their codes, and finally, the entire research team convened to amalgamate their findings. When team members did not agree on the meaning of an extract, they chose to double-code it. In this way, collaborative coding honours individual viewpoints, enhances understanding through dialogue, and allows divergent interpretations to co-exist.

Following Long et al. (2020), we "resist drawing a discursive closure of feminist collaboration. It is important to keep the principles of feminist collaboration specific enough to be actionable yet vague enough for feminist collaboration to be agile" (496). Our collection illustrates the variances in feminist collaborations across different contexts.

## VOLUME OUTLINE

Throughout this collection, authors delve into the specificities of how they facilitated participatory data analysis processes with participants and how different types of collaborative research teams co-analyze data as a feminist praxis.

In chapter one, Nadha Hassen and Sarah Flicker carefully detail a multi-phase photovoice project with racialized residents who use greenspaces in Toronto, Canada. Hassen and Flicker frame their approach to analyzing resident photographers' images as a type of "collaborative sensemaking." Since the authors undertook the project during COVID-19, they printed out and mailed the dataset to participants, who then gathered for virtual participatory data analysis meetings. Hassen and Flicker's chapter contributes to the growing body of scholarship on strategies for shifting visual methods from in-person to virtual mediums, such as photovoice (Chen 2023), object elicitation (Schwarz 2023), and participatory video (Marzi 2023). Beyond facilitating collaborative coding activities, Hassen and Flicker describe how they co-wrote a community report, responded to residents' critiques of their editing, and made changes to best reflect the contributions of everyone involved. Finally, the authors argue that committing to community-based participatory action research in the context of a doctoral dissertation is itself a feminist practice because it inherently challenges the kinds of knowledge production and the types of productivity that are typically valued in academia.

In chapter two, Nesa Bandarchian Rashti similarly adopts photovoice methodology as part of her doctoral dissertation. Her work, grounded in intersectional feminism and girlhood studies, makes explicit Black girls' experiences as refugees resettling in Montréal, Canada. Beyond the formal participatory data analysis phase in her study, Bandarchian Rashti positions the collective process of curating an exhibition of research findings as another form of collaborative analysis, wherein participants revisited their visual data and engaged one another in dialogue about how best to represent their experiences to the public. Bandarchian Rashti chronicles the steps she undertook to enact participatory data analysis with the refugee girls in her study, recounting her efforts to incorporate their voices, consider the implications of language and translation, and adopt a non-invasive approach to facilitation.

Grace Skahan's thoughtful analysis in chapter three illustrates the methodological and theoretical resonances between arts-based methodologies—in her case, clay-elicitation—and participatory data analysis. As a highly tactile method of data creation, clay-elicitation enables researchers to address sensitive topics and explore affective perspectives that may not otherwise emerge in response to structured interview questions, not unlike Constantino Dumangane Jr.'s (2022) use of "third object prompts." After individually sculpting clay creations with young men who were interested and involved in preventing gender-based violence, the author invited participants to co-analyze transcripts during a participatory data analysis session. Most participants chose not to or were unable to attend this follow-up meeting, a reminder that there are often constraints to sustained participation across multi-phase research studies. Nevertheless, the participants who did engage in the second study phase offered a nuanced portrait and dialogic analysis of gender-based violence prevention.

In chapter four, Milka Nyariro explores the possibilities of involving multiple sets of different participants to reply to the same photovoice prompts or to respond to images already taken by previous cohorts of participants. In Nyariro's case, recruiting several cohorts of participants was a necessary adaptation to working with transient populations that she could not re-engage in the analysis phase as she had originally planned. Instead, she recruited second and third cohorts to reflect on questions following an exhibition walk-through activity, and in doing so, created a unique space for "feminist dialogue." Nyariro demonstrates how adjusting one's study design can "actually uphold a feminist research ethics of care because flexible design allows research to be attentive to social situations and the lived realities of participants and researchers" (Miele et al. 2024, 139). Her focus on pregnant adolescents and young mothers in Nairobi, Kenya and the barriers they face completing their education is examined through the theoretical tradition of Black African girlhood studies.

Chapter five addresses both participatory data analysis with participants *and* collaborative data analysis with research teams. Drawing on feminist international development theories and policies, Geetanjali Gill describes an academic–non-governmental organization (NGO) collaboration, and their collective reasons for pivoting toward using participatory data analysis in conjunction with play-based methods. After undertaking participatory data *collection* in an initial project exploring gender roles in Mozambique, Rwanda, and Ghana, Gill chose to adopt participatory data *analysis* in subsequent projects in Uganda and Lebanon. However, she found that she could not fully realize her participatory agenda due to turnover among team members, time constraints, and conflicts between academic and programmatic priorities. Gill's highly reflexive chapter contemplates the strengths and challenges of collaborative and transnational research teams and offers pathways forward for researcher-practitioners working at similar intersections.

In chapter six, Sarah Flicker, Nadha Hassen, Jessica Fields, and 4theRecord detail their process of conducting and analyzing data from a large-scale survey, interactive timelines, and individual interviews on the topic of risk. 4theRecord is an intergenerational, international, and interdisciplinary research team comprising over two dozen members. Informed by intersectional feminist theories and praxis, Flicker et al. deliberately built diversity and equitable representation into their team's composition from the start. Moreover, the authors outline how they held space for and navigated tensions and disagreements during collaborative data analysis processes—notably, by challenging the need for "consensus" within thematic coding. Their chapter also highlights the importance of acknowledging the often-invisible labour of project managers, who provide training and support structures for student researchers and conduct in-person meetings to supplement virtual working environments, stave off isolation, and build team rapport. Importantly, this chapter and the two that follow "depart from prevailing norms that limit coauthorship and emphasize individual faculty ownership over research" by extending intellectual credit to undergraduate and graduate student team members (Bang-Jensen et al. 2023, 458).

In chapter seven, Catherine Vanner, Angelina Weenie, Claudia Mitchell, Meegwun Logan, Jillian Grace Goyeau, and Kathryn Kendal Ryan consider the feminist potentials of collective data analysis in collaborations between Indigenous and non-Indigenous researchers. Their approach to co-authorship shows the intentionality in their reflexive method, giving each team member a space to introduce themselves in relation to the project. In exploring how to teach about Missing and Murdered Indigenous Women, Girls, and 2SLGBTQQIA people (MMIWG2S), Vanner et al. move between theories of decolonial feminism and methods of reflective memoing. In this iterative process, each team member penned a one-page memo at the conclusion of the project, reflecting on their experiences contributing to the team's feminist and collective data analysis. Their chapter traces the themes arising from these memos, showing the importance of honouring individual positionality and doing work that feels personally and socially meaningful. Beyond the theoretical and methodological utility of memoing, Vanner et al. emphasize the value of professional skill building as a decolonial and feminist imperative for collaborative research teams.

Working within the fraught contexts of climate emergency and ecological grief, Mitchell McLarnon, Dawn Wiseman, Catherine Malboeuf-Hurtubise, L. Rebeca Esquivel, Terra Léger-Goodes, and Emma C. Cognet reflect on their collaborative approach to designing and analyzing a bilingual and mixed-method survey in chapter eight. While exploring how to prepare teachers for educating their students about the climate crisis, the authors drew inspiration from ecofeminist and intersectional feminist practices and assumed a non-hierarchical team approach to working with data. Among other goals, this involved disrupting power imbalances, embracing emotion, and making their labour visible. Team members' individual reflections, interspersed throughout the chapter, give voice to their experiences working across disciplines and with one another, as well as to the internal conflicts some of them felt along the way. What emerges from their collaboration is a sense of hope, not just for climate crisis interventions in education, but for the future of their research collaboration.

While our introductory chapter serves primarily as a literature review, our concluding chapter reflects on the experience of bringing this collection together, in line with the volume's deep commitment to *method*. As central to this reflexive account, we describe the feminist editing practices we strove to adopt, including our collaborative reviewing strategies and our approach to co-authorship. Looking back across the chapters, we highlight the emerging issues and future directions we envision for participatory and feminist researchers. For example, we point to synergies with visual research methods, underscore ethical and audience-based considerations, and revisit the role of relational joy and pleasure. Finally, we signal our hope that scholars will more widely employ participatory data analysis in feminist research, designing "a seat around the table" for participants, colleagues, and communities.

## AUTHORS' NOTE

"Constructing Feminist Identities through Visual and Participatory Methods" is supported by funding from the Social Sciences and Humanities Research Council.

## REFERENCES

Amauchi, Juliana F.F., Maeva Gauthier, Abdolzaher Ghezeljeh et al. 2022. "The Power of Community-Based Participatory Research: Ethical and Effective Ways of Researching." *Community Development* 53 (1): 3–20.

Askins, Kye. 2018. "Feminist Geographies and Participatory Action Research: Co-Producing Narratives with People and Place." *Gender, Place & Culture* 25 (9): 1277–1294.

Bang-Jensen, Bree, Bernadette Bresee, Sarah K. Dreier et al. 2023. "The Lab as a Classroom: Advancing Faculty Research through Undergraduate Experiential Education." *PS: Political Science & Politics* 56 (4): 455–462.

Brown, Nicole. 2022. "Scope and Continuum of Participatory Research." *International Journal of Research & Method in Education* 45 (2): 200–211.

Browne, Kath, Niharika Banerjea, Nick McGlynn et al. 2017. "Towards Transnational Feminist Queer Methodologies." *Gender, Place & Culture* 24 (10): 1376–1397.

Burkholder, Casey, Katie MacEntee, April Mandrona, Amelia Thorpe, and Pride/Swell. 2022. "Coproducing Digital Archives with 2SLGBTQ+ Atlantic Canadian Youth amidst the COVID-19 Pandemic." *Qualitative Research Journal* 22 (1): 24–41.

Byrne, Anne, John Canavan, and Michelle Millar. 2009. "Participatory Research and the Voice-Centred Relational Method of Data Analysis: Is It Worth It?" *International Journal of Social Research Methodology* 12 (1): 67–77.

Cahill, Caitlin. 2007a. "Doing Research *with* Young People: Participatory Research and the Rituals of Collective Work." *Children's Geographies* 5 (3): 297–312.

Cahill, Caitlin. 2007b. "Participatory Data Analysis." In *Participatory Action Research Approaches and Methods: Connecting People, Participation and Place,* edited by Sara Kindon, Rachel Pain, and Mike Kesby. Routledge.

Caretta, Martina A. 2016. "Member Checking: A Feminist Participatory Analysis of the Use of Preliminary Results Pamphlets in Cross-Cultural, Cross-Language Research." *Qualitative Research* 16 (3): 305–318.

Caretta, Martina A., and Yvonne Riaño. 2016. "Feminist Participatory Methodologies in Geography: Creating Spaces of Inclusion." *Qualitative Research* 16 (3): 258–266.

Chen, Jinwen. 2023. "Digitally Dispersed, Remotely Engaged: Interrogating Participation in Virtual Photovoice." *Qualitative Research* 23 (6): 1535–1555.

Code, Lorraine. 1995. "How Do We Know? Questions of Method in Feminist Practice." In *Changing Methods: Feminists Transforming Practice*, edited by Sandra Burt and Lorraine Code. University of Toronto Press.

Crenshaw, Kimberlé. 1989. "Demarginalizing the Intersection of Race and Sex: A Black Feminist Critique of Antidiscrimination Doctrine, Feminist Theory and Antiracist Politics." *University of Chicago Legal Forum* 1 (8): 139–167.

Datta, Ranjan, Nyojy U. Khyang, Hla Kray Prue Khyang, Hla Aung Prue Kheyang, Mathui Ching Khyang, and Jebunnessa Chapola. 2015. "Participatory Action Research and Researcher's Responsibilities: An Experience with Indigenous Community." *International Journal of Social Research Methodology* 18 (6): 581–599.

Drew, Sarah, and Marilys Guillemin. 2014. "From Photographs to Findings: Visual Meaning-Making and Interpretive Engagement in the Analysis of Participant-Generated Images." *Visual Studies* 29 (1): 54–67.

Dumangane Jr, Constantino. 2022. "Cufflinks, Photos and YouTube: The Benefits of Third Object Prompts When Researching Race and Discrimination in Elite Higher Education." *Qualitative Research* 22 (1): 3–23.

Ellingson, Laura L., and Patty Sotirin. 2020. *Making Data in Qualitative Research: Engagements, Ethics, and Entanglements*. Routledge.

Fields, Jessica. 2019. "The Racialized Erotics of Participatory Research: A Queer Feminist Understanding." In *Imagining Queer Methods*, edited by Amin Ghaziani and Matt Brim. New York University Press.

Fine, Michelle, and María E. Torre. 2019. "Critical Participatory Action Research: A Feminist Project for Validity and Solidarity." *Psychology of Women Quarterly* 43 (4): 433–444.

Folkes, Louise. 2023. "Moving beyond 'Shopping List' Positionality: Using Kitchen Table Reflexivity and In/Visible Tools to Develop Reflexive Qualitative Research." *Qualitative Research* 23 (5): 1301–1318.

Gottfried, Heidi, ed. 1996. *Feminism and Social Change: Bridging Theory and Practice*. University of Illinois Press.

Gough, Brendan. 2003. "Deconstructing Reflexivity." In *Reflexivity: A Practical Guide for Researchers in Health and Social Sciences*, edited by Linda Finlay and Brendan Gough. Blackwell Publishing.

Gringeri, Christina E., Stéphanie Wahab, and Ben Anderson-Nathe. 2010. "What Makes it Feminist? Mapping the Landscape of Feminist Social Work Research." *Affilia* 25 (4): 390–405.

Gubrium, Aline, and Krista Harper. 2013. *Participatory Visual and Digital Methods*. Routledge.

Guy, Batsheva, and Brittany Arthur. 2021. "Feminism and Participatory Research: Exploring Intersectionality, Relationships, and Voice in Participatory Research from a Feminist Perspective." In *The SAGE Handbook of Participatory Research and Inquiry*, edited by Danny Burns, Jo Howard, and Sonia M. Ospina. SAGE.

Haraway, Donna. 1988. "Situated Knowledges: The Science Question in Feminism and the Privilege of Partial Perspective." *Feminist Studies* 14 (3): 575–599.

Harding, Nicola A. 2020. "Co-Constructing Feminist Research: Ensuring Meaningful Participation while Researching the Experiences of Criminalised Women." *Methodological Innovations* 13 (2): 1–14.

Hayhurst, Lyndsay M.C., Audrey R. Giles, Whitney M. Radforth, and the Vancouver Aboriginal Friendship Centre Society. 2015. "'I Want to Come Here to Prove Them Wrong': Using a Post-Colonial Feminist Participatory Action Research (PFPAR) Approach to Studying Sport, Gender and Development Programmes for Urban Indigenous Young Women." *Sport in Society* 18 (8): 952–967.

Hesse-Biber, Sharlene N. 2012. "Feminist Research: Exploring, Interrogating, and Transforming the Interconnections of Epistemology, Methodology, and Method." In *Handbook of Feminist Research: Theory and Praxis, 2nd Edition*, edited by Sharlene N. Hesse-Biber. SAGE.

Hinton-Smith, Tamsin, Fawzia Haeri Mazanderani, Nupur Samuel, and Anna CohenMiller. 2022. "Co-Creating Cross-Cultural Approaches to Gender Mainstreaming in Higher Education: Experiences and Challenges in Developing an Interdisciplinary, International Feminist Knowledge-Exchange Research Approach." In *Leading Change in Gender and Diversity in Higher Education from Margins to Mainstream*, edited by Anna CohenMiller, Tamsin Hinton-Smith, Fawzia Haeri Mazanderani, and Nupur Samuel. Routledge.

Hundleby, Catherine E. 2012. "Feminist Empiricism." In *Handbook of Feminist Research: Theory and Praxis, 2nd Edition*, edited by Sharlene N. Hesse-Biber. SAGE.

Ingram, Leigh-Anne. 2014. "Re-Imagining Roles: Using Collaborative and Creative Research Methodologies to Explore Girls' Perspectives on Gender, Citizenship and Schooling." *Educational Action Research* 22 (3): 306–324.

Kindon, Sara, Rachel Pain, and Mike Kesby, eds. 2007. *Participatory Action Research Approaches and Methods: Connecting People, Participation and Place*. Routledge.

Liamputtong, Pranee. 2009. "Qualitative Data Analysis: Conceptual and Practical Considerations." *Health Promotion Journal of Australia* 20 (2): 133–139.

Liebenberg, Linda, Aliya Jamal, and Janice Ikeda. 2020. "Extending Youth Voices in a Participatory Thematic Analysis Approach." *International Journal of Qualitative Methods* 19: 1–13.

Lin, May. 2023. "'Actually Changing Our Way of Being': Transformative Organizing and Implications for Critical Community-Engaged Scholarship." *Social Sciences* 12 (10): 1–24.

Linabary, Jasmine R., Danielle J. Corple, and Cheryl Cooky. 2021. "Of Wine and Whiteboards: Enacting Feminist Reflexivity in Collaborative Research." *Qualitative Research* 21 (5): 719–735.

Long, Ziyu, Jasmine R. Linabary, Patrice M. Buzzanell, Ashton Mouton, and Ranjani L. Rao. 2020. "Enacting Everyday Feminist Collaborations: Reflexive Becoming, Proactive Improvisation and Co-Learning Partnerships." *Gender, Work & Organization* 27 (4): 487–506.

López, Ruth M., Esmeralda C. Valdez, Hope S. Pacheco, Maria L. Honey, and Raven Jones. 2020. "Bridging Silos in Higher Education: Using Chicana Feminist Participatory Action Research to Foster Latina Resilience." *International Journal of Qualitative Studies in Education* 33 (8): 872–886.

Lykes, M. Brinton, M. Emilia Bianco, and Gabriela Távara. 2021. "Contributions and Limitations of Diverse Qualitative Methods to Feminist Participatory and Action Research with Women in the Wake of Gross Violations of Human Rights." *Methods in Psychology* 4: 1–10.

Lykes, M. Brinton, and Rachel M. Hershberg. 2012. "Participatory Action Research and Feminisms: Social Inequalities and Transformative Praxis." In *Handbook of Feminist Research: Theory and Praxis, 2nd Edition*, edited by Sharlene N. Hesse-Biber. SAGE.

MacEntee, Katie, Caterina Kendrick, and Sarah Flicker. 2022. "Quilted Cellphilm Method: A Participatory Visual Health Research Method for Working with Marginalised and Stigmatised Communities." *Global Public Health* 17 (7): 1420–1432.

Maguire, Patricia. 1987. *Doing Participatory Research: A Feminist Approach*. University of Massachusetts.

Marzi, Sonja. 2023. "Participatory Video from a Distance: Co-Producing Knowledge during the COVID-19 Pandemic Using Smartphones." *Qualitative Research* 23 (3): 509–525.

Mason, Will. 2023. "On Staying: Extended Temporalities, Relationships and Practices in Community Engaged Scholarship." *Qualitative Research* 23 (3): 706–726.

Mauthner, Natasha S., and Andrea Doucet. 2008. "'Knowledge Once Divided Can Be Hard to Put Together Again': An Epistemological Critique of Collaborative and Team-Based Research Practices." *Sociology* 42 (5): 971–985.

McGregor, Hannah. 2022. *A Sentimental Education*. Wilfrid Laurier University Press.

Meer, Talia, and Alex Müller. 2023. "The Messy Work of Decolonial Praxis: Insights from a Creative Collaboration among Queer African Youth." *Feminist Theory* 24 (4): 555–579.

Mey, Erik, and Bettina van Hoven. 2019. "Managing Expectations in Participatory Research Involving Older People: What's in It for Whom?" *International Journal of Social Research Methodology* 22 (3): 323–334.

Miele, Rachelle, Jennifer Root, Rebecca Godderis, and Sonia Meerai. 2024. "Towards a Feminist Research Ethics of Care: Reflections, Lessons, and Methodological Considerations for Doing Research during a Pandemic." *Studies in Social Justice* 18 (1): 125–142.

Moore, Niamh, Rachel Thomson, and Ester McGeeney. 2023. "Putting Place Back into the Patriarchy through Rematriating Feminist Research: The WRAP Project, Feminist Webs and Reanimating Data." In *Temporality, Space and Place in Education and Youth Research*, edited by Julie McLeod, Kate O'Connor, Nicole Davis, and Amy McKernan. Routledge.

Nast, Heidi J. 1994. "Women in the Field: Critical Feminist Methodologies and Theoretical Perspectives." *The Professional Geographer* 46 (1): 54–66.

Nind, Melanie. 2011. "Participatory Data Analysis: A Step Too Far?" *Qualitative Research* 11 (4): 349–363.

Payne, Ashley N. 2023. "A Black Feminist Youth Participatory Action Research Photovoice Exploration of Black Girls and College Women." *American Journal of Community Psychology* 72 (1/2): 127–144.

Risman, Barbara J. 1993. "Methodological Implications of Feminist Scholarship." *The American Sociologist* 24 (3/4): 15–25.

Rosen, Rachel. 2023. "Participatory Research in and against Time." *Qualitative Research* 23 (3): 597–613.

Rouhani, Leva. 2019. "Using Digital Storytelling as a Source of Empowerment for Rural Women in Benin." *Gender & Development* 27 (3): 573–586.

Ryu, Yeonghwi. 2022. "Demystifying Participatory Analysis with Children: A South Korean Case of Migrant Children's Engagement in Analytic Works in Participatory Research." *International Journal of Qualitative Methods* 21: 1–15.

Schwarz, Kaylan C. 2023. "Pivoting Online in a Pandemic: Facilitating Object Elicitation Interviews with Canadian Craft Vendors." In *Facilitating Visual Socialities: Processes, Complications and Ethical Practices*, edited by Casey Burkholder, Joshua Schwab-Cartas, and Funké Aladejebi. Palgrave Macmillan.

Schwarz, Kaylan C., and J. Patrick Williams. 2021. "Introduction to the Social Construction of Identity and Authenticity." In *Studies on the Social Construction of Identity and Authenticity*, edited by J. Patrick Williams and Kaylan C. Schwarz. Routledge.

Snooks, Gina, Rosemary Nagy, Rebecca Timms et al. 2021. "Blending Feminist, Indigenous, and Participatory Action Research Methodologies: Critical Reflections from the Northeastern Ontario Research Alliance on Human Trafficking." *Feminist Formations* 33 (2): 160–184.

Stanley, Liz, ed. 2013. *Feminist Praxis: Research, Theory and Epistemology in Feminist Sociology*. Routledge.

Switzer, Sarah. 2020. "'People Give and Take a Lot in Order to Participate in Things': Youth Talk Back—Making a Case for Non-Participation." *Curriculum Inquiry* 50 (2): 168–193.

Thomas, Robyn, Janne Tienari, Annette Davies, and Susan Meriläinen. 2009. "Let's Talk about 'Us': A Reflexive Account of a Cross-Cultural Research Collaboration." *Journal of Management Inquiry* 18 (4): 313–324.

Thornton Dill, Bonnie, and Marla H. Kohlman. 2012. "Intersectionality: A Transformative Paradigm in Feminist Theory and Social Justice." In *Handbook of Feminist Research: Theory and Praxis, 2nd Edition*, edited by Sharlene N. Hesse-Biber. SAGE.

Walters, Rosie. 2020. "Relinquishing Control in Focus Groups: The Use of Activities in Feminist Research with Young People to Improve Moderator Performance." *Qualitative Research* 20 (4): 361–377.

Weaver, Brody, Amelia Thorpe, April Mandrona, Katie MacEntee, and Casey Burkholder. 2022. "Theorizing Non-Participation in a Mail-Based Participatory Visual Research Project with 2SLGBTQ+ Youth in Atlantic Canada." In *Facilitating Community Research for Social Change: Case Studies in Qualitative, Arts-Based and Visual Research*, edited by Casey Burkholder, Funké Aladejebi, and Joshua Schwab-Cartas. Routledge.

West, Nicole M. 2024. "Defining the Contours of a Participatory Action Research Counterspace Developed by, for, and about Black Women in Higher Education." *International Journal of Qualitative Studies in Education* 37 (5): 1542–1565.

Vaccaro, Mary-Elizabeth. 2023. "Reflections on 'Doing' Participatory Data Analysis with Women Experiencing Long-Term Homelessness." *Action Research* 21 (3): 332–350.

Vanner, Catherine. 2015. "Positionality at the Center: Constructing an Epistemological and Methodological Approach for a Western Feminist Doctoral Candidate Conducting Research in the Postcolonial." *International Journal of Qualitative Methods* 14 (4): 1–12.

Vanner, Catherine, Yasmeen Shahzadeh, Allison Holloway, Claudia Mitchell, and Jennifer Altenberg. 2022. "Round and Round the Carousel Papers: Facilitating a Visual Interactive Dialogue with Young People." In *Facilitating Community Research for Social Change: Case Studies in Qualitative, Arts-Based and Visual Research*, edited by Casey Burkholder, Funké Aladejebi, and Joshua Schwab-Cartas. Routledge.

von Unger, Hella, Anna Huber, Angela Kühner, Dennis Odukoya, and Herwig Reiter. 2022. "Reflection Labs: A Space for Researcher Reflexivity in Participatory Collaborations." *International Journal of Qualitative Methods* 21: 1–11.

Zreik, Thurayya, Rozane El Masri, Sandy Chaar et al. 2022. "Collaborative Coding in Multi-National Teams: Benefits, Challenges and Experiences Promoting Equitable Research." *International Journal of Qualitative Methods* 21: 1–8.

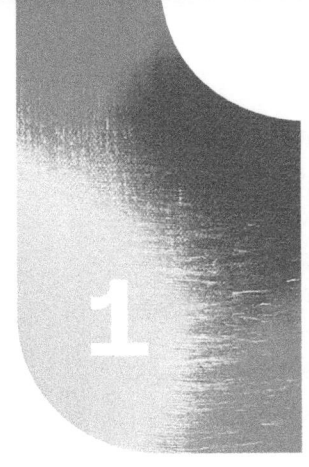

NADHA HASSEN AND
SARAH FLICKER

# COLLABORATIVE "SENSEMAKING"

Picturing a Feminist, Anti-Racist,
Community-Based Participatory
Action Research Dissertation

## INTRODUCTION

THIS CHAPTER OUTLINES the methodology of a dissertation focused on inequitable access to public urban greenspace during the COVID-19 pandemic. To begin, I (Nadha) briefly share *how* and *why* I came to this topic.[1] I provide a brief overview of the *Park Perceptions and Racialized Realities* project, which formed the basis of my dissertation, to situate this community-engaged and visual research study. Next, I chronicle seven key moments where feminist, anti-racist, and participatory analytical commitments were enacted. Throughout the chapter, I play with visual narratives to structure my writing, reflect its methodological underpinnings, and mirror the experiences of the residents who took part in the study.

I begin with my own positionality as one way of upholding a feminist and decolonial practice. In the tradition of Black and Brown

23

feminist scholars, I have long grappled with hyphenated identities and how these intersections influence my everyday realities (Ahmed 2017; hooks 1989; Lorde 2012; Piepzna-Samarasinha 2018). I am a woman of colour, a first-generation Sri Lankan immigrant and settler who migrated to Canada as a teenager. For most of my youth, I lived in an apartment in Abu Dhabi, in the United Arab Emirates with scarce access to outdoor space. As an adult in Toronto, I have enjoyed local parks, ravines, hydro corridors, and other publicly accessible open spaces. While these public greenspaces have been sites of healing, escape, and reflection for me, they have also been riddled with questions of belonging. While navigating these spaces, I have had racist, misogynistic, and xenophobic slurs hurled my way. I have also experienced less overt yet nevertheless hurtful instances of Othering and exclusion. The personal is political: it was my own embodied experiences of inequities that led me to this research (hooks 1989). I wanted to explore how issues of identity and intersecting social locations influence the possibilities of navigating public greenspaces. Moreover, the work felt urgent as possibilities for gathering indoors were hampered by a global pandemic.

## Project Overview

*Park Perceptions and Racialized Realities* is a feminist, anti-racist, community-based participatory action research (CBPAR) project that explores the experiences of racialized and Black, Indigenous, and People of Colour in public greenspaces using photovoice. I undertook this research study in collaboration with community organizations in two underserved, highly racialized neighbourhoods in Toronto, Canada: Jane-Finch and St. James Town. The study examines issues of access, equity, belonging, health, and well-being (see also Hassen et al. 2022).

Photovoice is a group process whereby community members use photography to capture their everyday experiences, collectively examine issues, and push for positive social change (Catalani and Minkler 2010; Wang and Burris 1997). Born as a feminist practice to study women's health needs, photovoice positions community members as experts of their own lived experience. When I initially conceptualized the project in 2019, I had planned to host collective visits to greenspaces and subsequent in-person focus group discussions. Due to COVID-19 physical distancing mandates, the study design had to be reimagined. I was inspired by photo-elicitation researchers, such as Marisol Clark-Ibáñez (2004), who had used individual interview formats to elicit the meanings behind photographs because it offered a more intimate approach. Ultimately, I chose to pursue a hybrid photovoice and photo-elicitation methodology that integrated the principles of photovoice (namely, anti-oppression, community co-ownership, collaboration, and action-orientation) with individual (or small group) Zoom interview formats to debrief experiences and build relationships.

From July to November 2021, eighteen racialized residents[2] went on over thirty-five individual greenspace visits to document their experiences in these neighbourhood spaces and collected over two hundred photos and videos. During over fifty-five online discussions (both individual and group), residents debriefed those encounters, shared perspectives on navigating public greenspaces as people of colour, and engaged in an iterative process of collective "sensemaking." Figure 1.1 describes the chronology of project activities. At each stage, all residents were paid an honorarium for their time and expertise.

The term "sensemaking" was adopted through conversations with a key knowledge mobilization partner, the Department of Imaginary Affairs,[3] a Toronto-based organization committed to imagining equitable futures. Scholars like Erin B. Carlson and Martina A. Caretta (2024) have employed the term "sensemaking" in a photovoice project to describe a process by which "stakeholders work together to articulate deeper, richer understandings of complex scenarios" (3) and then "strategize future action" (2). I conceptualize collaborative sensemaking as an ongoing and iterative process of meaning-making and analysis with community across all stages of a project, that attends to contexts, complexity, and nuance.

This chapter takes the form of a methodological reflection to support other students and scholars seeking to do similar participatory research. As I engaged in this research process, I too gathered images

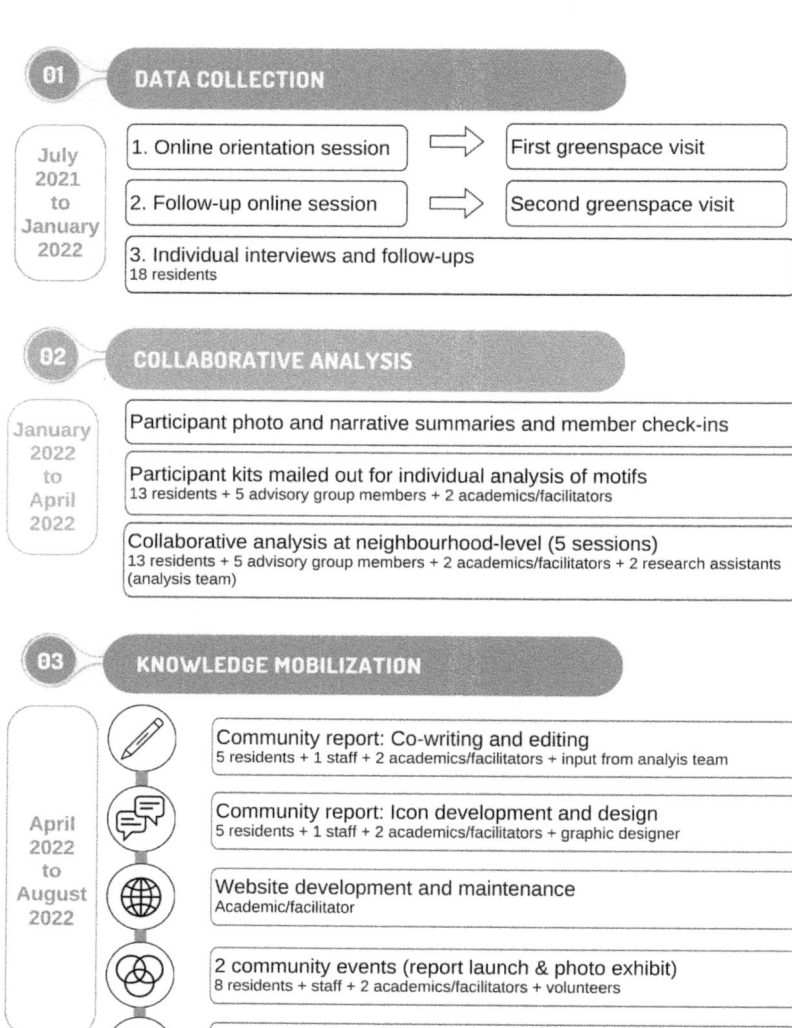

**01 DATA COLLECTION**

July 2021 to January 2022

1. Online orientation session ⟹ First greenspace visit

2. Follow-up online session ⟹ Second greenspace visit

3. Individual interviews and follow-ups
18 residents

**02 COLLABORATIVE ANALYSIS**

January 2022 to April 2022

Participant photo and narrative summaries and member check-ins

Participant kits mailed out for individual analysis of motifs
13 residents + 5 advisory group members + 2 academics/facilitators

Collaborative analysis at neighbourhood-level (5 sessions)
13 residents + 5 advisory group members + 2 academics/facilitators + 2 research assistants (analysis team)

**03 KNOWLEDGE MOBILIZATION**

April 2022 to August 2022

Community report: Co-writing and editing
5 residents + 1 staff + 2 academics/facilitators + input from analyis team

Community report: Icon development and design
5 residents + 1 staff + 2 academics/facilitators + graphic designer

Website development and maintenance
Academic/facilitator

2 community events (report launch & photo exhibit)
8 residents + staff + 2 academics/facilitators + volunteers

Travelling photo exhibit
2 academics/facilitators + Department of Imaginary Affairs + staff + residents

Ongoing

Advocacy: Meetings with decision-makers and presentations
Residents + staff + 2 academics/facilitators

**FIGURE 1.1** | Project timeline.

and field notes. I use photographs, taken by myself and others in the project, as timestamps to punctuate the study's trajectory. Through these pictures, I share and critically reflect on seven key stages where *Park Perceptions and Racialized Realities* took on an explicitly feminist, anti-racist, and participatory analytic approach. As a collection, they (somewhat imperfectly) document the research journey.

## An Intersectional Feminist and Anti-Racist Approach

Paul J. Fleming et al. (2023) outline the synergies between anti-racist principles and community-based participatory research (CBPR) noting that "the emancipatory roots that underlie CBPR draw from the epistemic traditions of oppressed communities of color and Indigenous communities across the globe that have sought to facilitate community empowerment and agency" (71). Gender, race, class, and their synergistic intersections (Crenshaw 1989) centrally influence people's experiences navigating public greenspaces. I drew on M. Ann Phillips's (1997) Feminist Anti-Racist Participatory Action Research (FARPAR) framework to integrate a more nuanced understanding of how power differentials relate to racism, sexism, and classism. While CBPR is in many ways inherently feminist and anti-racist, the explicit intersectional anti-racist lens of FARPAR moved me to "partner with racially marginalized communities to center their priorities" (71) and collaborate with them "as experts with valuable knowledge" (72). As Fleming et al. (2023) note, one of the ongoing challenges of anti-racist CBPAR remains how to operationalize such a project within an academic system that is extractive and steeped in structural racism. Early on, I committed to three key operational principles[4]: 1) embedding the project within community infrastructure through collaboration with existing and emerging community groups and leaders; 2) attending to power dynamics, structural contextual factors, and ethics; and 3) grounding the work in an intersectional, race-first analysis that unpacks the multiplicity of residents' experiences.

### Story Gathering Online: Who Am I? Who Are You?
### What Are We Doing Together?

Before I submitted my dissertation proposal, I assembled a community advisory committee comprised of members with lived or work
expertise that aligned with the project topic and goals. Nearly all were
racialized. Membership was fluid over the course of the project to
accommodate personal and professional changes. Nevertheless, the
advisory committee offered invaluable guidance, especially around
barriers to recruitment and participation. For example, they affirmed
the importance of open-ended questions (particularly around questions
of race), provided neighbourhood context, and validated my decision to
provide meaningful honoraria for residents' participation.

Data collection took place during the summer of 2021, at the
height of the COVID-19 pandemic, and in the wake of an intense
period marked by an international push for racial justice following the
murders of Breonna Taylor, George Floyd, and others. In a particularly
high-profile case, a white woman called the police on Christian Cooper,
a Black birdwatcher, while he was in Central Park, New York City. This
prompted ongoing public debates around who could safely access and
navigate greenspaces (Hassen 2021).

In the midst of this social and political moment, I began data
collection. I invited each resident to 1) attend two online training
sessions; 2) go on two greenspace visits and take photographs in
response to prompts; and 3) participate in an individual interview to
further unpack their photographs and experiences. As it was difficult
to coordinate schedules, I facilitated several online training sessions,
mostly one-to-one with residents and a couple of sessions in groups of
two or three. Residents who wished to engage further had the option to
participate in a series of group discussions to analyze the photographs
and plan knowledge mobilization activities.

The online orientation session included introductions, the
informed consent process, a land acknowledgement, a project overview,

honorarium information, training on the ethics of photography and processes involved in obtaining consent from those pictured, photography tips (considerations of light, contrast, perspective), safety considerations and guidelines, and instructions for their first greenspace visit. For this initial visit, I invited residents to take and send me three to five photographs about what they saw and how they felt on their visits and to record short explanatory audio and/or video clips. Greenspace visits integrated embodied ways of knowing, as described by Stephanie Springgay and Sarah E. Truman (2018), with the recognition that bodies do not move through or occupy spaces equally. As I could not be physically present with residents, I also took solo trips to greenspaces in each neighbourhood, took photographs, and reflected critically on these experiences. I noted my discomforts and what sparked moments of joy and calm. This exercise offered me a reference point and sense of connection to the resident photographers (Pink 2008).

The second online session focused on debriefing residents' experiences from the first greenspace visit, briefly discussing their photographs, providing a deeper understanding of photovoice and the possibilities of this project (including sharing a short video), discussing photography as a metaphor, and sharing the next set of prompts. For the second greenspace visit, I invited residents to photograph and think about what is safe/unsafe, inclusive/non-inclusive, welcoming/unwelcoming, and healthy/unhealthy. The sessions took approximately thirty to forty-five minutes each. Some went longer. I coordinated a few group sessions with two to three residents, but scheduling proved challenging during the height of the COVID-19 pandemic. This affirmed my decision to debrief the greenspace visits through individual interviews rather than try to hold a series of focus groups with all residents. Furthermore, I intentionally made space to build a foundation of rapport and trust, and to embed a feminist ethic of care (Hankivsky 2014). I grounded this research in the ethos of co-creation—coming together to make sense of complicated experiences that spanned both pain and joy. I offered parts of my story. This reciprocity opened a caring space. We often spoke beyond the allocated time, discussing everything from our families and housing to our careers and educational aspirations, health concerns, and other life transitions. It was important to take the time to build relationships and bring our whole selves to the table, grounding this as a feminist process.

Individual interviews began with residents describing their most memorable photograph and then meandering through their entire photo collection. Our dialogues became a process of co-constructing meaning. It was the first step in our collaborative participatory data analysis process marked by "joint theorizing" (Glaw et al. 2017, 7). To visually ground our discussions, I screenshared each photograph as they described it. All conversations were audio and video recorded on Zoom. The interview guide loosely followed Caroline Wang and Mary Ann Burris's (1997) SHOWeD process by inviting residents to elaborate on their visual submissions and share relevant stories. The goal was for residents to lead the analysis of their lived experiences, realities, and social worlds.

## Photograph and Story Check-Ins: Did I Capture This Accurately? Tell Me More, Please.

Participatory data analysis or collaborative "sensemaking" continued iteratively over several months. The next step entailed summarizing and collating verbal narratives and images. Drawing from the interviews, I used residents' own words, phrases, and titles to create short captions and consolidated them into personal slide decks for review (see sample slide in figure 1.2). Video submissions were flattened into screenshots. I encouraged residents to carefully review their deck and double-check the accuracy of the name ascribed (pseudonym, first name or full name), photograph titles, locations, key quotes, relevant context, and demographic information (e.g., racial identity, gender identity, age). Typically, participatory data analysis would take place in person. Ideally, we would have physically gathered with celebratory refreshments. Unfortunately, due to continued pandemic concerns that limited possibilities for in-person gathering, we had to find another way.

**NEGLECTING DIVERSE PEOPLE**
by Nathan

St. James Town

*"This greenspace is utilised by diverse people living in the neighbourhood and the bare minimum facilities in the space gives a feeling of neglect of such people."*

South Asian, Male, 45-54 years old
Living in Canada between 4-9 years
Location: St James Avenue and Ontario Street

**FIGURE 1.2** | Creating photo and narrative summaries.

## Participant Kits: Bridging Distance with Care

Photographs can be challenging to analyze because of the overwhelming amount of complex data that needs to be sorted and synthesized (Catalani and Minkler 2010). Drawing on Wang and Burris (1997), we developed a participatory analysis process that included selecting, contextualizing, and codifying photographs.

To facilitate virtual collaborative analysis, the entire collection of photographs and related stories (over two hundred in total) were printed and mailed to each member of the analysis team. The analysis team included me and Sarah, thirteen community residents, four advisory group members, and two research assistants (see figure 1.1). Each team member was tasked with individually reviewing the entire collection, grouping them by themes, and sharing their theme titles before we met so that we could compare and contrast what we saw in the collection.

Mailed packages included written instructions on how to engage in this individual sorting and categorizing exercise. I recorded a video with screensharing to outline this process and included an example from another CBPAR project (Switzer et al. 2017). Everyone was invited to identify motifs or "key themes" from the photograph collection and submit their initial musings.

**FIGURE 1.3** | Identifying motifs at home.
(Photograph provided by Zoi de la Peña, used with permission.)

We re-purposed our refreshment budget to provide everyone a twenty-five-dollar gift card to purchase and enjoy their own snacks during our virtual meeting. While there is little that can replace the relationship-building and camaraderie of sharing food in person, this was nevertheless an important act of care. I also included some tea packages from my mother's small business in each participant kit. Bridging distance in digital spaces can take greater effort and creativity. Often lost on Zoom are moments of personal interaction before, during, and after an in-person gathering. Instead, I made myself available to answer questions and checked in individually with everyone with task reminders and offers of support. Residents commented positively on these moments of care and personalization.

## Collaborative Analysis: Making Sense of It All Together

I aggregated the motifs submitted by each resident on two Google Jamboards, a collaborative digital whiteboard (see figure 1.4). I displayed one sticky note per idea for each neighbourhood. Next, I scheduled a series of synchronous Zoom discussions to consolidate and identify the most salient themes through consensus dialogue.

To maintain the place-based analysis, we structured these sessions as separate, parallel processes in each neighbourhood. These sessions were intended to promote critical dialogue and hear resident perspectives on what was most important to them (Wang and Burris 1997). Our main task was to review, compare, and contrast all the submitted suggestions for themes on the sticky notes and come to a consensus on a shared final list.

For many, our collaborative sensemaking sessions marked the first time that residents met each other, the advisory members, and Sarah. We began with introductions. As an icebreaker, I asked everyone to identify one of their favourite photos and explain why. This became an entry point for discussing neighbourhood greenspaces. Patterns began to emerge immediately: residents repeatedly highlighted some of the same photos.

It requires substantial skill to facilitate online sessions according to a feminist participatory framework that pays attention to issues of power dynamics, insider-outsider tensions, and group dynamics. For instance, some residents were hesitant to speak. Offering the Zoom chat alternative for engagement allowed these residents to message me privately and participate in written form throughout the sessions. The Google Jamboard has a function that also allowed folks to participate in non-verbal ways through moving sticky notes around and adding comments in real time.

Once we collectively consolidated themes, I divided residents into small breakout groups. Each group was assigned two themes and tasked with 1) developing a working definition for each theme, and 2) identifying some photos that they felt fit into this theme. Each breakout group had me, Sarah, or a member from the advisory group

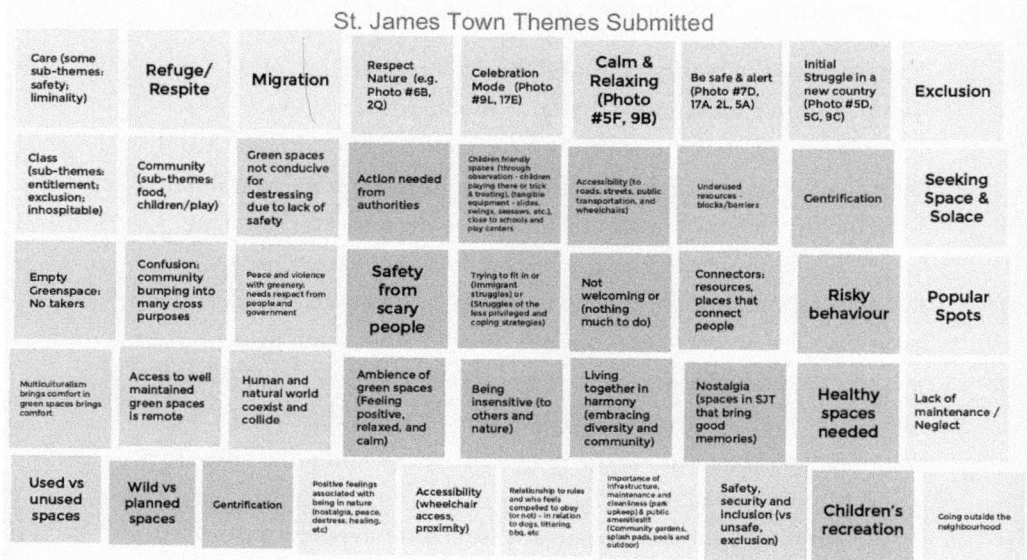

**FIGURE 1.4** | St. James Town analysis, before categorizing.

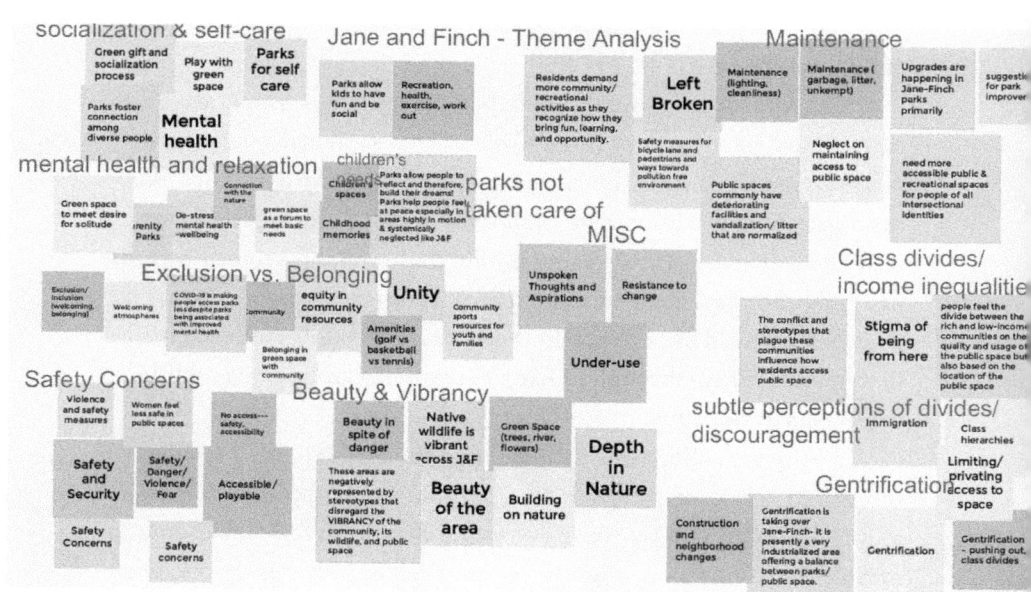

**FIGURE 1.5** | Jane-Finch analysis, after categorizing and dialogue.

to help facilitate the conversation and take notes. The small breakout groups were intended to facilitate greater participation. I intentionally worked with a resident who had been silent in the big group. Privately, she apologetically asked what gentrification meant. It was an important reminder for me to define terms, especially jargon, as part of our commitment to transformative community engagement as described by Julia Fursova et al. (2022). It was also a valuable reminder of the importance of creating smaller and more intimate spaces for frank discussions where people might feel less embarrassed to ask questions.

After this round of collaborative sensemaking sessions, I consolidated the themes, working definitions, and accompanying photographs, ensuring that every photograph was assigned to at least one theme. I brought these documents back to the groups for discussion and reflection, with the key questions: "Does this capture our conversations? What is missing?" I extended an open invitation to all analysis team members to continue their engagement by joining one of two new working groups that would take this work forward: a community report writing group and an event planning group.

## Collaborative Writing: Co-Writing Challenges, Ownership, and Finding a Collective Voice

The community report writing group was tasked with producing a highly visual, colourful, and engaging document to share our findings with residents, the broader neighbourhood community, advocates, and policymakers. Five residents from both neighbourhoods came forward to join the group. Through a series of recorded online meetings, we created an outline, divvied up writing tasks, and brainstormed key points for inclusion. To guide this collaborative process, I drew insights from Sarah Flicker and Stephanie A. Nixon (2016) on writing with community partners, such as clarifying the message and the audience, developing an outline as a form of engagement, and strategizing draft generation and revision.

At the first writing group meeting, residents came together to discuss the work completed to date by the two neighbourhood analysis teams. The meeting prompted discussions of the similarities and differences between both neighbourhoods. Residents from St. James Town emphasized the dearth of available greenspace, while Jane-Finch residents noted issues of access. Both identified inequities in the maintenance of neighbourhood greenspaces. I also shared publicly available statistics related to greenspace cover, population density, and neighbourhood demographics to contextualize the neighbourhood comparisons.

A lot of thought and conversation with residents went into whether to have one community report that included findings from both neighbourhoods, or to produce two separate reports. Ultimately, given capacity and resources, and in the interests of creating a stronger product that could serve to highlight the similarities between neighbourhoods, Sarah and I suggested writing one community report that would include neighbourhood-specific recommendations. We proceeded after getting buy-in from the writing group. Ultimately, this was an exercise in solidarity-building. The consolidated report proved to be a stronger output of the collaborative analysis process.

Finally, the group identified eight overarching themes. To facilitate co-writing, everyone identified themes that they would like to draft. I invited each person to write a short paragraph on their selected theme that considered the key messages and to identify five or six photographs they would like included in the report. I encouraged residents to represent a range of experiences, diverse demographics, and locations.

One of the challenges in co-writing is creating a unified voice. Indeed, residents wrote in a range of different lengths, styles, and tones. Finding a unified voice was one of the most significant obstacles to editing the report. I did some preliminary editing to bring each co-writer's paragraph and identified photographs together. I ensured that every resident photographer had at least one photo and/or quote included in the report. Having the advantage of a fresh pair of eyes, Sarah edited the report further, ensuring the writing held true to the data and reflected what the photographs and stories represented. A tension of the collaborative sensemaking process was that the residents (understandably) wrote about broader experiences that were not always explicitly grounded within the data captured for this study. Recognizing their interpretations as valid ongoing analysis, Sarah and I attempted to convey clear research findings that could be supported by the data, while making space for emerging community knowledge. The group had mixed reactions to our edited version. While some agreed that the edited report was stronger, others felt that their writing had been modified too much and were uneasy with the new version. In reflecting on the process, Sarah noted that with a photovoice project you would usually meet in person several times, but because of this missing step, she reflected that "we didn't have that social capital built up and I was read as a heavy-handed outsider."

We reiterated our commitment to producing a report that everyone on the team had ownership over and our shared intention to create a strong report. Through discussion with the writing group, we identified some tangible steps to move forward: 1) reframing from a passive voice (i.e., "residents described") to an active "we" voice; 2) explicitly stating in the introduction that the report was co-written by a group of community residents; 3) naming the systemic challenges and barriers residents faced; 4) changing the language from "participants" to "resident photographers" to move away from traditional research-focused language that further entrenches power dynamics; and 5) editing out jargon for accessible public dissemination. We shared these five changes with the writing group and sought every member's opinion and agreement before moving forward. This process of securing collective buy-in was a vital step in attending to and centring the voices of racialized residents whose concerns are often ignored or quelled by racist structures, both within research and in everyday interactions.

In finalizing the community report, several decision-points and processes embodied an intersectional feminist perspective by 1) ensuring clear writing processes and non-hierarchical authorship on the report cover; 2) saving all report versions so we did not lose anyone's original writing or ideas and could also backtrack if needed; 3) having clear check-in points; and 4) demonstrating accountability to the community's voices and stories. Before finalizing the report for graphic design, a penultimate draft was shared with everyone on the

**FIGURE 1.6** | The community report.

larger analysis team for their feedback and approval. Everyone who contributed in some way over the length of the project was contacted to determine how they would like to be acknowledged. Both a digital and physical copy of the report was shared with everyone who participated, along with a handwritten thank you note.

## Analysis through Design: Co-Creating Icons

Parallel to the writing process was the design of the community report. After sourcing quotes from graphic designers from our networks, we decided to hire a racialized student who was interested in the subject material. One of the tasks for the graphic designer was to work iteratively and collaboratively with our writing group to develop icons for each theme to be used in the report and photo exhibits. Drawing on Sarah Switzer and Sarah Flicker's work (2021), icon conceptualization supported our collective thematic theorizing.

For example, the initial proposed icon for the theme "access and accessibility" was a wheelchair. While physical accessibility was important, the group felt that the wheelchair icon did not represent the essence or entirety of the theme. Through collaborative discussions, the final design depicted a door that was slightly ajar, emblematic of how some spaces may be closed to some and open to others. Conceptualizing the icon for "exclusion" was the most challenging. The graphic designer presented us with several options. The first used barbed wire to depict exclusion, but for some residents, this invoked prisons. A second option was a golf course; this metaphor riffed on a resident's narrative who shared how a golf course near their home was an exclusionary greenspace that stoked class divides. However, several felt that the symbol was not widely legible. After a few more iterations, we agreed on the icon of a person behind a fence. Coming to consensus over the final icons helped our team not only to develop a visual brand, but also helped us to crystallize our collective interpretations of the data. By engaging in these conversations, the writing group was forced to expand on our interpretations of what each theme represented, pushing our analysis further to uncover deeper meanings.

FIGURE 1.7 | Final theme icons.

### Events and Photo Exhibits: Amplification through Partnerships, Centring Community Voices, and Lessons Learned

The event planning group curated a travelling photography exhibit and hosted two community launch events. Given the hyperlocal nature of these events organized in collaboration with community organizations and stakeholders, the event planning process was divided into two parallel processes, one for each neighbourhood.

Our collaboration with the Jane/Finch Centre[5] gave us access to a placemaking initiative called Corner Commons, which transforms a parking lot corner into a community space over the summer. Corner Commons gave us a central venue to host the event. This event planning group included two residents who designed the flyer, helped select photographs to showcase, and photographed the event. There were challenges with bringing this group together synchronously because of work and school schedules. Asynchronous planning meant that

**FIGURE 1.8** | Photo exhibit on shipping containers in St. James Town. (Photograph by author.)

I had to do a lot of coordinating to maintain momentum. In the other neighbourhood, two residents supported the event planning process and we collaborated with the St. James Town Community Co-operative.[6] One of the residents runs her own community organization, Auntie Amal Community Centre,[7] which provided catering and volunteers for the event.

A contributing factor to the success of the community events came from collaborating with community organizations, which made the process significantly easier to organize. The organizations were well established and shared resources like tents, tables, and sound systems. Without this in-kind support, our limited funding budget would have been stretched even more thin. The community organizations' knowledge about the neighbourhoods and the best setup for the outdoor events and exhibits was invaluable. For example, in St. James Town, the residents had the idea of using two outdoor shipping containers in a central greenspace to display the photographs. As several residents had also photographed and described this particular greenspace in the project, it seemed like the perfect location for display. Several residents and volunteers from the neighbourhood came together to assemble and dismantle this exhibit.

By this time in the project, a sense of fatigue with Zoom, email, and WhatsApp had settled in for me and for the residents. In-person meetings would have alleviated some of this difficulty, but the pandemic seemed unrelenting. I also faced limitations with my own health. Ultimately, I ended up taking the lead on the photo exhibits and developed a modular exhibit prototype to share with the entire team for feedback. I designed the prototype to be interactive and adaptable to multiple uses, budgets, and locations. From the prototype, I created a travelling photo exhibit that was featured at both community events and in several gallery exhibits. The process involved a "delicate balance of the researcher's personal creative expression, discretion, and attendance to the voices they are representing" (Capous-Desyllas and Bromfield 2018, 2). The curation process rested largely in my hands, and I felt uneasy deciding what was represented. I revisited all the photographs multiple times, considering who I might have missed, what fair representation looked like, and which photographs and narratives would convey the most salient findings. For example, I decided to forego a more visually striking photograph in favour of including all residents.

I would have preferred to develop the exhibit in a more participatory fashion with residents. Other scholars have noted this tension, asking, "Should we strive for full participation at each stage of a photovoice project?" (Wang et al. 1998, 85). However, aspirational expectations are not always feasible. I made it clear to residents that their participation was voluntary, and that, depending on their capacity, they could move in and out of the project. Feminist and anti-racist CBPAR is not about demanding participation at each research stage, but rather keeping the door open, providing invitations that do not require an affirmative response, and ensuring that residents know that they can rejoin at any time (van der Meulen 2011). Upon further reflection, my desire for engagement was in part a wish for more support. The task of coordinating several moving pieces was at times overwhelming. This feeling was exacerbated by doing everything online with limited to no in-person interactions. However, by doing a CBPAR dissertation and engaging with community advisory members and residents, I likely had more support than other doctoral students.

Furthermore, many of the residents faced structural barriers related to racism, migration, and economic inequities. The event planning teams were comprised entirely of racialized women. Considering the politics of labour, which often falls unevenly on racialized women, I was mindful of not over asking. Compensation was limited by budgetary constraints. I had to make space to pause and grapple with the underlying reasons behind my complicated feelings, bringing a critical feminist and anti-racist lens to the *process*. Continuous reflexivity regarding my role as researcher, the negotiation of power dynamics, a commitment to feminist and anti-racist principles, and the nuances that these processes entail demanded significant emotional labour that is not often accounted for or valued within traditional dissertations.

My commitment to moving the project forward and to respecting the residents, their pictures, and their stories pushed me to maintain momentum. I intentionally focused on community action and knowledge mobilization. Nevertheless, I was battling an underlying feeling of misplaced energy and attention. As a doctoral student, this commitment to community action was, at times, a lonely activity. Because of the ever-present pressures of academia, I had to remind myself of why I was committing months of my doctoral program to community and knowledge mobilization.

Consequently, I was consistently unsuccessful at carving out dedicated time to engage in dissertation writing activities; more immediate community-related activities always seemed to supersede these protected blocks of time. Fleming et al. (2023) describe the structural barriers of doing this type of anti-racist CBPAR work in academic institutions that operate within historically oppressive systems. Academia

**FIGURE 1.9** | Outdoor photo exhibit at Corner Commons, Jane-Finch. (Photograph provided by Isatu Barrie, used with permission.)

undervalues the forms of dissemination I was engaging in compared to academic publications, often misunderstanding anti-racist CBPAR as "too slow, underfunded, perceived as service or not perceived as rigorous science" (73). Fleming et al. (2023) also note significant structural barriers that first-generation, racially marginalized scholars and community partners face in receiving large-scale funding. Therefore, a commitment to CBPAR within this context is an inherently feminist and antiracist praxis. As the first person in my family to get a PhD, I had a hard time explaining my decisions to my immediate circle. When describing the knowledge mobilization activities to a loved one, I was asked the sincere question, "Are you saying that you don't *need* to do all this to get your PhD?" The short answer was yes. The longer response was that this effort is a crucial part of the CBPAR epistemology that questions why and how research is conducted. And while I didn't *need* to do CBPAR, given my research aims and values, I never felt it was an option not to do it.

**FIGURE 1.10** | Outdoor photo exhibit at St. James Town.
(Photograph provided by Ravi Ponnudurai, used with permission.)

The neighbourhood community events took place in August 2022. A media release announced the launch. We received significant media coverage as part of our media advocacy strategy to amplify community voices (Israel et al. 2010). Four residents spoke to the media and were featured on radio, television, and in print. Residents spoke to public audiences about our research findings, signaling their pride and co-ownership of the project. The events were successful venues for elevating community voices and receiving positive public feedback.

As Linda Liebenberg (2022) notes, the implementation of photovoice often falls short in the data analysis process and in the intentional use of dissemination activities. Through conversations with residents and the advisory group, I compiled a list of knowledge users we wanted to target and complementary knowledge mobilization activities to push for action and strategically share our findings. Michelle Fine and María Elena Torre (2019) note the multiple accountabilities inherent in this work. I too conceptualized knowledge mobilization in terms of

FIGURE 1.11 | Travelling photo exhibit, in collaboration with the Department of Imaginary Affairs as part of the "What if Parks Were Safe for Everyone" installation. (Photograph by author.)

accountability on multiple levels (individual, interpersonal, community, and policy) and with multiple audiences.

Even after analysis and knowledge mobilization activities conclude, accountability to community stories and transparency with residents is key. The capital that I might gain from academic publications may or may not be valuable in the same way to community residents. CBPAR involves a commitment to non-extractive research, that is in reciprocal relationship with communities. Non-extractive research includes developing long-term partnerships, co-ownership, legacy planning, and thinking about what comes next. Even in writing this chapter, I was torn about whether this should be a collaborative effort and/or whether I should invite community residents to be co-authors in the process. Sarah and I discussed the different options for how this chapter could be written collaboratively, in a non-tokenistic way. I grappled with the need to finish writing my dissertation in a timely manner alongside facilitating a process for meaningful co-authorship with residents. In this case, logistics, individual constraints, and the fact that the chapter is a reflection on the dissertation process resulted in the decision for me to write it—with Sarah's input—while acknowledging the important contributions of residents throughout.[8]

## CONCLUSION

There are multiple institutional and structural barriers to facilitating feminist and anti-racist CBPAR in academia, particularly within a doctoral program. The methodology of feminist and anti-racist CBPAR requires continuous reflexivity as well as a reciprocal engagement with racialized communities, an investment in collaborative "sensemaking" and co-creation, a recognition of often-unseen labour, and a commitment to adaptability and accountability. It is because of these underlying tenets that Fleming et al. (2023) describe CBPAR as a key driver in shifting institutional policies and encouraging anti-oppressive research that pushes for justice and equity.

My intention with this research was to facilitate a collaborative project that community residents and organizations could all lay claim to, resulting in something more than just my dissertation. Community residents showed up and kept showing up over the long haul. Residents spoke to the media and advocated for equitable greenspaces in racialized and underserved neighbourhoods. Residents co-authored the report and spoke at the community events in front of their neighbours. I intentionally designed the project, from the conception to conclusion, as rooted in anti-racist and feminist principles. Given the length of the project, residents' nearly continuous participation was another marker of how it successfully embodied feminist, anti-racist, and participatory principles.

Our focus on the collective process that took place online provides insight into the challenges and opportunities for fostering an inclusive, collaborative "sensemaking" process. By keeping in mind Liebenberg's (2022) critique that "voice in photovoice is not a given" (272), we intentionally fostered a process that centred racialized residents' voices. Our critical discussions and engagement resulted in community-owned products and exhibits that continue to push for material change. Neither the discussions nor the outputs would have been possible without listening to residents, respecting their perspectives, creating space for dialogue, and amplifying their role as co-creators and co-designers of knowledge, action, and change.

## AUTHORS' NOTE

The multiple pieces of this project would not have come together without the care, dedication, and insights of the residents, advisory committee, and other contributors to the *Park Perceptions and Racialized Realities* project. Deepest thanks to all. All photographs were included with permission. Funded by the York University-TD Community Engagement Centre's Catalyst Grant, Jane/Finch Centre, and York University. In-kind support for knowledge mobilization was provided by the St. James Town Community Co-op, Jane/Finch Centre, Auntie Amal Community Centre, and the Department of Imaginary Affairs. Nadha Hassen was supported by a SSHRC Vanier Scholarship, the Charles Caccia Graduate Award in Sustainable Development, and the Susan Mann Dissertation Scholarship.

## NOTES

1.  I have drafted this chapter in the first person, because it feels like the most direct and reflexive way to write about the research process that formed the basis of my dissertation. Sarah, my supervisor, is listed as a co-author because so many of these ideas were born out of conversations with her. Elsewhere, Sarah has written about her positionality as a white Jewish settler scholar doing research in solidarity with Indigenous communities (Flicker 2018). Her grandparents arrived in Canada as Holocaust survivors. While today she enjoys many of the privileges of whiteness (McIntosh 2018), she too comes from a family haunted by the horrors and violence of systemic racism. Today, she mothers racialized children. To speak back, she has spent her career devoted to studying and promoting health equity. Together, we

brainstormed an outline, reviewed drafts, and refined the arguments presented. Her words and intellectual contributions remain deeply embedded throughout.

2. In this chapter, I refer to participants as residents, arising from a group decision to centre community members' experiences.

3. The website for the Department of Imaginary Affairs is https://dia.space.

4. I also referenced the principles set up by the Jane Finch Community Research Partnership to guide ethical community-academic partnerships (https://janefinchresearch.ca/).

5. The website for the Jane/Finch Centre is https://www.janefinchcentre.org/.

6. The website for the St. James Town Community Co-operative is https://stjamestowncoop.org.

7. The website for the Auntie Amal Community Centre is https://auntieamalccorg.wordpress.com/.

8. Other chapters of the dissertation have been co-authored.

## REFERENCES

Ahmed, Sara. 2017. *Living a Feminist Life.* Duke University Press.

Capous-Desyllas, Moshoula, and Nicole F. Bromfield. 2018. "Using an Arts-Informed Eclectic Approach to Photovoice Data Analysis." *International Journal of Qualitative Methods* 17 (1): 1–14.

Carlson, Erin Brock, and Martina Angela Caretta. 2024. "Collaborative Sensemaking through Photos: Using Photovoice to Study Gas Pipeline Development in Appalachia." *Qualitative Research* 24 (2): 367–390.

Catalani, Caricia, and Meredith Minkler. 2010. "Photovoice: A Review of the Literature in Health and Public Health." *Health Education & Behavior* 37 (3): 424–451.

Clark-Ibáñez, Marisol. 2004. "Framing the Social World with Photo-Elicitation Interviews." *American Behavioral Scientist* 47 (12): 1507–1527.

Crenshaw, Kimberlé. 1989. "Demarginalizing the Intersection of Race and Sex: A Black Feminist Critique of Antidiscrimination Doctrine, Feminist Theory and Antiracist Politics." *University of Chicago Legal Forum* 1 (8): 139–167.

Fine, Michelle, and María Elena Torre. 2019. "Critical Participatory Action Research: A Feminist Project for Validity and Solidarity." *Psychology of Women Quarterly* 43 (4): 433–444.

Fleming, Paul J., Lisa Cacari Stone, Melissa S. Creary et al. 2023. "Antiracism and Community-Based Participatory Research: Synergies, Challenges, and Opportunities." *American Journal of Public Health* 113 (1): 70–78.

Flicker, Sarah. 2018. "Unsettling: Musings on Ten Years of Collaborations with Indigenous Youth as a White Settler Scholar." In *Disrupting Shameful Legacies*, edited by Claudia Mitchell and Relebohile Moletsane. Brill Sense.

Flicker, Sarah, and Stephanie A. Nixon. 2016. "Writing Peer-Reviewed Articles with Diverse Teams: Considerations for Novice Scholars Conducting Community-Engaged Research." *Health Promotion International* 33 (1): 152–161.

Fursova, Julia, Denise Bishop-Earle, Kisa Hamilton, and Gillian Kranias. 2022. "'Participation—with What Money and Whose Time?' An Intersectional Feminist Analysis of Community Participation." *Community Development Journal* 58 (3): 453–471.

Glaw, Xanthe, Kerry Inder, Ashley Kable, and Michael Hazelton. 2017. "Visual Methodologies in Qualitative Research: Autophotography and Photo Elicitation Applied to Mental Health Research." *International Journal of Qualitative Methods* 16: 1–8.

Hankivsky, Olena. 2014. "Rethinking Care Ethics: On the Promise and Potential of an Intersectional Analysis." *American Political Science Review* 108 (2): 252–264.

Hassen, Nadha. 2021. "6 Ways to Approach Urban Green Spaces in the Push for Racial Justice and Health Equity." *The Conversation*, June 10. http://theconversation. com/6-ways-to-approach-urban-green-spaces-in-the-push-for-racial-justice-and-health-equity-160227.

Hassen, Nadha, Darryl D'Souza, Sayem Khan et al. 2022. "Park Perceptions and Racialized Realities in Two Toronto Neighbourhoods." York University. https://www.yorku.ca/ euc/research-projects/park-perceptions/publications/.

hooks, bell. 1989. "Choosing the Margin as a Space of Radical Openness." *Framework: The Journal of Cinema and Media* 36: 15–23.

Israel, Barbara A., Chris M. Coombe, Rebecca R. Cheezum et al. 2010. "Community-Based Participatory Research: A Capacity-Building Approach for Policy Advocacy Aimed at Eliminating Health Disparities." *American Journal of Public Health* 100 (11): 2094–2102.

Liebenberg, Linda. 2022. "Photovoice and Being Intentional about Empowerment." *Health Promotion Practice* 23 (2): 267–273.

Lorde, Audre. 2012. *Sister Outsider: Essays and Speeches.* Crossing Press.

McIntosh, Peggy. 2018. "White Privilege and Male Privilege." In *Privilege: A Reader*, edited by Michael S. Kimmel and Abby L. Ferber. Routledge.

Phillips, M. Ann. 1997. "Feminist Anti-Racist Participatory Action Research: Research for Social Change around Women's Health in Brazil." *Canadian Woman Studies/ Les Cahiers de La Femme* 17 (20): 100–105.

Piepzna-Samarasinha, Leah Lakshmi. 2018. *Care Work: Dreaming Disability Justice.* Arsenal Pulp Press.

Pink, Sarah. 2008. "Mobilising Visual Ethnography: Making Routes, Making Place and Making Images." *Forum Qualitative Sozialforschung/Forum Qualitative Social Research* 9 (3): 1–17.

Springgay, Stephanie, and Sarah E. Truman. 2018. *Walking Methodologies in a More-than-Human World.* Routledge.

Switzer, Sarah, and Sarah Flicker. 2021. "Visualizing DEPICT: A Multistep Model for Participatory Analysis in Photovoice Research for Social Change." *Health Promotion Practice* 22 (2): 50S–65S.

Switzer, Sarah, Sarah Flicker, Soo Chan Caruosone et al. 2017. "Picturing Participation: Exploring Engagement in HIV Service Provision, Programming and Care." https://www.picturingparticipation.com/_files/ugd/23c716_ 6452a3fd985e4fa5ac6c640158c48e23.pdf.

van der Meulen, Emily. 2011. "Participatory and Action-Oriented Dissertations: The Challenges and Importance of Community-Engaged Graduate Research." *The Qualitative Report* 16 (5): 1291–1303.

Wang, Caroline, and Mary Ann Burris. 1997. "Photovoice: Concept, Methodology, and Use for Participatory Needs Assessment." *Health Education & Behavior* 24 (3): 369–387.

Wang, Caroline C., Wu Kun Yi, Zhan Wen Tao, and Kathryn Carovano. 1998. "Photovoice as a Participatory Health Promotion Strategy." *Health Promotion International* 13 (1): 75–86.

NESA BANDARCHIAN RASHTI

# PARTICIPATORY DATA ANALYSIS IN A PHOTOVOICE PROJECT WITH REFUGEE GIRLS

## INTRODUCTION

IN THIS CHAPTER, I map out the steps I took to facilitate a participatory data analysis workshop within a photovoice project that explored refugee girls' and young women's engagement in resettlement programs in Montréal, Canada.[1] Resettlement programs are offered to ease the transition of refugees and provide access to key services such as mental health and education (Morland and Levine 2016). Such programs, offered by not-for-profit organizations, are particularly important for adolescent girls and young women, enabling them to acquire key social, educational, and employment skills during a critical period of their psychological and social development (Samuels et al. 2017). The main objective of my study was to give refugee girls and young women an opportunity to narrate their stories and experiences of resettlement in Quebec, using photovoice as a participatory visual method. The main argument of this chapter revolves around participatory data analysis and its various approaches. The chapter also discusses challenges such as ensuring that all voices are included, particularly those of marginalized participants.

## Photovoice

Caroline Wang and Mary Ann Burris (1997) coined the term "photovoice" to refer to a research process in which participants take photographs to identify and represent critical issues, with the broader goal of enhancing their communities.[2] Photovoice enables people to record and reflect their community's strengths and concerns, promotes critical dialogue about important issues, and endeavours to reach policymakers (Wang et al. 1998). In developing their SHOWeD method for carrying out photovoice research, Wang et al. (1998) pose the following questions for participants to discuss: "What do you See here? What's really Happening here? How does this relate to Our lives? Why does this situation, concern, or strength exist? What can we Do about it?" (80).

Photovoice has meaningful resonances with feminist theoretical frameworks, specifically building upon Patricia Maguire's (1987) feminist participatory approach and Paulo Freire's (1970) notion of *conscientization*, the idea that a new awareness of one's self-in-context can lead to social change. Furthermore, photovoice is a research tool that is meant to amplify the voices of marginalized groups, including women and girls (Mitchell et al. 2017). For instance, scholars have employed photovoice to explore girls' perceptions of water and sanitation access (Sajan Virgi and Mitchell 2011), pregnant teenagers' and young mothers' experiences re-entering formal education (Nyariro 2021), girls' perceptions of physical education (Rivard 2015), and girls' perceptions of feeling safe and unsafe as well as of feeling strong and not so strong (Mitchell 2015). My research specifically builds on the work of scholars who have utilized photovoice with war-affected populations. For example, Eric Green and Bret Kloos (2009) used photovoice with twelve internally displaced youth residing in a camp in Uganda who deployed digital cameras to take photos of everyday life in their communities. More recently, Neila Miled (2020) conducted a photovoice project with a group of ten Muslim girls from refugee backgrounds to explore their sense of belonging in Western Canada. These studies demonstrate that photovoice can serve as a constructive tool to assist refugee children and youth to describe and analyze their lived experiences, as photographs and narratives facilitate "knowledge production, as opposed to knowledge gathering" (Veale 2005, 254).

Even though photovoice can generate a rich amount of data on participants' thoughts, reflections, and experiences, it sometimes fails to meet its "emancipatory aims" because it does not eliminate power imbalances between the researcher and participants (Switzer and Flicker 2021). Furthermore, while the data collection and knowledge dissemination phases are often participatory, the data analysis and interpretation phases may be mostly researcher-driven (Switzer and Flicker 2021). Melanie Nind (2011) observes that while the potential to include participation throughout the whole research process is "boundary-less," many photovoice researchers do not take this potential into account. In this chapter, I contribute to visual and participatory scholarship by outlining the steps I took to facilitate participatory data analysis in a photovoice project with a group of refugee girls and young women.

## FRAMING THE PROJECT: GIRLHOOD STUDIES

My study draws from the main tenets of girlhood studies, which adopts a feminist viewpoint on girls' childhoods and adolescences (Mitchell et al. 2008). Girlhood studies acknowledge that children, girls, and young women are independent, agentic individuals who can choose for themselves, create their own narratives, and address issues of self-representation (Mitchell et al. 2008). According to April Mandrona (2016), the starting point of girlhood studies is "research and engagement with girls, for girls, and by girls" that draws attention to and seeks to remedy their "absence and voicelessness" in studies that impact their lives (1).

Scholars' understanding of knowledge creation in research has evolved over time. Marnina Gonick (2003) suggests that "the process of knowing" takes place "within a complex collaboration" between the researcher and participants and is shaped by power dynamics that exist in the research setting (60). In the field of girlhood studies, Relebohile Moletsane et al. (2008) highlight the importance of recognizing these power dynamics and advocate for an approach that is focused on working with, for, and by girls. This approach acknowledges the need for crossing disciplinary boundaries as well as bridging cultural and age differences to ensure that the research is inclusive and empowering for all participants. By acknowledging factors like gender and power, girlhood scholars can develop a deeper understanding of the experiences of girls and young women and help to promote greater social justice and equality (Krause et al. 2017).

Girlhood scholars increasingly draw on the work of Kimberlé Crenshaw (1989) to consider the intersections of race, class, religion, and other identities. For instance, Catherine Vanner (2019) highlights the importance of considering how "varying social processes" shape the experiences of girlhood and asserts that such processes are especially complex for girls of colour and other marginalized or racialized populations (20). As we can see in recent work exploring intersectionality within girlhood studies, Black girlhood has become a distinct field of study in and of itself (Rogers 2022; Scott 2022; Smith-Purviance and Jackson 2022).

My project is located within what Claudia Mitchell and Jacqueline Reid-Walsh (2008) refer to as "girl method," which means working "*with* girls" as opposed to "*about* girls," and which seeks to provide a place where participants can express their agency and power (17). In addition, intersectionality is a key component for understanding the experiences of refugee girls and young women after resettlement, since they may experience various forms of discrimination due to their gender, age, citizenship status, and race. Thus, intersectionality guides my understanding of how the girls' identities intersect with systems of subordination and oppression specific to Quebec society.

## Positionality

The participants in this study were refugee girls and young women from Haiti, Venezuela, Brazil, and the Democratic Republic of Congo. They all identified as Black, and their experiences were shaped by intersecting factors such as race, gender, and migration status. I believe that in the eyes of the refugee girls in my study, I held an "outsider" status. I am a West Asian middle-class woman, and at the time of data collection, I was in my early thirties. Before coming to Canada in 2017, I lived in Rasht, the largest city on Iran's Caspian Sea coast. My first language is Persian, and I learned English as my second language. Being an outsider meant that I might not easily understand participants' attitudes, behaviours, and values. James Banks (1998) notes that in cross-cultural research, being an insider who shares the same culture, language, and social background with participants is necessary for conducting successful fieldwork. This is primarily due to insiders' ability to gain participants' trust and build a positive relationship with them (Sharrif 2014). However, as Narendar Manohar et al. (2019) suggest, outsider status can be an advantage for researchers because they tend to seek more explanation to understand the context of participants' experiences.

All the participants identified as Black, so race played an influential role in the research process. Ruth Frankenberg (2004) suggests that who we are shapes the questions we ask, the responses we receive, and the knowledge we produce from those responses. According to Thomas Fletcher (2014), a lack of awareness about the importance of race in the research process can have negative consequences, such as "distorting the voice" of participants and marginalizing their perspectives. He explains that this can "[reinforce] the centrality of white ideologies and practices; whilst deifying 'whiteness' and assuming this perspective can best explain all number of experiences" (249). As a non-Black feminist researcher, I tried to repeatedly reiterate to participants that they are knowledge holders who have the power to raise awareness about the issues affecting their lives.

Researchers' understanding of girls' and young women's experiences will be superficial unless their voices are included in various research stages. Reducing power imbalances between researchers and participants requires researchers to pay attention to the notion of reciprocity. According to Kimberly Huisman (2008), reciprocity is based on the idea that researchers and participants have equal value and importance to the research process, and that the research needs to be beneficial for both parties. Since reciprocity is intertwined with reflexivity, throughout the research process I considered how my own identities and life experiences affect the way I see and experience the world as an adult researcher and how they give meaning to participants' stories, issues, and concerns.

## HOW HAS PARTICIPATORY DATA ANALYSIS BEEN ADDRESSED IN THE LITERATURE?

Participatory data analysis has been taken up by scholars in various ways. Virginia Braun and Victoria Clarke (2006) developed a six-step thematic analysis process which involves becoming familiar with the data, generating initial codes, identifying themes, reflecting on themes, identifying the relationship between themes, and producing a report.[3] Importantly, the accessibility and flexibility of this approach makes it possible for participants who do not possess formal research training to be involved in some steps of the analysis process (Braun and Clarke 2006).[4] Linda Liebenberg et al. (2020) build on Braun and Clarke's work in developing a participatory thematic analysis process to actively involve participants in all steps of the data analysis. They argue that including participants in data analysis challenges inequitable power dynamics between participants and researchers and acknowledges both parties as experts with skills, knowledge, and insights to contribute to research findings. Liebenberg et al. employed participatory thematic analysis in a photovoice project with a group of Indigenous youth in three Canadian communities to explore the spaces and places where they felt supported when facing risks. The researchers concluded that including participants in data analysis shaped and guided the findings and ensured that participants' voices remained central.

Recognizing that community members can bring rich expertise to the analysis process, Sarah Flicker and Stephanie Nixon (2015)
introduced the DEPICT model to involve participants with varying
levels of research expertise. The model includes six sequential steps:
Dynamic reading, Engaged development of codebooks, Participatory
coding, Inclusive reviewing of categories, Collaborative analysis, and
Translation (Flicker and Nixon 2015). Sarah Switzer and Sarah Flicker
(2021) employed the DEPICT model to analyze the participant-generated
photos and narratives related to the diverse conceptualizations of
engagement within three HIV organizations in Toronto, Canada.
According to the researchers, the primary benefit of using this model
was democratizing data analysis, which allowed the participation of
diverse groups of stakeholders.

The level of participation in participatory data analysis can vary.
While participants' reflections and insights are included in all steps
of analysis in the DEPICT model, in other studies their involvement is
limited to one step of data analysis. For example, Ndumiso Ngidi (2020)
conducted a participatory visual study with twenty-seven adolescents
who identified as orphans, using a combination of drawings, photographs, collages, storyboards, and written reflections to understand
and communicate their vulnerability to sexual violence. Participants
contributed to the data analysis process by writing captions to explain
their visual work and by verbally explaining their visuals to other participants during group discussions. Afterwards, the researcher utilized
thematic analysis to analyze the storyboards and written reflections.
Although the analysis utilized participants' interpretations, their
involvement was contained to one phase.

Whether the researcher includes participants in all steps or in
just a few steps of the data analysis phase, the approach must align with
the research objectives and study context (Bergold and Thomas 2012).
For example, Ruth Barley and Lisa Russell (2019) were interested in the
identities, hopes, and feelings of children and youth living in Northern
England, and they chose to explore this topic through two longitudinal
ethnographies. They designed a participatory analysis tool to facilitate
the children and youth working alongside the researchers to review the

data extracts. Longitudinal ethnography was well-suited to this study context as it allowed the researchers to establish a trusting relationship with the participants over time.

## STUDY PHASES

I divided my project into four phases: photovoice workshops, a community-based exhibition, individual interviews, and participatory data analysis (figure 2.1). I conducted all phases of the study at Maison d'Haïti, a non-profit organization in Montréal. Founded in 1972, Maison d'Haïti is a community and cultural organization dedicated to promoting the integration of immigrants, asylum-seekers, and refugees into Quebec society. The organization develops and delivers programs related to education, literacy, womanhood, and parenting (Maison d'Haïti 2021).

To address the needs of immigrant and refugee women and girls, the organization employs a feminist approach focused on empowering women. This is achieved by fostering spaces for open discussion and debate, as well as by encouraging both individual growth and collective action for change.

In 2019 and 2020, I was a volunteer at Maison d'Haïti and had the opportunity to work with refugee youth and children at the centre. As such, the girls and young women who attended the workshops and participated in this study had previously met me in my capacity as a volunteer.

I applied purposive sampling to recruit a group of adolescent refugee girls and young women at Maison d'Haïti. Purposive sampling is a type of non-probability sampling where researchers select participants based on a specific purpose or criterion. I recruited nine participants between the ages of fourteen and twenty-four from Congo, Haiti, Venezuela, and Brazil. While their durations of stay in Quebec differed, all of them had arrived as refugee claimants after 2017. As most participants preferred to communicate in French, I hired an interpreter to help me communicate with them.

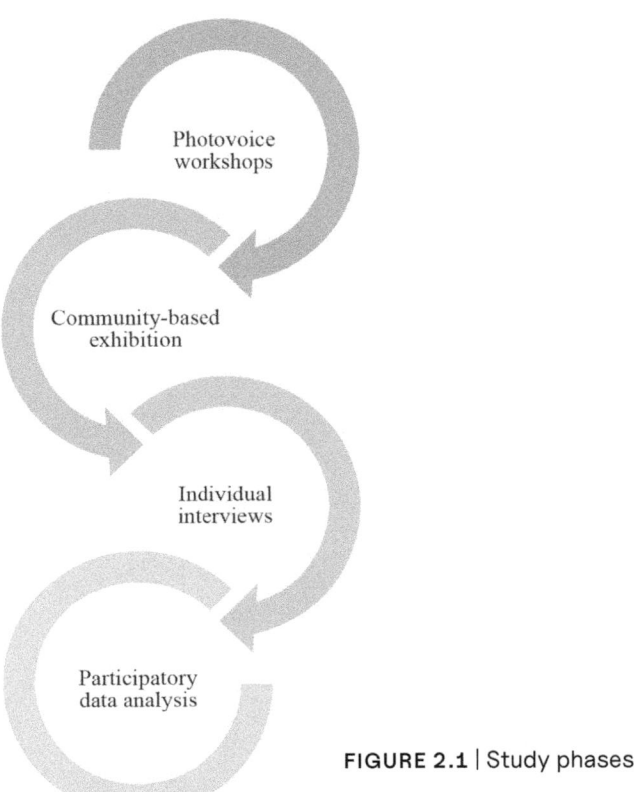

Photovoice
workshops

Community-based
exhibition

Individual
interviews

Participatory
data analysis

**FIGURE 2.1** | Study phases.

## Phase One: Photovoice Workshops

Participants attended five photovoice workshops where I taught them about photovoice methodology and its objectives, the importance of visual ethics, and the project more generally. During the workshops, I provided participants with two prompts: "Take pictures that show your struggles and challenges in Quebec" and "Take pictures that show the solutions for these issues." Before taking the photos, participants worked in small groups to brainstorm what issues, challenges, and solutions they might wish to capture. I gave participants one week to

**FIGURE 2.2** | Group's poster narrative.

(Photograph by author.)

**FIGURE 2.3** | Participant's photograph and caption.

(Photograph by author.)

take photographs in response to the prompts. In the next workshop, I divided participants into three small groups to create poster-narratives (figure 2.2). Poster-narratives consist of a series of photographs accompanied by captions or text that explain the meaning or significance of the images. In an individual activity, participants selected one photo that best represented their challenges as an adolescent refugee or young woman in Quebec and added a one-sentence caption to explain the image's significance (figure 2.3).

## Phase Two: Community-Based Exhibition

I worked with participants to plan a public community exhibition to be held at Maison d'Haiti. My goal for the event was to raise awareness about the resettlement experiences of refugee girls and young women in Quebec and to initiate public conversations about the issues and challenges they faced. I did not initially consider the workshop where we collectively prepared the community exhibition as part of the participatory data analysis process. However, I later recognized that the preparation workshop and the participatory data analysis workshop were closely related because participants went through the visual dataset and worked together to select the photographs and poster-narratives they felt best represented their experiences in Quebec. In addition to selecting works for exhibition, participants engaged in discussions about the intended audience of the exhibition, as demonstrated by the following dialogue:

> P7: We should definitely invite parents because in Haitian community parents always say you have food, you have house, you have school, so you have no problem. If they come they will learn having food and house is not enough for having a good life.
> P5: Yeah, parents should also be educated so learn about teenagers' problems.
> P1: I totally agree! They should learn about our fight.

**P7:** I like the word fight.

**Nesa:** How about the title of our exhibition?

**P1:** I vote for our fight.

**P7:** Un combat pour les adolescents.

Here, participants are highlighting two key points. First, they emphasize the importance of involving parents to broaden their understanding of the challenges faced by teenagers, beyond the basic necessities of food, shelter, and education. Second, they express a strong desire for the exhibition to convey the concept of "fight" or "combat," emphasizing the struggles and issues faced by adolescents, with one participant suggesting the title *Un combat pour les adolescents* (*A fight for adolescents*). By involving the participants in this collective decision-making process, the exhibition was tailored to be accessible and engaging to the targeted audience as well as meaningful and relevant to the participants themselves.

Once participants had agreed on the exhibition title, they shared their reflections on what to include in the curatorial statement. A curatorial statement refers to the printed text that curators typically employ to "interpret, justify, and explain" to the audience what their exhibition is about (Kompatsiaris 2020, 1). Participants created a curatorial statement that highlighted the importance of listening to the voices of adolescent girls and young women, fostering collaboration, addressing social issues, and taking an active role in shaping their experiences to create positive change. Ultimately, the curatorial statement was an important demonstration of the power of art and collective storytelling in amplifying the voices and experiences of adolescent girls and young women in the process of resettlement (figure 2.4).

*Un combat pour les adolescents* aimed to shed light on the experiences of adolescent girls and young women during resettlement in Quebec. It called attention to the roles of parents, educators, researchers, and community members in shaping their experiences and emphasized the potential for collective action and social change. It is important to note that while researchers can encourage participants' attendance and collaboration, participants might not be interested in or available for all

**FIGURE 2.4** | Participants developed the curatorial statement and title together.

(Photograph by author.)

planned activities. For example, even though all participants had been part of planning the exhibition, only three out of nine attended.

## Phase Three: Individual Interviews

I conducted individual interviews with participants where they shared their thoughts and reflections about the photovoice workshops, allowing me to gain deeper insight into their experiences of the research process thus far. The questions were designed to gather information and reflections from participants regarding their workshop experience, migration experiences, reasons for coming to Canada, personal challenges, integration barriers, awareness of rights, and recommendations for supporting adolescent girls and young women. The questions aimed to explore various aspects of the participants' perspectives, experiences, and opinions related to these topics.

### Phase Four: Participatory Data Analysis

Following the interviews, I held a two-hour workshop on participatory data analysis where participants analyzed the photographs and poster-narratives. I decided to only work with the visual data; participants did not have access to interview transcripts. I made this decision for several reasons. First, by prioritizing the photos and poster-narratives, I ensured that participants' attention was focused on the implicit meanings of the visual data they generated. Second, by excluding the interview transcripts, I avoided the risk of losing participants' engagement and involvement, since they found the visual data more compelling. Finally, because most of the interview transcripts revolved around the photos and poster-narratives, by excluding them from the workshop, I gave participants another chance to revisit the photographs they had previously produced and add to their narratives and stories. Overall, this workshop provided participants with an engaging and powerful experience, ensuring their active participation and ownership in the interpretation of the visual data. In the next section, I will detail the specific steps I took to facilitate the participatory data analysis workshop.

## WHAT DOES PARTICIPATORY DATA ANALYSIS *LOOK* LIKE?

### Step One: Getting Started

I showed participants the twenty-seven photos and four poster-narratives through a slideshow (figure 2.5). I began the workshop with a photo that had been taken in one of the photovoice workshops (figure 2.6). I selected this photo of two holding hands as a starting point since it had been widely discussed by participants in the photovoice workshops and it had received the attention of many people during the exhibition. I asked participants to reflect on what they saw in the photo and what message they felt it contained. Participants offered explicit answers such as "hands" but also implicit answers such as "compassion" and "solidarity."

**FIGURE 2.5** | Projecting the photo images.

(Photograph by author.)

Next, I asked the group to respond to the broader question "What does our visual data mean?" To help them become familiar with the concept of participatory data analysis, we discussed how, like verbal and written data, visual data does not speak for itself, so we must speak for it (Darby 2018). Participants then worked in pairs to answer questions about the importance of their involvement in the research process: "Why is it better for this study to have your involvement?" and "How does your involvement change the outcome of the study?" Participants noted that they enjoyed having the opportunity to "speak for themselves" and to "decide what works for them." One of the participants mentioned that by participating in projects such as this, girls may come to believe they are "capable" and prove to others that they are not "a child." While participants' responses varied, they all embraced the idea of having agency and autonomy to influence the outcome of the study.

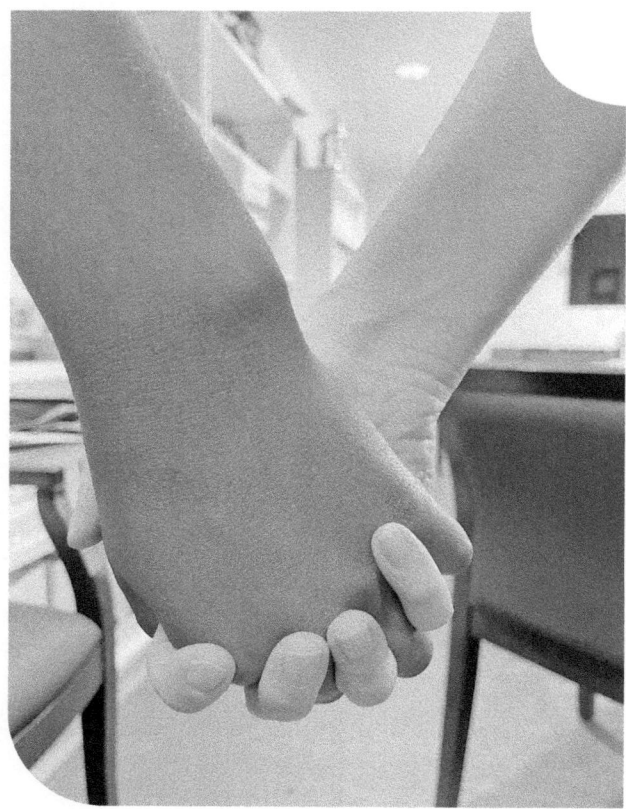

**FIGURE 2.6** | Photograph by participant.
(Used with permission.)

## Step Two: Initial Exploration

According to Liebenberg et al. (2020), analysis should accurately reflect the focus of the research question. For this reason, I encouraged participants to recall the research questions that framed the study: "What issues and challenges do you face daily as a refugee?" and "What solutions do you think can solve these issues and challenges?" I placed participants in small groups and handed everyone a sticky note and coloured markers. Participants observed all the photos and poster-narratives displayed on the slideshow and reflected on the issues and challenges they could see in the visuals. The goal of this step was to allow each participant to get a sense of the data before beginning a systematic process of analysis. After going through the photos, participants spent a few minutes taking brief notes and developing their initial ideas (Liebenberg et al. 2020). Everyone shared their ideas in small groups, and one person from each group volunteered to summarize their discussion for the larger group.

During the initial discussion, participants mainly talked about the impact of discrimination on their daily lives:

> P1: We talked about reaction to Black people. For example, if someone sees someone Black, they think they are street gang or something like that. That's why [the poster] says you cannot judge me before you know me.
>
> P8: We find racism in a lot of photos. This is an important message. Refugee girls experience racism.

In this conversation, participants highlighted the centrality of racism as something they all agreed affects their daily life at school and in society. During these activities, I was present to answer questions and clarify any issues or confusion, but otherwise, I tried to allow the conversations to unfold without much interruption or active facilitation. While I adopted a minimum interruption approach of facilitation that aimed to create a safe space for participants to express their perspectives and experiences, a continuous challenge was how to employ questioning techniques without imposing my own view. As noted by Yeonghwi Ryu (2022), there is a risk that the participants in our group would simply provide answers that they believed the researcher wanted to hear, rather than expressing their authentic perspectives. To counteract this, I employed a strategy of sharing my own experiences that had shaped my knowledge, particularly as an international student in Quebec. At the same time, I openly acknowledged my limited understanding of the girls' unique experiences.

## Step Three: Discussion of Themes

I encouraged participants to return to the photos on the slideshow once more and put similar or seemingly related photos together to organize the data (Brooks and Hesse-Biber 2014). I gave participants time to categorize the photos individually and additional time to discuss the themes that emerged with the larger group. In the previous photovoice and community exhibition preparation workshops, I learned that giving participants more time to complete tasks was beneficial because they were able to notice significant details in the photos and find new insights into their meanings. As one participant noted, when they had enough time, they could "think about the questions many times" and find a "new answer each time."

The purpose of the thematic discussion step was for participants to reach an agreement about the main themes. This was particularly important because it helped to ensure that all participants were on the same page and shared a common understanding of the main themes. Moreover, consensus regarding the main themes made it easier to build a common language and framework for my own analysis and interpretation of the transcripts. However, it is worth mentioning that in cases where participants disagreed with each other or an individual idea dominated the discussion, I gave participants more time and encouraged group consensus.

The main themes that participants identified included financial issues, police brutality, mental health, education, and language issues. It is notable that participants were not only generating themes based on the explicit visual content within the photographs, but also on the social, economic, and political issues that underlie them. For example, participants interpreted a picture of a trash can overflowing with garbage (figure 2.7) as a symbol of mental health issues affecting adolescents. In another example, participants interpreted two pictures of Black people as indicative of the ways police brutality affects the mental and physical health of Black youth.

**FIGURE 2.7** | Photograph by participant.

(Used with permission.)

## Step Four: Reflection

I guided participants through the "So What?" phase of the analysis process by posing three questions: "What can we do with the themes on the board?" "How do these themes relate to larger projects for refugees?" and "Who needs to learn about these issues?" In answering these questions, participants discussed the importance of sharing findings with non-profit organizations such as Maison d'Haiti:

> **P8:** [These organizations] work with immigrants. It would be good if they were aware of their concerns so that they could better support them. And during the consultation tables to be able to make proposals to the government. They can also reassure them, give them moral and psychological support at no cost because many experience a lot of stress throughout their immigration and integration process.

Participants also mentioned that even a simple program can improve the well-being of refugee girls and make them feel less isolated and lonely. In addition, they emphasized the role of government in facilitating refugees' integration and resettlement. Thus, through participatory data analysis, participants were able to reflect upon the issues they had previously recognized and generate solutions to tackle them.

In the final activity, I gave each participant a piece of paper where they could share their final thoughts and answer the following: "What have you learned about yourself or your problems from participating in this research?" I reminded them that they were free to write in any language and could even sketch or draw their thoughts instead of writing (figures 2.8 and 2.9). The statements participants wrote reflected the importance of promoting equality and creating a safe space where individuals could feel comfortable expressing themselves. They also highlighted the need for inclusive spaces that simultaneously value diversity and empower participants to share their thoughts and experiences.

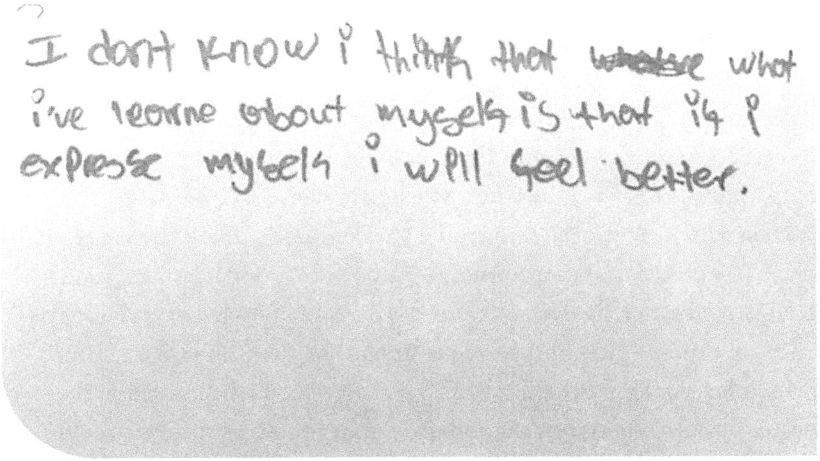

FIGURE 2.8 | Participants wrote their reflections in the last activity.

(Photograph by author.)

FIGURE 2.9 | Participants wrote their reflections in the last activity.

(Photograph by author.)

## DISCUSSION

By employing participatory data analysis in the photovoice project with refugee girls, I saw that this method has several feminist and intersectional implications. First, actively involving participants in data analysis ensures that their voices are heard in every step of the decision-making process. Second, by recognizing that knowledge and expertise go beyond conventional frameworks, participatory data analysis acknowledges and values the unique knowledge and experiences of refugee girls and young women. Third, in line with feminist principles, participatory data analysis can effectively challenge the power dynamic between the researcher and participants (Liebenberg et al. 2020). By actively involving participants in the process of data analysis and interpretation, this approach disrupts traditional hierarchies and empowers individuals who are typically relegated to the role of passive subjects. In this context, challenging power structures means giving participants agency and control over the research process and transforming them from mere subjects to active partners in shaping research outcomes. This empowerment not only amplifies the voices and perspectives of the participants but also leads to a more equitable distribution of power between the researcher and participants, fostering a collaborative and inclusive research environment. Fourth, by examining the unique challenges refugee girls and young women face, I gained a better understanding of how their various identities shape their lives. For example, one participant noted that her ability to access education is limited both because she is expected to fulfill house chores and care for her younger siblings and because her family is experiencing financial hardship. Participatory data analysis thus contributes to more inclusive, equitable, and impactful research outcomes by amplifying the voices of the participants, valuing their knowledge, challenging power dynamics, facilitating intersectional analysis, and promoting empowerment.

The participatory data analysis workshop led to conversations that would not have happened otherwise, resulting in a deeper level of understanding of the issues that refugee girls and young women face after resettlement in Quebec. Without engaging participants in data analysis, the findings of the study would have been solely interpreted by me, but I felt it was critical to centre the voices of refugee girls and young women since one of the main objectives of the study was to highlight *their* needs and concerns. In addition, I brought participants' attention to the solutions that could potentially meet their needs and challenges such as access to education and creating a circle of trust.

One criticism of involving participants in data analysis is the possibility that they will be bored and uninterested (Vaccaro 2023). During the process, I found that participants were genuinely interested in taking part in analysis and interpretation as they kept asking and answering questions and were eager to participate in the discussions. However, because of various life circumstances, it was not always easy to have their full attention and engagement. For instance, one partici- pant mentioned that her mom was pregnant, and she had to go home early to babysit her younger brother and help with the housework. To overcome this challenge, I employed a variety of activities such as individual reflection, group discussion, and large group conversations to encourage their participation.

Working with a group in a participatory way also helped me realize how difficult it can be to record and transcribe overlapping speech, as participants frequently spoke over each other and at the same time. As soon as the workshop ended, I wrote fieldnotes about my observations and experiences, which helped me to clarify the audio recordings. It is also important to note that most of the discus- sions in the participatory data analysis workshop were in French, and the interpreter translated my questions and participants' answers. However, while transcribing the audio recording, I realized that in some cases my interpretation (based on my limited understanding of French) was different from what had been translated. To tackle this issue, I sometimes had to listen to the same sentence a couple of times or have further conversations with my interpreter to better understand what had been said in each context. Therefore, in cases where the interpreter is not available after the project ends the researcher might have to use other translation resources.

## CONCLUSION

There are various ways to conduct participatory data analysis. According to Nind (2011), these approaches can be formal or informal, structured or unstructured, but regardless, participants take an active role in making sense of the data. How can researchers ensure that everyone's voice has been included? Though one of the promises of participatory data analysis is to amplify the voices of otherwise silenced or marginalized populations, some participants may be more reserved and hesitant to share their perspectives. In this study, I attempted to encourage all participants to take part in discussions by focusing on collective rather than individual awareness. As a feminist researcher, I was committed to seeing through the eyes of the girls and young women themselves by prioritizing their voices and experiences rather than relying on my own assumptions and interpretations.

## AUTHOR'S NOTE

I would like to express my gratitude for the generous funding support provided by multiple organizations and institutions. Specifically, I acknowledge the financial support received from Fonds de recherche du Québec-Société et culture, Mitacs, the Interdisciplinary Research Team on Refugee and Asylum Seeker Families, and Jackie Kirk Fieldwork Support of McGill University.

## NOTES

1. Resettlement is the transfer of refugees from one place to another where they might be able to acquire permanent residency (United Nations High Commissioner for Refugees 2020).
2. Wang and Burris (1997) first used photovoice to understand the public health needs of fifty-three adult women in China. The participants used disposable cameras to capture images that reflected their daily lives and health concerns.

3. Thematic analysis is a process of coding and systematizing data to produce detailed descriptions of themes (Braun and Clarke 2006).
4. Later, Braun and Clarke (2021) suggested that researcher's reflexivity is an essential requirement for data analysis and noted that recursive engagement with the dataset can produce a more robust analysis. For this reason, they introduced reflexive thematic analysis to highlight the situated and subjective process of analysis that exists at the intersection of the researcher, the dataset, and the various contexts of interpretation.

## REFERENCES

Banks, James A. 1998. "The Lives and Values of Researchers: Implications for Educating Citizens in a Multicultural Society." *Educational Researcher* 27 (7): 4–17.

Barley, Ruth, and Lisa Russell. 2019. "Participatory Visual Methods: Exploring Young People's Identities, Hopes and Feelings." *Ethnography and Education* 14 (2): 223–241.

Bergold, Jarg, and Stephan Thomas. 2012. "Participatory Research Methods: A Methodological Approach in Motion." *Historical Social Research/Historische Sozialforschung* 4 (142): 191–222.

Braun, Virginia, and Victoria Clarke. 2006. "Using Thematic Analysis in Psychology." *Qualitative Research in Psychology* 3 (2): 77–101.

Braun, Virginia, and Victoria Clarke. 2021. *Thematic Analysis: A Practical Guide*. SAGE.

Brooks, Abigail, and Sharlene N. Hesse-Biber. 2014. "An Invitation to Feminist Research." In *Feminist Research Practice: A Primer, 2nd Edition*, edited by Sharlene N. Hesse-Biber and Patricia L. Leavy. SAGE.

Crenshaw, Kimberlé. 1989. "Demarginalizing the Intersection of Race and Sex: A Black Feminist Critique of Antidiscrimination Doctrine, Feminist Theory and Antiracist Politics." *University of Chicago Legal Forum* 1 (8): 139–167.

Darby, Fionnuala. 2018. "Belonging at ITB: The Use of Photovoice Methodology (PVM) to Investigate Inclusion and Exclusion at ITB Based on Ethnicity and Nationality from a Student Perspective." In *Transforming Our World through Design, Diversity and Education: Proceedings of Universal Design and Higher Education in Transformation Congress 2018*, edited by Gerald Craddock, Cormac Doran, Larry McNutt, and Dónal Rice, 611–623. IOS Press.

Fletcher, Thomas. 2014. "'Does He Look Like a Paki?' An Exploration of 'Whiteness,' Positionality and Reflexivity in Inter-Racial Sports Research." *Qualitative Research in Sport, Exercise and Health* 6 (2): 244–260.

Flicker, Sarah, and Stephanie A. Nixon. 2015. "The DEPICT Model for Participatory Qualitative Health Promotion Research Analysis Piloted in Canada, Zambia and South Africa." *Health Promotion International* 30 (3): 616–624.

Frankenberg, Ruth. 2004. "On Unsteady Ground: Crafting and Engaging in the Critical Study of Whiteness." In *Researching Race and Racism*, edited by Martin Bulmer and John Solomos. Psychology Press.

Freire, Paulo. 1970. *Pedagogy of the Oppressed*. Seabury Press.

Gonick, Marnina. 2003. *Between Femininities: Ambivalence, Identity, and the Education of Girls*. State University of New York Press.

Green, Eric, and Bret Kloos. 2009. "Facilitating Youth Participation in a Context of Forced Migration: A Photovoice Project in Northern Uganda." *Journal of Refugee Studies* 22 (4): 460–482.

Huisman, Kimberly. 2008. "'Does This Mean You're Not Going to Come Visit Me Anymore?' An Inquiry into an Ethics of Reciprocity and Positionality in Feminist Ethnographic Research." *Sociological Inquiry* 78 (3): 372–396.

Kompatsiaris, Panos. 2020. "Curators, Words and Values: The Branding Economies of Curatorial Statements in Art Biennials." *Journal of Cultural Economy* 13 (6): 758–771.

Krause, Kathleen H., Stephanie S. Miedema, Rebecca Woofter, and Kathryn M. Yount. 2017. "Feminist Research with Student Activists: Enhancing Campus Sexual Assault Research." *Family Relations* 66 (1): 211–223.

Liebenberg, Linda, Aliya Jamal, and Janice Ikeda. 2020. "Extending Youth Voices in a Participatory Thematic Analysis Approach." *International Journal of Qualitative Methods* 19: 1–13.

Maguire, Patricia. 1987. *Doing Participatory Research: A Feminist Approach*. University of Massachusetts.

Maison d'Haïti. 2021. "Intégration." https://www.mhaiti.org/web/integration/.

Mandrona, April. 2016. "Ethical Practice and the Study of Girlhood." *Girlhood Studies: An Interdisciplinary Journal* 9 (3): 3–19.

Manohar, Narendar, Pranee Liamputtong, Sameer Bhole, and Amit Arora. 2019. "Researcher Positionality in Cross-Cultural and Sensitive Research." In *Handbook of Research Methods in Health Social Sciences*, edited by Pranee Liamputtong. Springer.

Miled, Neila. 2020. "Can the Displaced Speak? Muslim Refugee Girls Negotiating Identity, Home and Belonging through Photovoice." *Women's Studies International Forum* 81: 1–12.

Mitchell, Claudia. 2015. "Looking at Showing: On the Politics and Pedagogy of Exhibiting in Community-Based Research and Work with Policy Makers." *Educational Research for Social Change* 4 (2): 48–60.

Mitchell, Claudia, Naydene De Lange, and Relebohile Moletsane. 2017. *Participatory Visual Methodologies: Social Change, Community and Policy*. SAGE.

Mitchell, Claudia, and Jacqueline Reid-Walsh, eds. 2008. *Girl Culture: An Encyclopedia*. Greenwood Press.

Mitchell, Claudia, Jacqueline Reid-Walsh, and Jackie Kirk. 2008. "Welcome to This Inaugural Issue of Girlhood Studies: An Interdisciplinary Journal (GHS)." *Girlhood Studies: An Interdisciplinary Journal* 1 (1): vii–xv.

Moletsane, Relebohile, Claudia Mitchell, Ann Smith, and Linda Chisholm. 2008. *Methodologies for Mapping a Southern African Girlhood in the Age of Aids*. Brill.

Morland, Lyn, and Tarima Levine. 2016. "Collaborating with Refugee Resettlement Organizations: Providing a Head Start to Young Refugees." *National Association for the Education of Young Children* 71 (4): 69–75.

Morse, Janice M. 2008. "Confusing Categories and Themes." *Qualitative Health Research* 18 (6): 727–728.

Ngidi, Ndumiso D. 2020. "Being an Adolescent Orphan in the Context of Sexual Violence: A Participatory Visual Methodology Study in and around a Township Secondary School in Kwazulu-Natal, South Africa." PhD diss., University of KwaZulu-Natal.

Nind, Melanie. 2011. "Participatory Data Analysis: A Step Too Far?" *Qualitative Research* 11 (4): 349–363.

Nyariro, Milka. 2021. "'We Have Heard You but We Are Not Changing Anything': Policymakers as Audience to a Photovoice Exhibition on Challenges to School Re-Entry for Young Mothers in Kenya." *Agenda* 35 (1): 94–108.

Rivard, Lysanne. 2015. "Gender, Physical Education, and Sport Bringing Forward Rwandan Girls' Perspectives on Their Lived Experiences of Physical Activity and Sport in Secondary Schools." PhD diss., McGill University.

Rogers, Dehanza. 2022. "Hostile Geographies." *Girlhood Studies: An Interdisciplinary Journal* 15 (1): 24–49.

Ryu, Yeonghwi. 2022. "Demystifying Participatory Analysis with Children: A South Korean Case of Migrant Children's Engagement in Analytic Works in Participatory Research." *International Journal of Qualitative Methods* (21): 1-15.

Sajan Virgi, Zainul, and Claudia Mitchell. 2011. "Picturing Policy in Addressing Water and Sanitation: The Voices of Girls Living in Abject Intergenerational Hardship in Mozambique." *International Education* 40 (2): 40–57.

Samuels, Fiona, Nicola Jones, and Bassam Abu Hamad. 2017. "Psychosocial Support for Adolescent Girls in Post-Conflict Settings: Beyond a Health Systems Approach." *Health Policy and Planning* 32 (5): v40–v51.

Scott, Renee N. 2022. "Taking on the Light: Ontological Black Girlhood in the Twenty-First Century." *Girlhood Studies: An Interdisciplinary Journal* 15 (1): 1–16.

Shariff, Fauzia. 2014. "Establishing Field Relations through Shared Ideology." *Field Methods* 26 (1): 3–20.

Smith-Purviance, Ashley, and Sarah Jackson. 2022. "Toward Black Girl Futures: Rememorying in Black Girlhood Studies." *Girlhood Studies: An Interdisciplinary Journal* 15 (3): 67–83.

Switzer, Sarah, and Sarah Flicker. 2021. "Visualizing DEPICT: A Multistep Model for Participatory Analysis in Photovoice Research for Social Change." *Health Promotion Practice* 22 (2): 50S–65S.

United Nations High Commissioner for Refugees. 2020. "UNHCR, the UN Refugee Agency." https://www.unhcr.org/resettlement.html#:~:text=Resettlement%20is%20 the%20transfer%20of,of%20the%20three%20durable%20solutions.

Vaccaro, Mary-Elizabeth. 2023. "Reflections on 'Doing' Participatory Data Analysis with Women Experiencing Long-Term Homelessness." *Action Research* 21 (3): 332–350.

Vanner, Catherine. 2019. "Toward a Definition of Transnational Girlhood." *Girlhood Studies: An Interdisciplinary Journal* 12 (2): 115–132.

Veale, Angela. 2005. "Creative Methodologies in Participatory Research with Children." In *Researching Children's Experience: Approaches and Methods*, edited by Sheila Greene and Diane Hogan. SAGE.

Wang, Caroline, and Mary A. Burris. 1997. "Photovoice: Concept, Methodology, and Use for Participatory Needs Assessment." *Health Education & Behavior* 24 (3): 369–387.

Wang, Caroline C., Wu K. Yi, Zhan W. Tao, and Kathryn Carovano. 1998. "Photovoice as a Participatory Health Promotion Strategy." *Health Promotion International* 13 (1): 75–86.

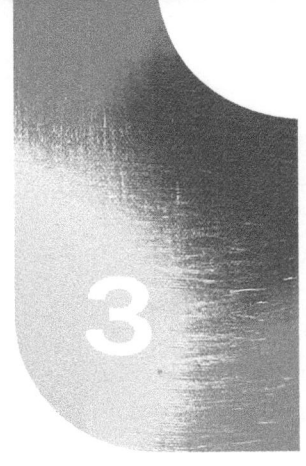

3

GRACE SKAHAN

# SCULPTING POSSIBILITIES FOR FEMINIST PRAXIS

Participatory Data Analysis and Clay-Elicitation
with Young Men Involved in Gender-Based
Violence Prevention

## INTRODUCTION

IN EVE TUCK'S "Suspending Damage: A Letter to Communities"
(2009), she calls for a moratorium on damage-centred research. Tuck,
an Indigenous feminist scholar, is referring to the ways in which
researchers often focus on documenting the pain and suffering of those
experiencing oppression as a means to rectify injustices. Tuck invites
researchers to question themselves about how documenting disenfran-
chised communities' pain actually helps those communities. Perhaps
most saliently, she states that it may not be the research itself that will
shift a community's experience of a particular issue, but that critical
thinking about who is asking the research questions, how the data is
being collected, and *who is doing the analysis* can ensure that research
processes work toward the end goal of bettering social conditions.

Tuck's (2009) generative letter shifted my perspective and my practical understanding of what it means to do research for feminist and social justice purposes. For my master's thesis, on which this chapter is based, I initially planned to work with young women to better understand the sites in and around Montréal high schools where gender-based violence happens. Tuck's invitation to researchers propelled me to think more deeply about how the process of developing research findings—and the findings themselves—might better serve affected communities. With Tuck's invitation in mind, my interest in working with young women metamorphosed into an interest in using participatory methods to work with young men involved in gender-based violence prevention.

If we understand that the solution to ending gender-based violence is partially rooted in men themselves taking on more prevention work (Hendra et al. 2013; Jewkes et al. 2015; Women and Gender Equality 2019; Peacock and Barker 2014), how can participatory research support men in doing this work? By examining the experiences of young men coming together to discuss gender-based violence prevention in the context of participatory data analysis, this chapter explores how positioning participants as active agents in examining and collectively discussing data supports the work of feminist research by providing participants with an opportunity to learn from each other, learn from the research they are analyzing, and imagine new ways forward. I also explore how clay-elicitation as an embodied, tactile, and arts-based method holds feminist potential for research and social change.

My research aimed to better understand what factors lead young men to become interested in gender-based violence prevention, gender equality, and feminism, and to what extent men's pathways to these interests are informed by gender-transformative and intersectional principles (Skahan 2022). In phase one, I carried out one-on-one sessions with each of the six project participants using an arts-based methodological technique called clay-elicitation, combined with semi-structured interview questions. In phase two, I conducted a participatory data analysis session with two of the six research participants. In using participatory methods for my research on and with young men, I aimed to contribute to knowledge on gender-based violence prevention and explore how to engage men in prevention work as part of the research process.

I am a woman in my early thirties who did research on and with men between the ages of eighteen and twenty-four. Being an outsider with regards to gender and age means that some of my research participants may have not felt as comfortable opening up to me as they might have otherwise. It also means that there may be blind spots in this research that would be more obvious to someone who is younger, or a man. I am also an insider to this research in some ways, as most participants in this study were white, university educated, able-bodied, and from middle-class backgrounds. I share many of the same demographic groups as participants, as I am also white, middle-class, able-bodied, and university educated. These demographics are important to consider as they shape the perspective from which I examine the issues explored in this chapter.

Because of the nature of gender-based violence, my lived experience as a woman has made it so that I have unique and, in some ways, insider insights into this subject. I experience the consequences of men not being actively aware of or engaged with gender-related issues. I am doing this work in part because violence has, in varying and multiple ways, affected me and almost every close woman, non-binary, trans, or queer person in my life.

## MEN'S INVOLVEMENT IN GENDER-BASED VIOLENCE PREVENTION

In the 1970s, gender-based violence began to gain prominence as a topic of interest within feminist movements. At the time, and for decades after, the role that men should play in these movements was a topic of debate (Messner et al. 2015). Not everyone within feminist organizations agreed on how and if men should participate in this work. In more recent decades, those involved in feminist initiatives have come to more of a consensus on the importance of men's involvement (hooks

2004; Messerschmidt 2018; Messner et al. 2015). Today, on the national and international stage, Women and Gender Equality Canada and the United Nations Commission on the Status of Women both recognize the need to fully engage men and boys to truly advance gender equality (Women and Gender Equality 2019). Scholars and activists also agree that engaging men and boys in gender-based violence prevention and gender equality movements is foundational to these urgent fights for justice. Such scholars and activists have offered various rationales; for example, while not all men commit violence and although men are also sometimes the victims of patriarchal violence (Peacock and Barker 2014), broader patterns of reported violence in Canada and globally suggest that most violence is perpetrated by men (Burczycka 2019; Casey and Smith 2010; Flood 2010; World Health Organization 2021). Scholars suggest that it is men's ethical responsibility to be interested and involved (Pease 2008) and that "relationships based on equality and mutual respect are far more satisfying than those based on fear and domination" (Peacock and Barker 2014, 582). In bell hooks's book *The Will to Change: Men, Masculinity, and Love* (2004), she argues that sexist violence will not end unless men are part of feminist resistance.

Scholars have identified the link between constructed notions of masculinity and violence as another reason for men to be involved in violence prevention. Harmful ideas of masculinity and gender uphold gendered violence and can affect the health and well-being of people of all genders (Flood 2011; Peacock and Barker 2014). Most visibly, we see extreme demonstrations of masculinity in mass horrors such as gun violence (Willer et al. 2013). Men and boys have a key role in addressing the association between masculinity and violence, because when men are actively engaged in combating problematic gender norms and practices in everyday life, they are actively sculpting new forms of masculinity. Men's involvement has the potential to redefine hegemonic gender norms and relations in which masculinity is defined as superior to femininity (Connell and Messerschmidt 2005; Messerschmidt 2018).

Researchers also examine how men listen more willingly to other men (Flood 2006; Piccigallo et al. 2012). Men's privilege across economic, social, and political spheres uniquely and strategically positions them to challenge problematic gender relations and advance feminist agendas. Nevertheless, appealing to this hierarchy as a reason to get men involved risks reproducing the very hierarchy it hopes to dismantle (Colpitts 2020; Walsh 2015). While men can be powerful allies in the struggle against gender-based violence, using this ascribed superior position as a pedestal from which they can act risks reproducing patriarchal ideas instead of tearing them down. Leveraging men's power for advancing gender-based violence prevention has potential, for men tend to hold disproportionate influence within structures and systems that maintain gender-based violence. Men's engagement in violence prevention must recognize the systemic, constructed, and structural nature of gender-based violence (Colpitts 2020), avoid reinscribing men in a dominant position, and be informed by those most affected by this violence.

Arguably, when men are involved and interested in gender-based violence prevention, it removes some of the work from women's shoulders. This is noteworthy because it is often women who end up sensitizing men close to them to gender-based violence (Casey and Smith 2010; Messner et al. 2015; Peretz 2017; Piccigallo et al. 2012; Skahan 2022). When women are the primary people who raise awareness of gender-based violence, this may place the burden of educating men on the women who have experienced such violence. Researchers have also found that not many men are trained in how to thoughtfully respond to disclosures, which can further harm survivors of violence (Piccigallo et al. 2012). The responsibility of women to educate men to reduce gender- and sexual-based violence is mirrored in the societal burden placed on women to avoid risk and assault in the first place, propping up the idea that gender-based violence is a women's problem and potentially further absolving men of the responsibility to act.

## PARTICIPATORY RESEARCH AS FEMINIST PRAXIS

Praxis is a critical dimension of feminist research and social change. Liz Stanley (2013) defines feminist praxis in the context of research as "a continuing shared commitment to a political position in which 'knowledge' is not simply defined as 'knowledge *what*' but also as 'knowledge *for*'" (15, emphasis original). Stanley (2013) conceives of feminist praxis not as one specific feminist position or method, but rather as a research labour process that is committed to creating knowledge for changing social conditions. She uses the word "praxis" to reject theory/research binary thinking and to emphasize that "a focus on feminist research labour processes shifts the epistemological basis of the completed research" (Stanley 2013, 14). In other words, focusing on how we do research will impact what will come of it. One such feminist research praxis can be found in participatory research.

Participatory research centres notions of control, power, and equity throughout research processes (Cornwall and Jewkes 1995). Participatory research methods and feminist praxis have significant overlapping values: a concern for social inequalities and a desire to redress these (Lykes and Hershberg 2012); a commitment to building equitable knowledge about the complexities of intersectional realities and identities (Fine and Torre 2019); and a focus on changing the world and not only studying it (Stanley 2013). Transformative feminist praxis, much like participatory research, emphasizes the importance of examining the processes of "doing" (Lykes and Hershberg 2012).

If we consider that praxis is not only studying issues but also taking action to remedy them, then participatory data analysis's processes of collaboratively discussing and analyzing ideas and their feminist potential, implications, and tensions are particularly resonant. In a small-scale project such as mine, engaging in participatory data analysis can provide a venue for participants to study issues while also taking action to make change.

## Situating Clay-Elicitation within Feminist Research Methods

Participatory visual research methods have the potential to allow for making meaning in ways that align with feminist values of social change (Finley 2008; Keifer-Boyd 2011; Mitchell et al. 2017). In a broad sense, visual methodologies increase participants' voices in research processes and reduce power imbalances, since they intentionally create a space that allows participants to reflect on what they have expressed through a visual medium (Barton 2015; Mitchell et al. 2017). Feminist researchers who use visual methodologies have noted the generative and transformative potential of such methods in feminist research. For example, they have highlighted the ways in which visual methodologies allow participants and researchers to act collaboratively within research projects (Lykes and Crosby 2015; Wang and Burris 1997), use creative means to construct alternative and subversive ways of knowing, and creatively express things which are either complicated or painful to verbalize (Lykes and Crosby 2015). Visual methodologies can also help those who do not read or write in the same or in dominant languages to express themselves and uncover knowledge that is less obvious to those who are not "insiders" (Wang and Burris 1995). Elicitation techniques (Harper 2002), included under the umbrella of visual methodologies, can be useful in discussing sensitive topics because these techniques move the attention of the interview to an external object and can help reduce and/or make evident power imbalances between the researcher and the researched (Barton 2015; Dumangane Jr. 2022).

In this study I used clay-elicitation to gather data. I gave participants a block of clay and asked them to make something in response to a prompt, followed by interview questions. My choice to use clay arose from my personal experiences and reflect how I understand meaningful knowledge to be created. Clay-elicitation is a method I feel connected to; I am a ceramicist and have processed various difficult experiences through art therapy using clay as a medium. Clay easily takes on new yet familiar shapes in my hands that reflect the simple yet deeply meaningful everyday components of my life. The malleability and adaptability of clay as a potential therapeutic and tactile means of processing experiences and emotions offers a powerful avenue for creating knowledge.

Arts-based research methods are rooted in the tradition of art therapy (Coemans et al., 2015). Miche Fabre Lewin (1997), a researcher and artist, discusses how the embodied essence of art therapy allows women to recreate their own environments. By extension, this embodied process can empower them to take back control of their bodies:

It is this interactive relationship with the materials and process of making objects, as well as the image's capacity for making visible the invisible which has far-reaching implications for psychological and embodied liberation. Art therapy, with its process of mark-making and modelling, and in its creation of visible, material images and objects offers a powerful medium for reconnecting ourselves with physical objects and consequently with our own bodies. (Fabre Lewin 1997, 121)

Making visible that which is painful or difficult to express holds transformative potential. Hearing about men's stories of wanting to break free from patriarchal and restrictive norms around gender and masculinity and watching them use clay to create material representations of where, when, or how they first began to question notions of gender and power, suggests that the embodied feminist potential of clay as a research method extends beyond women.

Nehama Grenimann and Michal Bat Or (2021) used clay in their research on understanding behaviours in the context of Israeli fathers' mental states, while Tricia Ong et al. (2020) used clay in their research on the reproductive health knowledge of women in Nepal who had been trafficked. These scholars discuss how clay effectively moves participants to tap into memories and to represent visually what can be difficult to express in words. Art therapy researchers have noted this benefit as well and add that clay can help patients express complicated emotions because of its visual and tactile dimensions. The direct contact of clay with one's hands can allow for expression that is not mediated or filtered through the mind and provides a rich avenue for deepening an understanding of our own unconscious or of thoughts that are difficult to articulate (Nan and Ho 2017; Sholt and Gavron 2011).

The benefits of various art therapy processes for connecting to one's feelings may have unique benefits for men, given that they are often socialized to have less of a vocabulary for and ability to express emotions (American Psychological Association, Boys and Men Guidelines Group 2018; Vick 2007). Randy Vick (2007), an art therapist, found through clinical observation that men often need time to process emotions, and suggests that art therapy can provide this time through the act of creation. The tactile, embodied nature of clay-elicitation may provide an outlet for men to express themselves in the context of research and holds rich potential for generating knowledge on a deeply complex and emotional topic like gender-based violence.

## THE STUDY

The project involved six participants between the ages of eighteen and twenty-four. They were either in university or had recently graduated. Five identified with the term "young man" and one identified as trans masculine. I recruited participants through McGill University's Institute for Gender, Sexuality and Feminist Studies' listserv and by word of mouth. Data was collected between March and June 2022.

The first phase of my data collection involved one-on-one interviews combined with clay-elicitation, which lasted approximately one hour. I began by asking participants to mold something out of clay in response to the prompts, "How did you first develop an interest in gender equality/feminism/gender-based violence prevention?" and "What life experiences brought you to be interested in this subject (education, family, friends, pop culture...)?" I left them by themselves for fifteen minutes while they worked with the clay. When I returned, I asked participants to explain what they had made, and to reflect on the process and significance of their creation. Finally, I asked participants to create a caption or a title for their work. I then asked further interview questions around their interest in gender-based violence prevention, gender equality, and feminism more broadly.

Four of the six participants created one or more small human figurines which, they explained, represented the diverse social settings they found themselves in, the people they were surrounded by, and the impacts these individuals had on their developing interest in gender issues. The other two creations were a garden, which the participant explained represented a non-gendered space in their family, and a house, which the participant explained represented the impact his family had on him growing up. At the end of each one-on-one session, I photographed the clay creations.

After the clay-elicitation sessions and before the participatory data analysis session, I completed an initial analysis of the data using theoretical thematic analysis (Braun and Clarke 2006). In theoretical thematic analysis, the prevalence of a pattern does not necessarily make it more important or valid, nor is there a minimum number of times that an observation or pattern must be present for it to be considered a theme. The researcher has agency in deciding how the coding process is done, but it is important to maintain consistency in the coding method (Braun and Clarke 2006). To develop themes, I examined the data for observations and patterns that helped reveal something about my research questions. I also looked for latent themes (Braun and Clarke 2006), meaning that I was not simply looking at what my participants were explicitly saying, or the associated surface meanings, but also how the data related to wider structures that had previously been theorized.

During the coding process and the thematic analysis of the clay-elicitation interview sessions, I looked at the photographs of participants' clay creations as a reference, but I prioritized analyzing the ways participants had described what they had made. This was an intentional choice I made to maximize my participants' voices.

## PLANNING THE PARTICIPATORY DATA ANALYSIS SESSION

I conducted the participatory data analysis portion of my research approximately three months after the clay-elicitation sessions. The analysis involved several stages. In the first stage, I produced excerpts from the clay-elicitation sessions transcripts, redacting any personally identifiable information. I extracted the excerpts that I thought were most relevant to my research questions, as it would not have been possible to ask participants to read through interview transcripts in their entirety, given the limited amount of time that we had together.

I invited all six of the participants to come together for the participatory data analysis session, however, only two of my participants, Seth and John (these are pseudonyms), were able to join me. Seth and John collectively looked at the interview and clay-elicitation data during this session. Although this session was intended to regroup all six of the initial research participants to enhance their voices in the research process and to provide an opportunity for them to discuss the issues at hand, some participants could not join because of conflicting schedules and commitments. If this were a larger scale research project, the scheduling issues may have been more easily mitigated given a presumably longer time span for project completion. It is also possible that despite my intention to regroup all participants, they were simply not interested in participating further in the research. This possibility is a tension inherent to participatory data analysis and participatory research more broadly. Though I had hoped that participants would find the process interesting beyond the small remuneration they were offered, the project remained my own and was not necessarily a priority for those involved, nor was returning to analyze the data necessarily an appealing invitation.

## STEPS FOR PARTICIPATORY DATA ANALYSIS

When Seth and John arrived at the participatory data analysis session, they introduced themselves to each other and I invited them to help themselves to the light refreshments I had brought. I then moved through several steps in the analysis process:

1.  I went through a short presentation I had prepared, which included my research objectives and questions as well as a brief overview of my literature review on men's pathways to gender-based violence prevention.
2.  I provided Seth and John with printed photos of the creations that each person had made and a redacted set of transcript excerpts. I indicated the creators' pseudonyms on the photos,

so that participants could connect the transcripts to the photos, should they choose to do so. I showed participants photos of the clay creations because while I did keep the clay creations, many of them cracked or broke when they dried and no longer resembled their original shape. In this sense, photographs represented a truer version of what participants had made.

3.  I gave Seth and John time to read through the transcripts. I asked them to individually identify words or phrases that were significant to the research questions and I encouraged them to highlight sections of the text and/or take notes using markers.

4.  I asked Seth and John to share their initial reactions to the data and the words, phrases, ideas, and themes that they had identified as salient across the transcripts and photos of clay creations.

5.  I shared my preliminary interpretation of the findings, and I asked for their feedback and insights on my analysis.

6.  I closed the session by asking Seth and John to share any thoughts or feelings they had about the entire process.

I recorded and transcribed both phases of the study.

## FINDINGS RELATED TO PARTICIPATORY DATA ANALYSIS

I considered the participatory data analysis session as both a chance to collectively analyze the data but also as another opportunity for data collection, producing an additional set of transcripts. Collectively, Seth and John were able to offer further thoughts on the findings by building on what they observed in the first set of transcripts and photos. During this session, Seth and John identified similar themes to the ones that I had initially identified, helping to confirm my preliminary analysis. They had the chance to explain certain concepts to each other in more depth and to offer answers to each other's questions. In reading through the data and looking at photos of the clay creations, they picked up on wider patterns that were either present or missing across the data and were able to connect the data to their own experiences. Examining the lives of individuals provided John, Seth, and myself some insight into how people's day-to-day lives are shaped by systems that either contribute to or challenge structural violence.

## Participatory Data Analysis as a Forum for Learning

Bringing men together in the context of this research project allowed them to discuss critical issues related to gender-based violence amongst themselves and to gain a deeper understanding of the concept's complexity. At several moments during the participatory data analysis, Seth elaborated on certain ideas in response to comments from John. Seth was six years older than John and displayed a nuanced understanding of issues related to gender-based violence.

At one point, Seth expressed surprise that there was very little discussion of consent in participants' transcripts or clay creations. John commented that perhaps it was because if a person is interested in feminism, they have already "checked the consent box." Seth then brought up a crucial point: "I think the point that you made about guys who are already interested in these things—in their head they've already checked that box, I think that's very true, I think it's also true that a lot of guys in their head check that box, but in real life may not necessarily." John replied: "Yeah for sure. I would hope that if feminism is truly something they care about and like they live it correctly even though I don't necessarily believe there is a correct way to live it then that way the box is already checked, then again I guess that's odd to say."

Seth helped John to consider that unequal, problematic, and violent relations can be reproduced anywhere, by anyone; even by those interested or invested in promoting social change. Just because someone is interested in gender-based violence prevention, it does not automatically mean that they have a comprehensive and working understanding of consent.

At another point during the session, John was reflecting on the transcripts and commented that he expected research participants to be more surprised at the lack of men interested in gender-based violence prevention and feminism. John grew up in a household with four women and for him, caring about gender issues felt natural. In response to this, Seth said:

> I have a male friend who literally said to me, "I have no interest in developing female friendships," and another who in a joking way, but it was still pretty shocking, he said "women are surplus to demands." No, he said, "I see women as non-entities," or something like that, very jarring language. And 'cause I'm the same [as you], it's easy to get caught up in my bubble and be kind of like, I care about these people, I'm obviously going to care about these issues that affect them, but interactions like that remind me that for some people, they very much do not have those voices in their lives and when they do see or interact with women it's only in a sexual context.

I added that some participants, in explaining their pathways to becoming interested in gender-based violence, had said that even without the impactful people or moments on their journey, they hoped that they would have felt enough basic empathy to care about gender issues and feminism and that it would have come naturally anyway. John responded by saying "Yeah, that makes sense," and then Seth went on to talk about how men are often socialized out of feeling deeply and being empathetic. The participatory data analysis provided a moment of informal peer-to-peer learning for participants on gender-based violence prevention.

## Comparing Experiences and Imagining Ways Forward

In the participatory data analysis session, Seth and John were able to compare their experiences with each other and with the participants who were unable to attend to identify what was "conspicuously absent" (Schwarz 2021) from the dataset. The earlier example of Seth expressing surprise that there was little discussion of consent in the transcripts or clay creations exemplifies how participants gained a wider understanding of how their experience fit into broader patterns of men coming to be interested in gender-related issues.

In seeing their own stories reflected in others' stories, participants were able to question wider societal structures and deepen their own understanding of their personal experiences. Seth saw similarities in an anecdote from one participant who talked about being "spoon fed" harmful ideas related to gender by people he admired on the internet in his early teen years. In reflecting on the similarities between his experiences and that of another participant, he noted that that period coincided with "all the Hillary backlash, locker room talk, Access Hollywood tapes" and Trump's electoral campaign. He said:

> It's possible too that conservatives, social conservatives, Republicans, needed language in order to defend a candidate and celebrities that they liked and so that language started trickling down into everybody's everyday lives, and so people who didn't previously know how to articulate these more conservative opinions were suddenly being delivered these talking points.

In looking through the data, Seth connected his own experiences and that of others with the wider socio-political context of the period that he was talking about.

At one point, John noted that like him, many participants spoke of influential women in their lives who impacted their interest in gender issues. He said, "Everyone's roots of feminism came from women... which I think is a bit sad, that the concept of feminism has to come from a woman." Although he did not articulate exactly why, John recognized this as being problematic and representing something that merited further consideration. Seth also commented on the impact of family relationships on men's pathways, which was evident in the clay creations. Four out of the six creations were directly related to home life: a garden, a house, a participant's sister, and a participant surrounded by women in his life. Later in the conversation, John contemplated how one teaches the relevance of issues relating to gender when a person has not experienced something "really major" to make them realize their ethical obligation to live in ways that align with feminist values.

Following that, Seth commented on the lack of education around emotional literacy, and John responded with "preach on that." Seth then noted, "so many people are walking around without any of these emotional skills, communication skills, all of these things that are so important and necessary to building support for these matters." This led Seth and John to talk about important directions for the future of gender-related work. Seth said: "If it's moving beyond women, I'm honestly not gonna expect a lot of men to take up this mantle and fight this fight so I think it might be the institutions, and we've seen that, Tim talked about it, and someone else talked about feminist lit class they had taken." Tim (also a pseudonym) was one of the participants in this study. After looking across the data, Seth noted that institutional action represented perhaps the most important avenue for widening and deepening men's involvement in gender-related causes.

## DISCUSSION

Men explaining concepts related to gender-based violence to each other and noticing patterns among their relationships to questions of gender hold important implications for working toward a more just future. When men engage in discussions and reflections on these topics, they take on work that is otherwise done by women or not done at all. Engaging in these discussions offers men the chance to learn more about these subjects and to map ways forward through positive peer-to-peer influence.

## Men Learning From Each Other

Doing participatory data analysis in the context of this study gave participants a deeper understanding of issues around gender-based violence and the need for men's involvement. In reading through the transcripts, participants were able to identify patterns among respondents, and our discussions revealed unanswered questions and areas of contention. For example, Seth helped John understand that being interested in gender-based violence prevention or feminism does not mean that one has a practical and working understanding of consent. Recognizing this is vital for anyone interested in gender-based violence. At another point, Seth provided concrete examples from his life, which seemed to expand John's understanding of how some men express little or no care about gender issues and can be complicit in perpetuating harmful ideas around gender. These examples suggest that participatory data analysis can potentially serve as an informal forum for men to learn from each other and to gain a better understanding of where and how other men situate themselves in relation to concepts of feminism and gender.

## Men Mapping Ways Forward

Discussing gender-based violence in a group setting can help men work through difficult questions related to gender-based violence. During the participatory data analysis sessions, participants were able to reframe their own experiences within a wider context. Seth and John wondered about how best to teach gender-based violence prevention, the role of women close to them in teaching it, and the role of institutions in providing this education. Participants also pointed to things they perceived to be missing from this research, such as explicit mentions of consent. Through discussion, they thought about and problematized men's pathways to becoming interested in these issues, and they considered sustainable ways forward, such as not relying on women to do this work and the need for socio-emotional literacy education. The participatory data analysis session supported men in doing gender-based violence prevention work and provided a space for feminist praxis as men contributed to building knowledge not just for the sake of knowing, but for change (Stanley 2013).

## CONCLUSION AND IMPLICATIONS

This research was limited in the extent to which it was participatory due to time constraints and the small scale of a master's research project. Participatory data analysis provided a way to centre participants' voices and to accurately represent what they were saying. However, due to the small amount of time I had with my research participants, the depth to which they could analyze the data and extract corresponding themes was limited. The transcripts they looked through were redacted and extracted by me in advance, so participants did not get a full contextual understanding. Furthermore, only two out of the original six participants were able to participate. Under other circumstances, I would have tried to engage my participants for a longer session, or over a period of several weeks, but due to the scope and size of this project, we only gathered for a single session.

Nevertheless, the participatory data analysis session yielded some important lessons. Returning to Tuck's (2009) invitation, participatory data analysis may offer one avenue for doing research for social justice and feminist purposes that is useful to affected communities. This method of analysis is often hailed for democratizing research and centring participants' voices (Liebenberg et al. 2020; Salmon 2007). This is true and it is part of what makes this method valuable, appropriate for feminist research, and useful. However, in the case of this study, it is important to highlight the praxis dimension of participatory data analysis and its implications for research on allyship development. Seth and John's involvement—learning more about gender-based violence from each other and contributing to findings in this research—constitutes feminist praxis. The tactile, embodied nature of clay-elicitation in phase one also offered a way for participants to begin to sculpt a better future for themselves and others, both literally and figuratively.

Pairing clay-elicitation and participatory data analysis creates avenues for men to get involved in gender-based violence prevention while simultaneously troubling issues of gender-based violence, prevention, and intervention. When participants are active agents in examining and collectively discussing data, they can further anti-violence goals by relieving the burden on women to do this work, deepening men's knowledge, and collectively continuing to imagine and work toward change.

## REFERENCES

American Psychological Association, Boys and Men Guidelines Group. 2018. "APA Guidelines for Psychological Practice with Boys and Men." http://www.apa.org/about/policy/psychological-practice-boys-men-guidelines.pdf.

Barton, Keith C. 2015. "Elicitation Techniques: Getting People to Talk About Ideas They Don't Usually Talk About." *Theory and Research in Social Education* 43 (2): 179–205.

Braun, Virginia, and Victoria Clarke. 2006. "Using Thematic Analysis in Psychology." *Qualitative Research in Psychology* 3 (2): 77–101.

Burczycka, Marta. 2019. "Section 2: Police-Reported Intimate Partner Violence in Canada, 2018." https://www150.statcan.gc.ca/n1/pub/85-002-x/2019001/article/00018/02-eng.htm.

Casey, Erin, and Tyler Smith. 2010. "'How Can I Not?' Men's Pathways to Involvement in Anti-Violence against Women Work." *Violence against Women* 16 (8): 953–973.

Coemans, Sara, Qingchun Wang, Joyce Leysen, and Karin Hannes. 2015. "The Use of Arts-Based Methods in Community-Based Research with Vulnerable Populations: Protocol for a Scoping Review." *International Journal of Educational Research* 71: 33–39.

Colpitts, Emily. 2020. "Men, Masculinities, and Responses to Rape." In *Rape Culture 101: Programming Change*, edited by Geraldine Cannon Becker and Angel Dionne. Demeter Press.

Connell, R.W., and James W. Messerschmidt. 2005. "Hegemonic Masculinity: Rethinking the Concept." *Gender and Society* 19 (6): 829–859.

Cornwall, Andrea, and Rachel Jewkes. 1995. "What Is Participatory Research?" *Social Science & Medicine* 41 (12): 1667–1676.

Dumangane Jr., Constantino. 2022. "Cufflinks, Photos and YouTube: The Benefits of Third Object Prompts When Researching Race and Discrimination in Elite Higher Education." *Qualitative Research* 22 (1): 3–23.

Fabre Lewin, Miche. 1997. "Liberation and the Art of Embodiment." In *Feminist Approaches to Art Therapy*, edited by Susan Hogan. Routledge.

Fine, Michelle, and María Elena Torre. 2019. "Critical Participatory Action Research: A Feminist Project for Validity and Solidarity." *Psychology of Women Quarterly* 43 (4): 433–444.

Finley, Susan. 2007. "Arts-Based Research." In *Handbook of the Arts in Qualitative Research: Perspectives, Methodologies, Examples, and Issues,* edited by J. Gary Knowles and Ardra L. Cole. SAGE.

Flood, Michael. 2006. "Changing Men: Best Practice in Sexual Violence Education." *Women against Violence: An Australian Feminist Journal* 18: 26–36.

Flood, Michael. 2010. "Where Men Stand: Men's Roles in Ending Violence against Women." http://www.ncdsv.org/images/WR_WhereMenStandMen'sRoles InEndingVAW_Long_2010.pdf.

Flood, Michael. 2011. "Building Men's Commitment to Ending Sexual Violence against Women." *Feminism and Psychology* 21 (2): 262–267.

Grenimann Bauch, Nehama, and Michal Bat Or. 2021. "Exploring Paternal Mentalization among Fathers of Toddlers through a Clay-Sculpting Task." *Frontiers in Psychology* 12: 1–14.

Hanes, Michael J. 2007. "'Face-to-Face' with Addiction: The Spontaneous Production of Self-Portraits in Art Therapy." *Art Therapy* 24 (1): 33–36.

Harper, Douglas. 2002. "Talking about Pictures: A Case for Photo Elicitation." *Visual Studies* 17 (1): 13–26.

Hendra, John, Ingrid FitzGerald, and Dan Seymour. 2013. "Towards a New Transformative Development Agenda: The Role of Men and Boys in Achieving Gender Equality." *Journal of International Affairs* 67 (1): 105–122.

hooks, bell. 2004. *The Will to Change: Men, Masculinity, and Love.* Beyond Words/Atria Books.

Jewkes, Rachel, Michael Flood, and James Lang. 2015. "From Work with Men and Boys to Changes of Social Norms and Reduction of Inequities in Gender Relations: A Conceptual Shift in Prevention of Violence against Women and Girls." *The Lancet* 385 (9977): 1580–1589.

Keifer-Boyd, Karen. 2011. "Arts-Based Research as Social Justice Activism: Insight, Inquiry, Imagination, Embodiment, Relationality." *International Review of Qualitative Research* 4 (1): 3–19.

Liebenberg, Linda, Aliya Jamal, and Janice Ikeda. 2020. "Extending Youth Voices in a Participatory Thematic Analysis Approach." *International Journal of Qualitative Methods* 19: 1–13.

Lykes, M. Brinton, and Alison Crosby. 2015. "Participatory Action Research as a Resource for Community Regeneration in Post-Conflict Contexts." In *Methodologies in Peace Psychology,* edited by Diane Bretherton and Siew Fang Law. Springer.

Lykes, M. Brinton, and Rachel M. Hershberg. 2012. "Participatory Action Research and Feminisms: Social Inequalities and Transformative Praxis." In *Handbook of Feminist Research: Theory and Praxis, 2nd Edition,* edited by Sharlene N. Hesse-Biber. SAGE.

Messerschmidt, James W. 2018. *Hegemonic Masculinity: Formulation, Reformulation, and Amplification.* Rowman & Littlefield.

Messner, Michael A., Max A. Greenberg, and Tal Peretz. 2015. *Some Men: Feminist Allies in the Movement to End Violence against Women.* Oxford University Press.

Mitchell, Claudia, Naydene De Lange, and Relebohile Moletsane. 2017. *Participatory Visual Methodologies: Social Change, Community and Policy.* SAGE.

Nan, Joshua K.M., and Rainbow T.H. Ho. 2017. "Effects of Clay Art Therapy on Adults Outpatients with Major Depressive Disorder: A Randomized Controlled Trial." *Journal of Affective Disorders* 217: 237–245.

Ong, Tricia, David Mellor, and Sabrina Chettri. 2020. "Clay as a Medium in Three-Dimensional Body Mapping." *Forum Qualitative Sozialforschung/Forum Qualitative Social Research* 21 (2): 1–28.

Peacock, Dean, Gary Barker, and Jeff Hearn. 2014. "Working with Men and Boys to Prevent Gender-Based Violence: Principles, Lessons Learned, and Ways Forward." *Men and Masculinities* 17 (5): 578–599.

Pease, Bob. 2008. "Engaging Men in Men's Violence Prevention: Exploring the Tensions, Dilemmas and Possibilities." *Australian Domestic and Family Violence Clearinghouse* 17: 1–20.

Peretz, Tal. 2017. "Engaging Diverse Men: An Intersectional Analysis of Men's Pathways to Antiviolence Activism." *Gender & Society* 31 (4): 526–548.

Piccigallo, Jacqueline R., Terry G. Lilley, and Susan L. Miller. 2012. "'It's Cool to Care about Sexual Violence': Men's Experiences with Sexual Assault Prevention." *Men and Masculinities* 15 (5): 507–525.

Pollack, William. 1998. *Real Boys: Rescuing our Sons from the Myths of Boyhood*. Holt.

Salmon, Amy. 2007. "Walking the Talk: How Participatory Interview Methods Can Democratize Research." *Qualitative Health Research* 17 (7): 982–993.

Schwarz, Kaylan C. 2021. "'Gazing' and 'Performing': Travel Photography and Online Self-Presentation." *Tourist Studies* 21 (2): 260–277.

Sholt, Michal, and Tami Gavron. 2006. "Therapeutic Qualities of Clay-Work in Art Therapy and Psychotherapy: A Review." *Art Therapy* 23 (2): 66–72.

Skahan, Grace. 2022. "Using Clay-Elicitation to Explore Men's Pathways to Gender-Based Violence Prevention." Master's thesis, McGill University.

Stanley, Liz, ed. 2013. *Feminist Praxis: Research, Theory and Epistemology in Feminist Sociology*. Routledge.

Trombetta, Robert. 2007. "Art Therapy, Men and the Expressivity Gap." *Art Therapy* 24 (1): 29–32.

Tuck, Eve. 2009. "Suspending Damage: A Letter to Communities." *Harvard Educational Review* 79 (3): 409–427.

Vick, Randy M. 2007. "The Boy Is Father to the Man: Introduction to the Special Issue on Men in Art Therapy." *Art Therapy* 24 (1): 2–3.

Walsh, Shannon. 2015. "Addressing Sexual Violence and Rape Culture: Issues and Interventions Targeting Boys and Men." *Agenda* 29 (3): 134–141.

Wang, Caroline, and Mary Ann Burris. 1997. "Photovoice: Concept, Methodology, and Use for Participatory Needs Assessment." *Health Education & Behavior* 24 (3): 369–387.

Willer, Robb, Christabel L. Rogalin, Bridget Conlon, and Michael T. Wojnowicz. 2013. "Overdoing Gender: A Test of the Masculine Overcompensation Thesis." *American Journal of Sociology* 118 (4): 980–1022.

Women and Gender Equality Canada. 2019. "Calling Men and Boys In: What We Heard: Report from the Roundtables on Engaging Men and Boys to Advance Gender Equality." https://women-gender-equality.canada.ca/en/consultations/Men_Boys.pdf.

World Health Organization. 2021. "Violence against Women." https://www.who.int/news-room/fact-sheets/detail/violence-against-women.

MILKA NYARIRO

# MULTI-PARTICIPATORY
# DATA ANALYSIS

A Feminist Approach for Working
with Transient Populations

## INTRODUCTION

IN THIS CHAPTER, I discuss how I navigated the process of participatory data analysis with three different sets of participants. The aim of
this study was to explore barriers to school continuation and re-entry
for pregnant adolescents and young mothers. Evidence shows that
despite countries in sub-Saharan Africa adopting school re-entry
policies to mitigate school dropout among pregnant adolescents and
young mothers, most remain out of school after pregnancy (Onyango et
al. 2015). I conducted the research in Korogocho in two phases between
2017 and 2019. Korogocho is the second-largest slum in Kenya after
Kibera, twelve kilometres from Nairobi's central business district
area. According to Chi-Chi Undie et al. (2009), a typical living unit
in Korogocho is a ten-by-ten single room made with timber and mud
walls and waste material from tin cans used as roofing. Korogocho

is characterized by high rates of unemployment, insecurity, physical, sexual, and domestic violence, and teenage pregnancy; poor housing and infrastructure; and the absence of essential services such as schools, health facilities, childcare, and clean water (African Population and Health Research Center 2002a, 2002b; Emina et al. 2011; Undie et al. 2009).

I recruited three cohorts of forty pregnant adolescents and young mothers throughout the two phases of the study—fifteen in phase one (cohort one) and twenty-five in phase two (fifteen in cohort two and ten in cohort three). I travelled to Kenya for phase one of the study in September 2017 and conducted a photovoice study with cohort one. In this phase, the fifteen participants produced over one hundred photographs from the photovoice study, which I used to curate the photovoice exhibition for phase two. I travelled back to Kenya for phase two of the study in September 2019, where I recruited two additional cohorts of pregnant girls and young mothers who participated in the participatory data analysis. These additional cohorts led to the methodological invention of multi-participatory data analysis, which is the main contribution of this chapter. The two cohorts of young mothers in phase two continued the participatory data analysis started by cohort one in phase one of this study. They also conducted separate photovoice studies, which are not included in the participatory data analysis of this chapter.

I did not *plan* to recruit a second and third cohort of participants—the need for this pivot emerged as a methodological necessity when I returned to the field site and could not reach the individuals who had participated in the first phase. While participatory methodologies such as photovoice often assume that engagement with the same participants will span across all research phases, this is not always possible—especially when doing research with highly transient populations. Here, I offer my reflections on working with transient populations in the hopes that other researchers may learn from my approach to participatory data analysis. Across all three cohorts of participants, I aimed for continuity while also inviting new and emergent perspectives.

## LOCATING PARTICIPATORY RESEARCH
## AS A FEMINIST METHODOLOGY

Over the past two decades, arts-based participatory and visual methodologies have gained popularity with researchers working with vulnerable groups such as children, girls, and young women (De Lange et al. 2015; MacEntee 2015; Rivard 2016; Rivard and Mitchell 2013). Michael Gallagher (2008) defines participatory methods "as a diverse set of techniques bound together by a common concern for actively involving research subjects in the construction of data" (139). In practice, participants may have a role in setting the research agenda, taking part in data collection and analysis, and making decisions about the use and outcomes of the study (Brown 2022). When engaging with participatory methodologies, participants actively help to construct the research rather than being "objects" of study.

Arts-based participatory and visual methodologies include activities such as cellphilms (Burkholder 2018; MacEntee 2015; MacEntee et al. 2016), collages (Gerstenblatt 2013; Hernández-Leo et al. 2006; Kagola and Khau 2020), participatory videos (Lamb 2021; Mahadev 2015), drawing (Literat 2013; Mitchell et al. 2011; Ngidi and Moletsane 2018), and many others. Some scholars like Melvin Delgado (2015) and Sandra Weber (2014) argue that arts-based participatory and visual methodologies are guided by feminist and community-based research principles, which seek to interrogate hierarchical, elitist, and positivist methods. Mary-Elizabeth Vaccaro (2023) adds that "using art in participatory processes offers ways for women to examine their own lived experience, reflect creatively on social action and through doing so, enriches the writing of research and the vivifying of dissemination" (336).

Relebohile Moletsane et al. (2015) are among the researchers who have applied arts-based, participatory, and visual methodologies to research with girls and young women. They demonstrate that these methodologies can enable girls and women to take up activist and advocacy roles in their communities to address pressing social issues that affect them, such as gender-based violence (see also De Lange and Mitchell 2016; Moletsane et al. 2008). Although some participatory researchers advocate for involving participants throughout the research cycle from conceptualization to dissemination, such involvement is only sometimes possible. Likewise, not all participatory research includes participatory data analysis.

## POSITIONALITY

I am a woman born in rural western Kenya and I became a young mother in the first year of my undergraduate studies. Despite attaining my educational goals, I had to navigate many challenges in a higher education system that was not structured to accommodate the needs of young mothers. Both my lived experience as a student and young parent and my own mother's commitment to social justice for girls and women through her career as a social worker contributed to my interest in feminist research. Aside from patriarchal norms and values that put girls and women in subordinate positions, those who live in low-resource settings also contend with systemic barriers that minimize their lived experiences. As an academic, I have long conducted research with girls and women who live in low-resource urban settings to explore their health and educational challenges and to highlight the ways in which they navigate barriers in their lives. My lived and professional experiences provide a point of commonality for understanding the experiences of the young mothers who participated in my study and underscore the importance of collaborating with girls and women in analyzing issues that affect them as central to finding sustainable solutions.

Although there are contextual differences between rural and low-resource urban settings in Kenya, the two share some commonalities: both have low rates of enrolment and educational attainment for girls and higher rates of unplanned teenage pregnancies compared to the general Kenyan population. In Kenya, as in other developing country contexts, low-resource urban spaces are not integrated into national planning and often need more adequate public services, amenities, and infrastructure (Undie et al. 2009).

## THEORETICAL CONCEPTUALIZATIONS: BLACK AFRICAN GIRLHOOD STUDIES

Girlhood studies draws from perspectives in women's studies, feminist studies, sexuality studies, and childhood and youth studies, all of which take a rights-based approach to participants' voice and agency (Alanen 2005; Cieslik and Simpson 2013; Mitchell and Reid-Walsh 2008). Girlhood studies emerged as a scholarly domain in the 1990s, partly responding to concerns that women's studies and childhood studies did not adequately address the problems girls face in relation to the intersections of age, gender, sexuality, and race, among other categories (Rivard 2015). Central to girlhood studies is the issue of recovering girls' historically silenced voices and histories (Vanner 2019). To counter the ways that men and other older members of society silence girls' voices and disempower them from decision making about their own lives, feminist scholars strive to do research with, about, and for girls (Caron 2016; Kirk and Garrow 2003; Rivard 2015).

Building on Black girlhood studies (Epstein et al. 2017; Halliday 2019; hooks 1996), Jen Katshunga (2019) argues for a Black *African* girlhood studies approach that centres the voices and experiences of Black African girls and young women on the continent and in the diaspora, arguing that the current discourses of Black girlhood/s are North American and Western centred and exclude African girls in scholarly conversations. I adopt Katshunga's (2019) Black African Girl Approach (BAGA) as a conceptual framework to acknowledge the continued marginalization of African girls' voices, not only in the established girlhood studies literature (Gonick and Gannon 2014; Forman-Brunell 2010; Helgren and Vasconcellos 2010; Mitchell 2016), but also in the developing scholarship on Black girlhood studies (Field et al. 2016; Halliday 2019). I juxtapose BAGA's acknowledgement of the agentic power of Black African girls against development discourses that have historically presented them as submissive, oppressed, lacking agency, and in perpetual need of saving (notably, by white women or girls). The young mothers who participated in my study show that Black African girls have always had agency; they need only the space to speak about the issues that affect them and how they want to be supported. Likewise, Annah Kamusiime's (2023) work with young mothers in a poor urban setting focuses on young mothers' agency. She argues that the frequent erasure of African girls and young mothers is a result of researchers leaving them out of research processes as knowledge creators.

## WHAT IS PARTICIPATORY DATA ANALYSIS?

Many scholars who adopt participatory research approaches have documented the processes of undertaking participatory data *collection* without documenting how researchers and participants engage in participatory data *analysis* (Nind 2011). Participatory data analysis is a continuous and collaborative process that involves participants and researchers working together to sort, interpret, and organize the data, bringing to the fore what they perceive as most important (Byrne et al. 2009; Clarke et al. 2018; Geurts and Joldersma 2001; Tilley et al. 2021). Elizabeth Tilley et al. (2021) and Vaccaro (2023) both highlight that data analysis is the stage at which some aspects of the data are emphasized and privileged more than others. This process is power-laden, "drawing particular voices to the fore while others disappear in the background" (Tilley et al. 2021, 568). Tilley et al. (2021) argue that academics tend to assume greater power in the data analysis stage of the research, a notion that participatory data analysis seeks to disrupt by democratizing and diversifying the voices involved in the process.

The principles of participatory data analysis align with feminist prioritizations of girls' and women's perspectives in data analysis, enabling participants to highlight which findings are a priority (Neill et al. 2021; Rix et al. 2021, 2022; Vaccaro 2023). For instance, in her research with homeless women in Canada, Vaccaro (2023) adopts a feminist participatory action research approach, positioning women as co-theorizers of social change. While emphasizing the value of including women in the processes of participatory data analysis, Vaccaro (2023) also acknowledges the difficulty of forging meaningful research collaborations with highly transient individuals. In Vaccaro's (2023) study, like in mine, many of the participants who initially participated in a semi-structured interview could not participate in a second arts-based participatory phase.

Participatory data analysis integrates principles of equity, diversity, and inclusion into research processes by valuing diverse voices and perspectives. In this study, I included a diverse group of educational stakeholders from the local community—parents, business owners, teachers, daycare owners, and local administrative and religious leaders—as well as young mothers experiencing barriers to school continuation and completion, despite the presence of a school continuation and re-entry policy in Kenya. Because participatory data analysis considers local priorities and perspectives, these processes may lead to nuanced understandings of complex social issues and more appropriate recommendations for action (Gallagher 2008). Related to these values, Myriam Gervais and Lysanne Rivard (2013) adopted a SMART framework in their photovoice study with women farmers in Rwanda, which prioritizes the following criteria: Socio-cultural context informs the procedures; Making participants' priorities the central focus of the consultation question; Analysis process includes women's analysis; Results disseminated by women through a participatory exhibition; and Timeframe adapted to participants' schedule drives the logistical process.

## WORKING WITH DIFFERENT COHORTS OF YOUNG MOTHERS TO ANALYZE A PHOTOVOICE EXHIBITION: A MULTI-PARTICIPATORY DATA ANALYSIS APPROACH

This chapter draws from my doctoral study (Nyariro 2021a), in which I used photovoice to explore barriers to school re-entry, continuation, and completion among forty pregnant adolescents and young mothers across three study phases. From the onset of the study, I experienced challenges in systematically selecting and recruiting participants. Instead, I used snowball sampling to locate pregnant girls and young mothers. Snowball sampling is normally used by researchers when the study population is difficult to access. It involves identifying the first participant(s), who then refers the researcher to subsequent participants through informal networks until reaching the desired number of participants (Naderifar et al. 2017; Woodley and Lockard 2016). I adopted the following criteria in identifying and recruiting participants: at the time of the study, they had to be out of school because of pregnancy/young motherhood, be between thirteen and nineteen years old, and live in Korogocho.

## METHODOLOGY

My study drew heavily from photovoice techniques. Photovoice was developed by Caroline Wang and colleagues, who worked in public health settings with women farmers in the rural province of Yuhan, China (Wang and Burris 1994, 1997; Wang et al. 1996). Photovoice is a visual methodology in which participants use cameras to visually capture their lives (Wang et al. 2004). It is also a participatory approach that empowers historically marginalized groups like young mothers (Capous-Desyllas and Forro 2014; Delgado 2015; Liebenberg 2018). Researchers typically train participants how to use cameras, take "ethical" photographs, and engage with study prompt(s) in a workshop setting (Boog 2003). Participants take photographs in their community and return for a storytelling session, during which they verbally describe and write captions to explain why they took each photograph and what it means to them.

### Cohort One

Phase one of my doctoral study involved a photovoice study with fifteen young mothers who I recruited via snowball sampling. I began by asking the participants to collectively identify the problems they faced in their community. In response, the young mothers mentioned a lack of employment, extreme financial insecurity, and school discontinuation because of early pregnancy and motherhood. From this initial photo-voice study, I developed the photovoice prompt: *"What challenges do you face as pregnant girls and young mothers in this community?"* I trained the young mothers on photovoice methodology. After dividing the young mothers into smaller groups of four or five, they went into the community to take photographs representing their challenges. Together, the fifteen young mothers produced over one hundred photographs.

When they returned, participants continued to work in smaller groups. I asked them to choose three or four of their "best" photographs and describe what each photo meant to them. Next, participants used glue sticks to paste the photos they had selected onto a cardboard paper and added a caption to each photo. I adopted the SHOWeD[1] guide to facilitate a post-participatory data analysis group reflection (see Johnston 2016; Liebenberg 2018; Liebenberg et al. 2020; Wang and Burris 1994; Wang et al. 1996). Some of the questions I adopted from the SHOWeD guide were: "What did you want to illustrate when you took the picture?" and "What is occurring in this photo?" In other words, small groups of participants were reviewing and helping each other to interpret their own photographs rather than the photographs of the larger group.

Each small group produced a "photo narrative," also referred to as "poster narratives" (Mitchell 2011), which they presented to the larger group using the selected images and captions mounted on poster board. I used these visual narratives to conduct a thematic analysis to identify common and emerging themes in the photographs, which I then used to curate a photovoice exhibition to engage different audiences and stakeholders for phase two. Three common themes that emerged as barriers to school re-entry and completion across the various data sets of photo narratives produced by the three groups of the young mothers in this study were: 1) a lack of efficient, clean, and affordable daycares; 2) a lack of social and family support; and 3) poverty.

## Cohort Two

As a feminist methodology, photovoice adheres to the principle that researchers ought to return findings to participants for verification and confirmation whenever possible. This approach is meant to enhance the accuracy of the data while strengthening collaboration and transparency between researchers, participants, and their communities (Tilley et al. 2021). In my case, as I began to organize a public photovoice exhibition in the Korogocho community, I wanted to re-engage the same young mothers who had created it in 2017 during phase one of the study. I hoped to conduct a second level of participatory data analysis by offering participants another chance to reflect on their images and share additional feedback before they were displayed to community members and policymakers (Nyariro 2021b).

However, when I returned to Kenya for phase two in September 2019, I was unable to locate the first cohort of participants through the telephone numbers they had provided or through door-to-door household visits. This was not entirely unprecedented; participant attrition is a common challenge in Korogocho because of high migration rates within slum settlements (African Population and Health Research Center 2002a, 2002b; Emina et al. 2011). Young women are especially likely to move to other urban areas to look for jobs or to live with relatives. For pregnant girls and young mothers, moving out of the slum settlements also provides an escape from the ostracization they face for being young mothers within their current communities.

I resolved to recruit a second cohort of fifteen additional young mothers using snowball sampling, following the same selection and inclusion criterion I used to recruit the first cohort. I call this second cohort "shadow participants." Although the second cohort of participants did not participate in the photovoice study, the shadow participants facilitated recognizability of the dataset since they had some demographic and life experiences in common with the first. In my case, recruiting the second cohort of young mothers was possible only because teenage pregnancy is a common phenomenon in Korogocho. The second cohort of shadow participants partook in phase two.

**FIGURE 4.1** | Young mothers in the second cohort looking at the photovoice exhibition created by young mothers in first cohort. (Photograph by author.)

Phase two of the study was a participatory data analysis of the photovoice exhibition, which involved an exhibition walk-through activity with the second and third cohorts of participants. After developing an exhibition of the photographs generated by the initial cohort of young mothers in phase one, I invited the second and third cohorts of participants to view them and respond to the same prompt: *"What challenges do you face as pregnant girls and young mothers in this community?"* I asked these participants to identify images from the exhibit that resonated with their experiences as young mothers in Korogocho. In doing so, they had the opportunity to place their responses in conversation with the images they had just viewed, comparing and contrasting their own lived experiences with those represented in the exhibit.

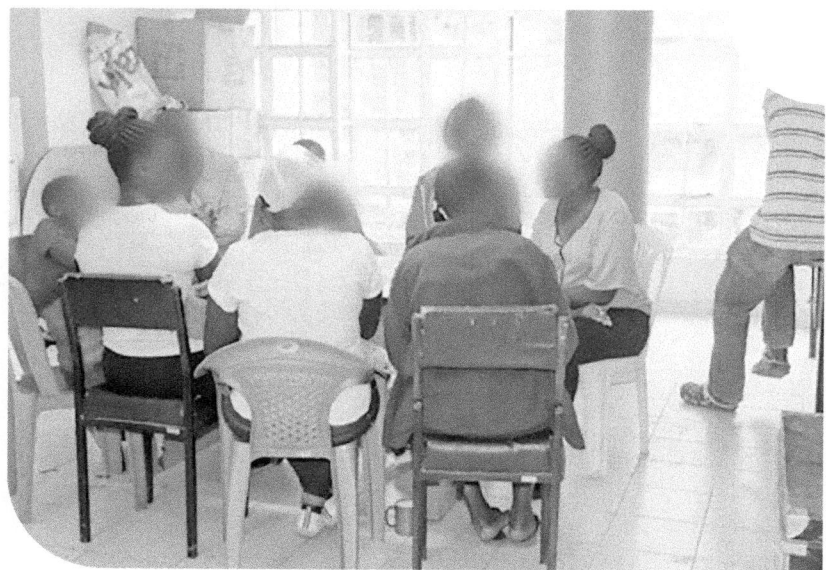

**FIGURE 4.2** | Representatives from local community-based organizations during the consultation workshop.

(Photograph by Hope Nyariro, used with permission.)

## Cohort Three

Photovoice is both a feminist and community-based methodology. Therefore, beyond seeking input from participants, photovoice encourages engaging participants' communities in mapping challenges and finding local solutions through participatory analysis and community reflections (Naderifar et al. 2017). To that end, I held a workshop with seven representatives from local community-based organizations whose work supports girls' education and sexual reproductive health. As part of this workshop, I invited the community representatives to walk through and respond to the photovoice exhibition. Community representatives contributed to my participatory data analysis by highlighting some contextual challenges they routinely see in practice: lack of access to contraceptives, lack of accessible childcare, and intergenerational poverty. The community representatives also brought forward a methodological concern, noting the absence of Islamic pregnant girls' and young mothers' voices and perspectives from the dataset. There is a significant Islamic community in Korogocho, and community representatives argued that Islamic pregnant girls and young mothers face unique challenges compared to the young mothers who created the photovoice exhibition, due to cultural and religious differences.

Following the recommendation of the community representatives, I recruited a third cohort of participants from the Islamic community to contribute to the participatory analysis of the photovoice exhibition. Recruiting young mothers from the Islamic community was challenging, even with the snowballing technique that was effective with the first cohort in phase one and the second cohort in phase two. First, I had to attain approval to allow the community mobilizers to enter the community and speak to the heads of the households and the young mothers. To do this, two Islamic community representatives contacted the village elders on my behalf, and the village elders contacted the community council and Imam. Without the Imam's permission, my first attempt to recruit young mothers from the Islamic community was unsuccessful. Some members of the Islamic community were wary about the presence and intention of non-Muslims and researchers (seen as foreigners) in the community. The young Islamic mothers who were seen speaking with the community mobilizers were threatened with eviction from the community and repatriation to the northern part of Kenya, from which many of the families had migrated. Such threats initially stopped young mothers from participating in the study. After negotiations through the male Muslim community representatives who had participated in the workshop, and with permission from the Imam, the community mobilizers finally gained entry to the community and access to the young mothers. In the end, they recruited ten young mothers from the Islamic community who participated in participatory data analysis of the photovoice exhibition.

The young mothers from the Islamic community added unique perspectives to the challenges young mothers face in Korogocho. In their participatory data analysis session, they highlighted that in addition to the issues presented in the first cohort's photovoice exhibition,

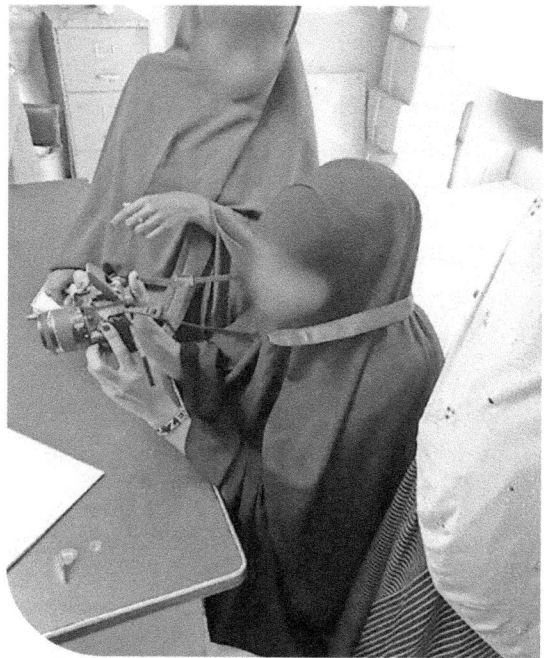

**FIGURE 4.3** | Young mothers from the Islamic community during a photovoice workshop.

(Photograph by author.)

they were forced to marry by their families as a way of restoring family and community honour. Their analysis also revealed that the young Islamic mothers' male family and community members oversaw the decisions about their lives. However, like the other young mothers, the young Islamic mothers are active agents who engage in economic activities to provide for themselves and their children.

While I had not anticipated needing to recruit a second and third cohort of young mothers to complete the participatory data analysis process, the shadow participants verified many of the challenges faced by the first cohort of young mothers living in low-resource urban settings while nuancing and expanding on challenges specific to young mothers' intersectional identities.

**FIGURE 4.4** | Young mothers from the Islamic community creating their photo narratives/poster narratives.

(Photograph by author.)

## REFLECTIONS ON THEMES ARISING FROM MULTI-PARTICIPATORY DATA ANALYSIS

In this final section, I reflect on what I have learned about the importance of participatory data analysis and how these processes can engender voice and agency among girls and women, focusing on particularly vulnerable segments of the population.

### Voice

Voice is the ability to express one's opinion openly and publicly, individually or as a collective. Lisa A. Mazzei (2016) describes voice "as a process of couplings and connections, as a process of differentiation in a shift away from the ontological unit of the individual to the forces at work producing voice as an entanglement" (153). One of the aims of participatory research is to centre the voices of the participants and those of their communities. During the participatory data analysis processes in this study, I was aware of the potential power imbalances and wanted to ensure that I prioritized the voices of young mothers to speak about their lived experiences. For example, the young mothers themselves selected places in the community to take pictures, chose what to photograph, and selected the images that they thought best described the challenges they faced.

The young mothers who contributed to the multi-participatory data analysis mentioned that, for the first time, they felt that they were in a position to speak for themselves regarding the challenges they contended with daily. One young mother in phase one said: "This is the first time that someone has come to this community to speak to us [pregnant girls and young mothers] about our problems. We always [just] see people coming here and talking to the others [the rest of the community] but not us. I am very happy that we spoke [about] the difficulties we face." Another young mother in phase one agreed with this sentiment: "In this community, we are never given a chance to talk about anything...People see us as bad girls...but in this workshop, we talked freely about everything."

In phase two, the young mothers commented on the ways the exhibition walk-through reflected their own lived experiences. One young mother said: "All the pictures show our daily problems in this community." Another young mother said: "I agree with the people who took these pictures, these are our exact problems." A third said: "I could have taken the same pictures if I was asked to." These excerpts speak to the temporal loss or lack of voice in the community when an adolescent girl becomes pregnant and then a mother. Here, I use the term "temporal" because the loss and gain of voice is not permanent and is influenced by several factors. Through their participation in the study's data analysis processes, the young mothers were able to find or reclaim their voices in ways that spoke to the issues that they felt were important in their lives and that continued to act as barriers to their school continuation and completion, as I discuss in my previous work (see Nyariro 2018).

## Agency

Agency refers to the capacity of an individual to act independently and make their own free choices. According to Richard N. Williams et al. (2021), agency means having power and self-direction to pursue happiness. Additionally, scholars define agency as individual autonomy: the ability to act as a force for change and to resist structural power (Eteläpelto et al. 2013). In this study, the pregnant adolescents and young mothers expressed their agency at individual and group levels. Kaisa Kärki (2018) connects agency and power, demonstrating that for an individual or group to exercise agency, there must be obvious evidence that they can exercise some level of power.

Contrary to the common assumption that young mothers lack agency, the participants in this study exercised agency by engaging in feminist dialogue through multi-participatory data analysis of a photovoice exhibition. I took an unconventional approach to participatory data analysis in that one cohort of participants created the visual dataset in a participatory way, and a second and third cohort of participants analyzed it in a participatory way. Importantly, multi-participatory data analysis via an exhibition walk-through was only possible because the first cohort of young mothers had given their informed consent to use their images for public display.

## CONCLUSIONS

Like other research approaches, participatory research involves sifting through data, organizing and making sense of it to highlight key findings, answer the research question(s), develop new theories, and offer newer ways of interpreting the world (Tilley et al. 2021). Unlike positivist research, participatory approaches seek to meaningfully involve stakeholders, communities, and participants to varying degrees and at various stages of the research. In my photovoice study with young mothers, I tried to engage participants in most of the research stages, but especially in data analysis. The process of facilitating participatory data analysis with a transient population of participants sparked multiple iterations of feminist conversations between three distinct groups of pregnant adolescent girls and young mothers, centring their voices in constructing their lived realities and bolstering their agency by not only speaking out about the challenges they face daily but by showing ways they have been resilient in maneuvering their lives amidst these challenges.

The need for a multi-participatory data analysis approach speaks to participants' transient circumstances in important ways. The first cohort contributed to the process of participatory data analysis by taking part in a photovoice study and analyzing the photographs taken to develop themes, which I used to create the photovoice exhibition that was analyzed by the second and third cohorts of participants. In addition to enabling some continuity within the process of participatory data analysis, the second and third cohorts acted as an audience to the photovoice exhibition created by the first cohort of participants and identified how the images in the exhibition resonated with their own lives and experiences. Additionally, both the second and third cohorts of young mothers participated in separate photovoice studies in which they talked about additional challenges and how they remained resilient (Nyariro, forthcoming).

Facilitating participatory data analysis with a transient group can pose challenges in participatory research, like the photovoice study in this chapter. A methodological innovation that developed from my study with the young mothers in Korogocho was the possibility of recruiting subsequent cohorts of participants using the same recruitment criteria for continuity. Involving the broader community in the participatory data analysis also helped me to identify a gap in my study regarding which voices were missing in the ongoing conversations about the challenges facing young mothers living in low-resource urban settings in Nairobi. Despite being a small settlement, this gap dispelled any assumptions of homogeneity within Korogocho and foregrounded the heterogeneous experiences of adolescent mothers living in the same setting.

The exhibition walk-throughs with the young mothers and the community members contributed to a collaborative process of data analysis, inviting reflections and conversations aimed at addressing the problem of teenage pregnancy and young motherhood in Korogocho (for example, highlighting the lack of efficient, clean, and affordable daycares). The young mothers in cohorts two and three were able to see how the lives of other young mothers mirrored their own through the images that they produced in the photovoice exhibition, while the exhibition walk-throughs offered community members the opportunity to learn about the challenges to school continuation and completion from the perspectives of the young mothers themselves.

While the multi-participatory data analysis approach emerged as a methodological necessity for my study, it could indeed be an intentional study design decision. Multi-participatory data analysis helps nuance and verify thematic findings and is a pragmatic solution to working with participants who cannot commit to recurring involvement. Moreover, grounding my work in Katshunga's (2019) Black African Girl Approach framed participants' stories as ones of agency and empowerment. Multi-participatory data analysis helped shape spaces where participants could speak for themselves on matters that affect them instead of being perceived as victims who need saving by their northern and western counterparts. By centring participatory data analysis and Black African girlhood studies, methodological decision making can work toward increasing inclusivity and providing an equitable space for all girls from diverse social and geographical backgrounds to develop their voice and agency (Nyariro, forthcoming).

## AUTHOR'S NOTE

I wish to acknowledge the support from McGill University through its International Graduate Mobility Award that funded phase one of the study and the International Development Research Center and Fonds de recherche du Québec Doctoral Award whose financial support enabled me to conduct phase two of the study. I acknowledge the McGill Third Century (M3C) Postdoctoral Fellowship through whose support I was able to write this chapter. I thank my Postdoctoral Fellowship mentors, Dr. Shelley Clark and Dr. Isabel Pike of the Department of Sociology for their guidance and support during its writing. My gratitude also goes to the editors, Dr. Claudia Mitchell, Dr. Kaylan Schwarz, and Rebekah Hutten for their review and insightful feedback throughout the process, from writing to publication. I also wish to acknowledge the young mothers from Korogocho for creating the time to participate in the study and the participatory data analysis that contributed to highlighting key socio-economic factors that continue to be barriers to school continuation and completion for out-of-school young mothers, despite the presence of policies that support their education.

## NOTE

1.  SHOWeD guide is a set of prompt questions: What do you See here? What is really Happening here? How does this relate to Our lives? Why does this condition Exist? and What can we Do about it? These questions guide the participatory analysis process and were first developed by Roy Shaffer (1983) in *Beyond the Dispensary*.

## REFERENCES

African Population and Health Research Center. 2002a. *Health and Livelihood Needs of Residents of Informal Settlements in Nairobi City*. APHRC.

African Population and Health Research Center. 2002b. *Population and Health Dynamics in Nairobi Informal Settlements*. APHRC.

Alanen, Leena. 2005. "Women's Studies/Childhood Studies: Parallels, Links and Perspectives." In *Children Taken Seriously: In Theory, Policy and Practice*, edited by Jan Mason and Toby Fattore. Jessica Kingsley Publishers.

Boog, Ben W.M. 2003. "The Emancipatory Character of Action Research, Its History and the Present State of the Art." *Journal of Community & Applied Social Psychology* 13 (6): 426–438.

Brown, Nicole. 2022. "Scope and Continuum of Participatory Research." *International Journal of Research & Method in Education* 45 (2): 200–211.

Burkholder, Casey. 2018. "Looking Back and Looking Around: Revisiting and Exploring Civic Engagement through Cellphilms with Ethnic Minority Youth in Hong Kong." PhD diss., McGill University.

Byrne, Anne, John Canavan, and Michelle Millar. 2009. "Participatory Research and the Voice-Centred Relational Method of Data Analysis: Is It Worth It?" *International Journal of Social Research Methodology* 12 (1): 67–77.

Capous-Desyllas, Moshoula, and Vanessa A. Forro. 2014. "Tensions, Challenges, and Lessons Learned: Methodological Reflections from Two Photovoice Projects with Sex Workers." *Journal of Community Practice* 22 (1/2): 150–175.

Caron, Caroline. 2016. "Placing the Girlhood Scholar into the Politics of Change: A Reflexive Account." In *Girlhood and the Politics of Place*, edited by Claudia Mitchell and Carrie Rentschler. Berghahn Books.

Cieslik, Mark, and Donald Simpson. 2013. *Key Concepts in Youth Studies*. SAGE.

Clarke, Charlotte L., Heather Wilkinson, Julie Watson, Jane Wilcockson, Lindsay Kinnaird, and Toby Williamson. 2018. "A Seat around the Table: Participatory Data Analysis with People Living with Dementia." *Qualitative Health Research* 28 (9): 1421–1433.

De Lange, Naydene, and Claudia Mitchell. 2016. "Community Health Workers as Cultural Producers in Addressing Gender-Based Violence in Rural South Africa." *Global Public Health* 11 (5/6): 783–798.

De Lange, Naydene, Claudia Mitchell, and Relebohile Moletsane. 2015. "Girl-Led Strategies to Address Campus Safety: Creating Action Briefs for Dialogue with Policy Makers." *Agenda: Empowering Women for Gender Equity* 29 (3): 118–127.

Delgado, Melvin. 2015. *Urban Youth and Photovoice: Visual Ethnography in Action*. Oxford University Press.

Emina, Jacques, Donatien Beguy, Eliya M. Zulu et al. 2011. "Monitoring of Health and Demographic Outcomes in Poor Urban Settlements: Evidence from the Nairobi Urban Health and Demographic Surveillance System." *Journal of Urban Health* 88 (2): 200–218.

Epstein, Rebecca, Jamilia Blake, and Thalia González. 2017. *Girlhood Interrupted: The Erasure of Black Girls' Childhood*. Georgetown University Law Center on Poverty and Inequality.

Eteläpelto, Anneli, Katja Vähäsantanen, Päivi Hökkä, and Susanna Paloniemi. 2013. "What Is Agency? Conceptualizing Professional Agency at Work." *Educational Research Review* 10: 45–65.

Field, Corinne T., Tammy-Charelle Owens, Marcia Chatelain, Lakisha Simmons, Abosede George, and Rhian Keyse. 2016. "The History of Black Girlhood: Recent Innovations and Future Directions." *The Journal of the History of Childhood and Youth* 9 (3): 383–401.

Forman-Brunell, Miriam. 2010. "Forward." In *Girlhood: A Global History*, edited by Jennifer Helgren and Colleen A. Vasconcellos. Rutgers University Press.

Gallagher, Michael. 2008. "'Power Is Not an Evil': Rethinking Power in Participatory Methods." *Children's Geographies* 6 (2): 137–150.

Gerstenblatt, Paula. 2013. "Collage Portraits as a Method of Analysis in Qualitative Research." *International Journal of Qualitative Methods* 12 (1): 294–309.

Gervais, Myriam, and Lysanne Rivard. 2013. "'SMART' Photovoice Agricultural Consultation: Increasing Rwandan Women Farmers' Active Participation in Development." *Development in Practice* 23 (4): 496–510.

Geurts, Jac L.A., and Cisca Joldersma. 2001. "Methodology for Participatory Policy Analysis." *European Journal of Operational Research* 128 (2): 300–310.

Gonick, Marnina, and Susanne Gannon. 2014. *Becoming Girl: Collective Biography and the Production of Girlhood.* Women's Press.

Halliday, Aria S. 2019. "Introduction." In *The Black Girlhood Studies Collection*, edited by Aria S. Halliday. Canadian Scholars.

Helgren, Jennifer, and Colleen A. Vasconcellos. 2010. "Introduction." In *Girlhood: A Global History*, edited by Jennifer Helgren and Colleen A. Vasconcellos. Rutgers University Press.

Hernández-Leo, Davinia, Eloy D. Villasclaras-Fernández, Juan I. Asensio-Pérez et al. 2006. "COLLAGE: A Collaborative Learning Design Editor Based on Patterns." *Journal of Educational Technology & Society* 9 (1): 58–71.

hooks, bell. 1996. *Bone Black: Memories of Girlhood.* Henry Holt and Co.

Johnston, Gloria. 2016. "Champions for Social Change: Photovoice Ethics in Practice and 'False Hopes' for Policy and Social Change." *Global Public Health* 11 (5/6): 799–811.

Kagola, Obakeng, and Mathabo Khau. 2020. "Using Collages to Change School Governing Body Perceptions of Male Foundation Phase Teachers." *Educational Research for Social Change* 9 (2): 65–80.

Kamusiime, Annah. 2023. "Young Mothers as Peer Researchers in a Collaborative Study." *Girlhood Studies: An Interdisciplinary Journal* 16 (1): 20–36.

Kärki, Kaisa. 2018. "Not Doings as Resistance." *Philosophy of the Social Sciences* 48 (4): 364–384.

Katshunga, Jen. 2019. "Contesting Black Girlhoods beyond Northern Borders: Exploring a Black African Girl Approach." In *The Black Girlhood Studies Collection*, edited by Aria S. Halliday. Canadian Scholars.

Kirk, Jackie, and Stephanie Garrow. 2003. "'Girls in Policy': Challenges for the Education Sector." *Agenda* 17 (56): 4–15.

Lamb, Pamela. 2021. "'We Need to Do Public Health Differently in This Community': A Reflexive Analysis of Participatory Video, Affective Relations, and the Policy Process." *Agenda* 35 (1): 42–53.

Liebenberg, Linda. 2018. "Thinking Critically about Photovoice: Achieving Empowerment and Social Change." *International Journal of Qualitative Methods* 17 (1): 1–9.

Liebenberg, Linda, Aliya Jamal, and Janice Ikeda. 2020. "Extending Youth Voices in a Participatory Thematic Analysis Approach." *International Journal of Qualitative Methods* 19: 1–13.

Literat, Ioana. 2013. "'A Pencil for Your Thoughts': Participatory Drawing as a Visual Research Method with Children and Youth." *International Journal of Qualitative Methods* 12 (1): 84–98.

MacEntee, Katie. 2015. "Using Cellphones in Participatory Visual Research to Address Gender-Based Violence in and around Rural South African Schools: Reflections on Research as Intervention." *Agenda* 29 (3): 22–31.

MacEntee, Katie, Casey Burkholder, and Joshua Schwab-Cartas. 2016. *What's a Cellphilm? Integrating Mobile Phone Technology into Participatory Visual Research and Activism.* Sense Publishers.

Mahadev, Rekha. 2015. "Making Silent Voices Heard: Using Participatory Video to Address Sexual Violence." *Agenda* 29 (3): 13–21.

Mazzei, Lisa A. 2016. "Voice without a Subject." *Cultural Studies ←→ Critical Methodologies* 16 (2): 151–161.

Mitchell, Claudia. 2011. *Doing Visual Research*. SAGE.

Mitchell, Claudia. 2016. "Charting Girlhood Studies." In *Girlhood and the Politics of Place*, edited by Claudia Mitchell and Carrie Rentschler. Berghahn Books.

Mitchell, Claudia, and Jacqueline Reid-Walsh. 2008. "Girl Method: Placing Girl-Centred Research Methodologies on the Map of Girlhood Studies." In *Roadblocks to Equality: Women Challenging Boundaries*, edited by Jeffrey Klaehn. Black Rose Books.

Mitchell, Claudia, Linda Theron, Jean Stuart, Ann Smith, and Zachariah Campbell. 2011. "Drawings as Research Method." In *Picturing Research: Drawing as Visual Methodology*, edited by Linda Theron, Claudia Mitchell, Ann Smith, and Jean Stuart. Sense Publishers.

Moletsane, Relebohile, Claudia Mitchell, and Naydene De Lange. 2015. "Gender Violence, Teenage Pregnancy and Gender Equity Policy in South Africa: Privileging the Voices of Women and Girls through Participatory Visual Methods." In *Gender Violence in Poverty Contexts: The Educational Challenge*, edited by Jenny Parkes. Routledge.

Moletsane, Relebohile, Ann Smith, and Linda Chisholm. 2008. *Methodologies for Mapping a Southern African Girlhood in the Age of Aids*. Sense Publishers.

Naderifar, Mahin, Hamideh Goli, and Fereshteh Ghaljaei. 2017. "Snowball Sampling: A Purposeful Method of Sampling in Qualitative Research." *Strides in Development of Medical Education* 14 (3): 1–6.

Neill, Ruth D., Paul Best, Katrina Lloyd et al. 2021. "Engaging Teachers and School Leaders in Participatory Data Analysis for the Development of a School-Based Mental Health Intervention." *School Mental Health* 13 (2): 312–324.

Ngidi, Ndumiso Daluxolo, and Relebohile Moletsane. 2018. "Using Drawings to Explore Sexual Violence with Orphaned Youth in and around a Township Secondary School in South Africa." In *Disrupting Shameful Legacies: Girls and Young Women Speak Back through the Arts to Address Sexual Violence*, edited by Claudia Mitchell and Relebohile Moletsane. Brill Sense.

Nind, Melanie. 2011. "Participatory Data Analysis: A Step Too Far?" *Qualitative Research* 11 (4): 349–363.

Nyariro, Milka. 2018. "Re-Conceptualizing School Continuation & Re-Entry Policy for Young Mothers Living in an Urban Slum Context in Nairobi, Kenya: A Participatory Approach." *Studies in Social Justice* 12 (2): 310–328.

Nyariro, Milka. 2021a. "Using Photovoice to Explore Barriers to School Continuation and Re-Entry for Pregnant Girls and Young Mothers Living in Poor Urban Settings in Sub-Saharan Africa." PhD diss., McGill University.

Nyariro, Milka. 2021b. "'We Have Heard You but We Are Not Changing Anything': Policymakers as Audience to a Photovoice Exhibition on Challenges to School Re-Entry for Young Mothers in Kenya." *Agenda* 35 (1): 94–108.

Nyariro, Milka. Forthcoming. "What Does Agency Look Like among Pregnant Adolescent Girls and Young Mothers?" *Girlhood Studies: An Interdisciplinary Journal*.

Onyango, George, Felix Ngunzo Kioli, and Erick Nyambedha. 2015. "Challenges of School Re-Entry among Teenage Mothers in Primary Schools in Muhoroni District, Western Kenya." *SSRN*. http://dx.doi.org/10.2139/ssrn.2546761.

Rivard, Lysanne. 2015. "Gender, Physical Education, and Sport: Bringing Forward Rwandan Girls' Perspectives on Their Lived Experiences of Physical Activity and Sport in Secondary Schools." PhD diss., McGill University.

Rivard, Lysanne. 2016. "From the Playing Field to the Policy Table: Stakeholder's Response to Rwandan Schoolgirls' Photographs on Physical Activity and Sport in Secondary Schools." In *Girlhood and the Politics of Place*, edited by Claudia Mitchell and Carrie Rentschler. Berghahn Books.

Rivard, Lysanne, and Claudia Mitchell. 2013. "Sport, Gender and Development: On the Use of Photovoice as a Participatory Action Research Tool to Inform Policy Makers." In *Pedagogies, Physical Culture and Visual Methods*, edited by Laura Azzarito and David Kirk. Routledge.

Rix, Jonathan, Helena Garcia Carrizosa, Simon Hayhoe, Jane Seale, and Kieron Sheehy. 2021. "Emergent Analysis and Dissemination within Participatory Research." *International Journal of Research & Method in Education* 44 (3): 287–302.

Rix, Jonathan, Helena Garcia Carrizosa, Kieron Sheehy, Jane Seale, and Simon Hayhoe. 2022. "Taking Risks to Enable Participatory Data Analysis and Dissemination: A Research Note." *Qualitative Research* 22 (1): 143–153.

Tilley, Elizabeth, Iva Strnadová, Sue Ledger et al. 2021. "'Working Together Is Like a Partnership of Entangled Knowledge': Exploring the Sensitivities of Doing Participatory Data Analysis with People with Learning Disabilities." *International Journal of Social Research Methodology* 24 (5): 567–579.

Undie, Chi-Chi, Abdhalah Kasiira Ziraba, Nyovani Madise, John Kebaso, and Elizabeth Kimani-Murage. 2009. "'If You Start Thinking Positively, You Won't Miss Sex': Narratives of Sexual (In)Activity among People Living with HIV in Nairobi's Informal Settlements." *Culture, Health & Sexuality* 11 (8): 767–782.

Vaccaro, Mary-Elizabeth. 2023. "Reflections on 'Doing' Participatory Data Analysis with Women Experiencing Long-Term Homelessness." *Action Research* 21 (3): 332–350.

Vanner, Catherine. 2019. "Toward a Definition of Transnational Girlhood." *Girlhood Studies: An Interdisciplinary Journal* 12 (2): 115–132.

Wang, Caroline, and Mary Ann Burris. 1994. "Empowerment through Photo Novella: Portraits of Participation." *Health Education Quarterly* 21 (2): 171–186.

Wang, Caroline, and Mary Ann Burris. 1997. "Photovoice: Concept, Methodology, and Use for Participatory Needs Assessment." *Health Education & Behavior* 24 (3): 369–387.

Wang, Caroline, Mary Ann Burris, and Xiang Yue Ping. 1996. "Chinese Village Women as Visual Anthropologists: A Participatory Approach to Reaching Policymakers." *Social Science & Medicine* 42 (10): 1391–1400.

Wang, Caroline, Susan Morrel-Samuels, Peter M. Hutchison, Lee Bell, and Robert M. Pestronk. 2004. "Flint Photovoice: Community Building among Youths, Adults, and Policymakers." *American Journal of Public Health* 94 (6): 911–913.

Weber, Sandra. 2014. "Arts-Based Self-Study: Documenting the Ripple Effect." *Perspectives in Education* 32 (2): 8–20.

Williams, Richard N., Edwin E. Gantt, and Lane Fischer. 2021. "Agency: What Does It Mean to Be a Human Being?" *Frontiers in Psychology* 12: 1–12.

Woodley, Xeturah M., and Megan Lockard. 2016. "Womanism and Snowball Sampling: Engaging Marginalized Populations in Holistic Research." *The Qualitative Report* 21 (2): 321–329.

5

GEETANJALI GILL

# PIVOTING TO PARTICIPATORY DATA ANALYSIS IN TRANSNATIONAL, COLLABORATIVE, NGO-ACADEMIC RESEARCH

## INTRODUCTION

IN THIS CHAPTER, I describe the methods, experiences, and lessons learned in carrying out participatory research with youth in two transnational, collaborative research projects involving the global non-governmental organization (NGO) Right to Play. We designed our projects in response to Right to Play's programmatic efforts to challenge gender inequalities. We also incorporated the organization's play-based philosophy and embraced feminist participatory research methods, emphasizing participation, inclusion, rights, and collaboration. While our first project used only participatory data collection, we pivoted to participatory data analysis in the second project.

While working as a gender and development consultant, I carried out several contracts with Right to Play's headquarters in Canada between 2018 and 2020. After joining academia as an Assistant

Professor in 2020, I initiated discussions with Right to Play about collaborative research, and the organization was immediately interested in exploring possibilities. Like most non-governmental organizations, they lacked the financial and human resources to initiate their own research studies. Our collaboration presented them with an opportunity to deeply examine their programmatic offerings for the benefit of their own organization and its programs, and to share their programmatic findings widely within development and academic circles. We created a transnational research team consisting of academics, Right to Play headquarters staff from the UK and Canada, and Right to Play national staff in various countries to design and carry out three collaborative projects, two of which are now completed and described in this chapter. In the second project, we also added a research scientist from a US donor organization to our team. Throughout this chapter, I use "we" and "our" to demonstrate the collaborative nature of the research decisions and "I" and "my" to insert my own personal reflections.

Given the practitioner background of the research team members (including myself) and that our research is designed to respond to the needs and priorities of Right to Play, our collaborative projects were guided by development practitioner perspectives on feminism. Canadian development organizations funded by Global Affairs Canada are required to conduct gender-based analyses, with the aim of identifying (and responding to) marginalized groups who experience intersecting inequalities based on sex, gender, age, location, class, ethnicity, and education status (Global Affairs Canada n.d.a). The Government of Canada's Feminist International Assistance Policy directs organizations to adopt gender-transformative, intersectional feminist, and empowering approaches (Global Affairs Canada 2017). A gender transformative approach addresses root causes of gender-based inequalities, and works to transform harmful gender roles, norms, and power relations (Pederson et al. 2015). Citing Kimberlé Crenshaw's (1989, 1990) foundational work on intersectionality, Global Affairs Canada (n.d.b) promotes the use of an intersectional feminist approach to understand and eliminate systemic discrimination on the basis of sex and gender identity, as well as on the basis of intersecting aspects of identity.[1] Right to Play (2021a) shares this commitment to ensuring that its programming contributes to greater gender equality.

In addition to development practitioner perspectives and federal feminist policy directives, our collaborative projects were influenced by decolonial feminist and gender studies frameworks. Feminist research often places the social construction of gender at the centre of the research inquiry (Lather 1991) and aims to challenge and equalize power structures by amplifying the voices and experiences of the less powerful (Collins 1991). Feminist postcolonial and decolonial scholars challenge the often binary approaches to achieving gender equality that are held by development agencies (Parpart and Parashar 2019). Feminist activists and advocates from the Global South are increasingly leading development programming and challenging "northern feminist thinking" (Kimotho et al. 2023, 54–55). To counter and broaden northern donor-driven views of feminism (such as those found in Global Affairs Canada's Feminist International Assistance Policy), we prioritized the voices of in-country research team members and participants in our study design, implementation, and understandings of gender transformation.

In our research projects, we emphasized collaborative and localized decision-making processes amongst the transnational research team members and research participants. Collaborative, participatory research can lead to "a new emphasis and respect for multiple voices/knowledge and grounded research" (Cottrell and Parpart 2006, 16). Intercultural dialogue, inherent in collaborative research, can also bring postcolonial perspectives and epistemologies to the forefront (Vanner 2015). Sylvanna Falcon (2016) proposes four criteria for nurturing and sustaining effective transnational feminist collaborations: 1) consciously negotiating imperial privilege; 2) building a research community; 3) supporting multilingualism; and 4) centring the role of projects, communities, and social movements to offer social critiques. In our projects, localized understandings of gender, intersectionality, and feminism provided by local academics, staff, and research participants shape research objectives, methods, and tools. Frequent transnational virtual meetings and in-country workshops were held to discuss implementation, findings, and data analysis; national staff played a key role in facilitating sessions in local languages; and research objectives were closely tied to the priorities of Right to Play programming at a local level.

## PARTICIPATORY RESEARCH

In participatory research, the voices of research participants (who are sometimes referred to as "co-researchers") are at the forefront of data collection, analysis, and the communication of findings (Guy and Arthur 2021). Participatory methodologies can be feminist when they aim to both interrogate/challenge and change the social conditions of marginalized girls and women in the interest of greater gender equality and justice (Gervais et al. 2018; Guy and Arthur 2021; Joyappa and Martin 1996). Participatory methodologies can also decolonize research by questioning who has power over knowledge production, dissemination, and management and by decentring those sources of power while centring people who have been marginalized (Iyer 2020; Lenette 2022). Recognizing and taking account of power differences embedded in relationships and the resulting ethical issues is particularly important when conducting participatory research with children and adolescents (Akerstrom and Brunnberg 2012; Akesson et al. 2014; Johnson and West 2021).

Some researchers have commented on the ability of those living on the margins of society to challenge how they are represented and to render themselves more visible through the use of visual, arts-based, performative, and play-based research methods (Blaisdell et al. 2019; Campo et al. 2019; Mitchell and Sommer 2016; Potts et al. 2022). Specific techniques include drawing, mapping, photography, video, collage, craft-making, drama, role play, music, poetry, dance, games, and puppetry (Bhatia et al. 2020; Blaisdell et al. 2019; Duncan 2021; Emmison 2021; Johnson and West 2021; Khuwaja et al. 2019; Mitchell et al. 2011; Percy-Smith 2021). Katie MacEntee and Claudia Mitchell (2011) position drawing with children as an "emancipatory approach" (97) that helps to challenge an oppressive status quo and critically analyze the everyday lives and perspectives of traditionally oppressed individuals and communities. The child-friendly context created with play-based methods can counteract intergenerational barriers between the researcher and research participants, centre children's creativity, and elicit children's voices (Blaisdell et al. 2019; Campo et al. 2019).

Youth-led, girl-led, and youth peer research studies using participatory methodologies explore issues from young people's perspectives and according to their priorities (Banati et al. 2021; Bill and Melinda Gates Foundation n.d.; McLean and Modi 2016; Mitchell et al. 2022). Trained in participatory methodologies by adult researchers, youth peer leaders assume a central role in data collection, analysis, and dissemination (McCleary-Sills 2011; Percy-Smith 2021; Porter 2016). Jeanette Akerstrom and Elinor Brunnberg (2012) describe the use of interactive research circles with adolescent girls in Scandinavian countries as a way to ensure close cooperation between researchers and participants throughout the entire research process. Lindsay McLean and Anny Modi (2016) discuss how girl-led research on girls' realities and journeys of "empowerment" in the Democratic Republic of Congo informs development programs. In a girl-led photovoice project in Sierra Leone, Plan International staff members taught girls how to use digital cameras to express their experiences, reflect on their views, identify themes, share their findings, and prepare advocacy plans (Plan International UK 2019).

It is vital that participatory research with children and adolescents includes both participatory data collection *and* analysis. Adopting an ethical and justice-oriented standpoint, Linda Theron et al. (2011) argue that adolescent participants should not only produce data through their drawings and discussions but also be involved in meaning-making and data analysis. As MacEntee and Mitchell (2011) note, involving children in coding and categorizing their drawings centres their voice, facilitates greater understanding, and engenders more democracy within research. Caroline Bradbury-Jones and Julie Taylor (2015) argue that children as researchers can be a "powerful conduit for other children's voices," and that with adequate preparation and training they are able to participate in and bring richness to data analysis and write up (161). According to Jane Coad and Ruth Evans (2008), involving children in data analysis processes enables a greater understanding of their perspectives and prioritizes their agendas in policy and practice.

For our research team, participatory research methodologies' potential to shed light on young people's perspectives and realities—while contributing to the organization's main purpose of building youths' agency, voice, and life skills—was a win-win situation. We contend that visual, arts-based, and performative research methods suit and build the creativity and skill level of youth participants. The sections that follow detail our rationale, experiences, challenges, and lessons learned in planning and carrying out collaborative, participatory research with youth.

## APPLYING RIGHT TO PLAY'S PLAY-BASED METHODS TO RESEARCH WITH YOUTH

Since Canada adopted the Feminist International Assistance Policy in 2017, Right to Play has prioritized understanding and measuring their programmatic impacts on gender equality, gender norms, youth agency, and empowerment. In 2020, as COVID-19 pandemic lockdowns affected many of the countries in which Right to Play works, the organization could no longer commission large-scale quantitative surveys and focus group discussions (their standard methodology for monitoring and evaluating programs), necessitating a methodological pivot toward small-scale, qualitative, and participatory methods. Right to Play's monitoring and evaluation staff also noted the inadequacies of quantitative surveys and focus group discussions in shedding light on the socio-cultural norms, beliefs, and attitudes of program participants.

Since Right to Play's programmatic niche is promoting play-based learning and play for the psycho-social well-being of marginalized children and youth, we decided to develop and use "playful," trauma-informed, and "empowering" research methods in our collaborative research projects. To achieve this, we asked Right to Play program staff—who are responsible for implementing projects with children and youth at local levels—to join Right to Play monitoring and evaluation staff on our research team. The involvement of program and field staff in research (previously the exclusive domain of monitoring and evaluation staff) was a considerable shift in the organization and led to several opportunities and challenges in the two collaborative research projects detailed below.

## Participatory, Play-Based Data Collection in Research Project #1

In the first research project, our transnational team sought to understand gender norm change amongst forty-eight girls and twenty-four boys (and their families) in education programs in Mozambique, Rwanda, and Ghana from 2021 to 2022. To make the best use of a small budget, I trained local university students and Right to Play country staff in each of the three countries to collect data.[2] I analyzed the data using NVivo software and consulted Right to Play country office staff on codes and findings.

In addition to carrying out one-on-one interviews with our research participants, we incorporated drawing exercises in the interviews. We first asked girls and boys to draw pictures representing their achievements, goals, and challenges while their parents and grandparents (or other caretakers across two generations) drew timelines of important events in their lives. The local university students then formulated interview questions from what they saw in the drawings. We decided to incorporate drawing into our data collection methods because Right to Play staff were already using drawing in their programmatic activities, materials were low-cost and readily available, and we hoped that drawing activities would better engage the research participants and enable them to speak openly.

The university students who collected data in the three countries and the Right to Play staff who assisted in sessions attributed the willingness of research participants to engage in open and honest discussions in interviews to the use of drawing. According to one university student in Ghana: "If I had gone straight to questions, I am sure I would have gotten more 'yes,' 'no,' or 'I don't know' answers, as well as silence. Because of the drawing, I was able to focus on a challenge that was important to the child in the interview." The richness of data that resulted from the drawing activities in this project encouraged the research team to expand its use of participatory data collection methods while piloting participatory data *analysis* in subsequent projects.

The pivot to participatory data collection *and* analysis methods for our second project was influenced by the core research team's desire to shift power from the researchers to the researched and contribute to empowerment processes for the organization's country office staff and the youth participants. Like Catherine Vanner (2015), who draws upon Joe Kincheloe and Peter McLaren (2005), we positioned ourselves as *bricoleurs*. We aimed to prioritize local contexts within the study design and implementation, minimize power imbalances within the research process, and maximize participants' feelings of empowerment, all while paying close attention to ethical and cultural considerations.

## Participatory, Play-Based Data Collection and Analysis in Research Project #2

Funded by the Global Women's Institute's Building Gender-based Violence Evidence grant at George Washington University, our second project used an array of play-based research methods to understand incidences of gender-based violence in humanitarian settings in Uganda and Lebanon from 2021 to 2023. The 260 participants included fifty-seven women and girls and thirty-eight men and boys in Uganda (fifteen to twenty-four years old), and ninety women and girls and seventy-five men and boys in Lebanon (twelve to twenty-four years old). All participants were living in refugee settlements and were participating in Right to Play's programs.

Ethical considerations are particularly important for researchers working with children who have been affected by adversity and conflict

(Akesson et al. 2014). We hoped that the use of playful participatory visual research methods would minimize the trauma that our research participants may have felt in the research process. We decided to prompt our research participants to speak about gender norms (not gender-based violence) and to broach the topic of gender-based violence only through the use of fictional vignettes.[3]

At the start of the project, we divided up tasks amongst the transnational research team. Right to Play staff in Uganda and Lebanon identified the research participants and locations for data collection, as well as local academics in each country to join the research team. Right to Play staff from the UK and Canada head-quarters, a researcher from the Global Women's Institute, and I held virtual sessions to discuss pre-existing participatory data collection and analysis methods and tools. All research team members completed the Canadian TCPS2 course on research ethics. Below, I describe our decisions and techniques for each project phase.

### STEP ONE:
### Country-Level Workshops to Develop and
### Pre-Test Data Collection and Analysis Tools

In February and March 2022, the research team attended workshops in Uganda and Lebanon to select and develop data collection and analysis tools, discuss the ethics of carrying out research with children and youth, and plan data collection and analysis sessions. Drawing upon pre-existing participatory methods and tools used by other non-governmental organizations to carry out research with children and youth (for example, Jones et al. 2019; Save the Children Norway 2008; McCleary-Sills et al. 2011; Global Women's Institute 2017), we discussed the suitability of tools to investigate gender-based violence in the context of refugee settlements and camps in Uganda and Lebanon. The research team also developed locally appropriate consent and assent processes for research participants.

Right to Play country staff played a key role in selecting the tools that they thought may be suitable for participants and research locations. Our selected participatory data collection tools and techniques included journaling and writing, drawing and mapping, and fictional vignettes followed by drama, role plays, and discussions. We also discussed how to involve youth in data analysis by asking them to reflect upon, compare, and contrast their drawings, writing, and role plays; to identify themes through free-listing and carrying out peer-to-peer interviews; to categorize, vote on, and rank themes; to match their drawings to themes; and to assign values to themes. Research team members carried out role plays to familiarize themselves with the data collection and analysis methods and subsequently tested the methods with girls and boys in local communities.

We held sessions in each country with five to six gender-specific groups of four to eight youths. Each one-and-a-half to two-hour long session included an icebreaker activity, one data collection tool, one data analysis tool, a discussion, and a closing game. Session facilitators provided prompts to participants who were drawing, mapping, writing, and carrying out role plays that explored gender roles in the household and community, aspirations, safety, and security in communities and schools, early marriage, decision making, agency, gender-based violence (only in the form of vignettes), and positive masculinity. Testing the tools enabled us to gauge participants' engagement and comfort levels, check the clarity of our instructions and suitability of our prompts, practice facilitation skills, and identify challenges and modifications needed for the tools.

While the tools were well received by participants, we discovered that some older youths were hesitant to draw, and the success of writing and journaling depended on the literacy levels of participants. We also learned that despite our efforts *not* to prompt the youth participants to discuss personal incidents of gender-based violence, some still voluntarily disclosed experiences of gender-based violence. This flagged a need to ensure that facilitators were knowledgeable about gender-based violence reporting, referral protocols, and trauma-informed approaches. The testing sessions also indicated a need to minimize the time spent playing games at the start or end of each session to allow sufficient time for both data collection *and* analysis. Following these in-country workshops, the research team drafted a manual detailing the use of the data collection and analysis tools, which also provided sample prompts, games, data analysis activities, ethical checklists, note-taking templates, and consent and assent scripts and forms (Right to Play 2023).

## STEP TWO:
### Participatory Data Collection Sessions

Due to socio-economic and linguistic barriers between research team members from Canada and the UK and the research participants in Uganda and Lebanon, we decided that team members from Right to Play's country offices in Uganda and Lebanon would be responsible for facilitating sessions with participants. In Uganda, graduates of Right to Play's programs (referred to as junior leaders)—some of whom came from the same local communities and spoke the same dialects as the research participants—assisted Right to Play staff in facilitating the sessions. While we had initially planned to carry out data collection *and* analysis in each session, facilitators reported an inability to fit both activities into a one-and-a-half to two-hour period. Therefore, we decided to carry out data collection first, and to organize follow-up data analysis sessions at a later time.

During data collection in Uganda and Lebanon, in-country research team members enthusiastically reported on the ability of the tools to facilitate open and fruitful discussion with research participants—including on sensitive topics—compared to standard interviews and focus group exercises. In both countries, the fictional vignettes were well received by participants. According to a male Right to Play staff member who facilitated sessions with boys in Uganda, "The vignettes and drawing tools helped in building trust and fostered a safe environment for the boys to disclose sensitive gender issues openly without reservations. The hypothetical nature of the fictional story made it simple for the boys to relate to typical community situations." The Ugandan research team found that drawing and mapping worked well for girls and boys of all ages, and that these activities resulted in animated discussions about safety and dangers in their communities. Facilitators in Uganda noted participants' eagerness to suggest ways to bring about positive change and action at individual, household, and community levels.

Research teams in Uganda and Lebanon modified some of the prompts in the manual and wrote fictional vignettes suited to the local context. For instance, the Uganda team wrote a story about domestic violence and positive masculinity, while the Lebanon team wrote a story about a girl who was forced into early marriage by her parents. The research team in Lebanon modified the writing and journaling tool to music lyric writing and song composition to cater to adolescents who had participated in Right to Play's music program. As these examples demonstrate, it is important for local research team members to have the agency to co-create, select, and modify research tools to suit their participants and local contexts.

### STEP THREE:
### Participatory Data Collection and Data Analysis Sessions

After several months of data collection, the research team took stock of the data collected in order to plan the participatory data analysis sessions. It became apparent that facilitators and observers of data collection sessions had not consistently taken notes, and some of the drawings and writing had not been safely stored. Many drawings and maps produced by participants were not accompanied by notes of the rich discussions that had taken place, and there were no notes on role-play activities. Staff turnover in Right to Play's Uganda office meant that new members of the research team as well as the junior leaders who were helping country staff to run sessions with participants did not receive adequate training on data collection and storage. Finally, with high programmatic workloads, Right to Play staff in both Lebanon and Uganda had started to combine data collection activities with program-matic activities in local communities, resulting in a lack of rigorous note-taking, data collection, and data storage.

While coming to terms with the weaknesses in our data, we began to discuss how to best carry out participatory data analysis with our participants moving forward. In-country research team members in Lebanon and Uganda found that some research participants who had taken part in data collection sessions were no longer living in the refugee and displaced persons settlement locations and could not be traced.[4] Given the fact that there would be a mix of previous and new participants taking part in data analysis sessions, and due to the scanty notes from previous sessions, we decided to carry out six additional sessions in each country that combined both data collection and analysis.

These subsequent sessions presented us with an opportunity to apply what we learned from previous data collection sessions. We could collect better quality data, practice using strict time controls during sessions to fit in both participatory data collection and analysis, and train new members of the Ugandan team on research methods. To prevent any further data loss, we agreed to use a simple note-taking template to keep track of what was said and done in sessions. We also decided to structure the timing of each session: fifteen minutes for an icebreaker or game, sixty minutes to instruct and carry out the drawing, mapping, or vignette activity, thirty to forty-five minutes for discussions and participatory data analysis, and an optional fifteen minutes for a closing game. All research team members participated in the subsequent sessions—both in-country and those from Canada and the UK. During the sessions, Canadian and UK research team members relied on the in-country team members to communicate with participants, translate, and take the lead in implementing sessions. Only in Uganda, where some of the youth research participants spoke English, were the core research team members able to assist with sessions and interact with research participants.

In addition to completing a data collection activity (drawing, mapping, or vignettes), facilitators asked participants to identify themes from their drawings, maps, and role plays, rank the importance or commonality of the issues captured in the data, and indicate how certain issues identified in the data (such as child marriage or gender roles) had changed over time. Participants worked in gender-specific groups while they were drawing, mapping, and planning role plays, as well as for the initial identification of themes and issues. In Lebanon, we asked girls and boys, aged fifteen to eighteen years, to work in pairs in gender-specific groups and to draw two images in response to a prompt about their aspirations for themselves versus their parents' aspirations for them. The youths presented and explained their drawings to their gender-specific groups and collectively considered and ranked the resources they would need to attain their aspirations and the barriers they might face.

To encourage richer discussions and cross-gender analyses, we brought girls' and boys' groups together for additional analysis of data in the same sessions. Girls and boys examined each other's drawings, maps, and lists of themes, and in some cases, they also watched and participated in each other's role plays. Perhaps because participants had previously taken part in mixed-gender programs, most felt free to discuss gender roles and norms in mixed-gender settings, appreciate each other's gendered challenges, and exchange ideas about why there were gendered differences in the household roles, beliefs, attitudes, and norms captured in their data. For instance, girls and boys in Uganda discussed reasons for the greater number of unsafe spaces marked on girls' maps compared to boys' maps and what could be done to make those spaces safer for girls.

### STEP FOUR:
### Collaborative Data Analysis

Once the data collection and analysis sessions were finished, the research team came together to upload notes and drawings to the analysis software, Dedoose.[5] We split into pairs to read through session notes, examine drawings, maps, and photos, and to discuss codes. Ugandan and Lebanese research team members developed a codebook and finished coding the data. In the coding process, we deferred to youth participants' ranking and analysis of themes and issues over those identified by research team members.

## LESSONS FOR COLLABORATIVE, NGO-DRIVEN RESEARCH

While Right to Play has previously hired academic research institutions to carry out evaluations and formative research, their engagement in collaborative research is new. Our collaborative research project in Uganda and Lebanon was driven by Right to Play's programmatic imperatives and their need to better understand gender norm change among their project participants. Right to Play research team members from Canada, UK, Uganda, and Lebanon were involved in all steps of the research process, including research design and dissemination of results. Our project "takes a positive and altruistic view of collaboration" (Aniekwe et al. 2012, 5) and employs a "joint learning model" (Roper 2002, 7) with a goal of sustainability, long-term partnership, and interdependency.

Our collaborative research projects were beneficial for all stakeholders in the ways described by Catherine Olivier et al. (2016), creating opportunities for mutual learning and complementarities of expertise, improved knowledge translation, and increased access to communities and policymakers. However, there were also some tensions and challenges that arose out of the collaborative project.

### Programmatic Versus Research Objectives

Our research project was designed to respond to Right to Play's programmatic and monitoring and evaluation needs, *as well as* to fill gaps in academic understanding of gender norm change and transformation. However, some Right to Play staff and team members were more familiar with the former than the latter and privileged this need in the research. This occasionally led to differences of opinion between research team members on what issues to probe with the participatory tools. For example, a staff member attending an in-country research workshop questioned the need to ask research participants about gender roles and norms when Right to Play was not currently implementing any gender-focused projects in that country.

Guided by their organizational mandate and programs, NGOs may prioritize the achievement of behavioural or policy change in a specific community (Rathgeber 2009). For instance, a new staff member who joined the research team was concerned by our inability to achieve adequate behavioural change amongst research participants in the project's timeframe, even though this objective was not in the scope of the research project. In addition, in-country research team members, for whom this was their first experience taking part in research, tended to conduct data collection and analysis sessions like they were program-oriented awareness sessions, lecturing youth participants instead of gathering their views. For instance, when Ugandan youth were asked to draw community maps indicating safe and unsafe spaces, one facilitator began the session by telling participants which places were safe and unsafe and where in the community they should and should not go. This hindered participants' ability to freely draw their maps from their own perspectives. Another facilitator used up most of a participatory data analysis session sensitizing participants on the meaning of gender-based violence instead of allowing participants to participate in data analysis. In-country research team members who carried out program-related work at Right to Play were clearly more comfortable with and accustomed to carrying out program-related tasks than research-related ones, alerting us to the importance of meaningful and ongoing training opportunities.

## Research Team Training and Staff Turnover

Our collaborative research projects used qualitative and participatory research methods. However, a survey of twenty Right to Play monitoring and evaluation staff in 2021 revealed that 85 percent were not confident in the use of qualitative tools to collect data on gender-based violence, nor confident in their ability to analyze qualitative data (Right to Play 2021b). Believing in the superiority of positivist research traditions, some research team members felt that research had to be top-down and quantitative. Some team members hesitated to accept participants' data analysis as "credible," and as a result, did not record what participants said in participatory data analysis sessions. While Right to Play program staff, coaches, and junior leaders who assisted in participatory data collection and analysis sessions were comfortable with the use of participation in *programs*, they required more training on how to apply participatory techniques in *research*. It also took some time for Right to Play staff who routinely carried out monitoring and evaluation tasks to accept a crossover to participatory research methods.

With the assistance of a researcher from Global Women's Institute (our donor), I delivered training on self-reflexivity, participatory data collection, analysis, and facilitation skills during the in-country workshops. Research team members also had access to a manual detailing data collection and analysis tools. While the training sessions and manual were indispensable, much more training and practice in participatory research was required, given that it was a new and challenging skill. In addition, changes in staffing at Right to Play meant that some session facilitators did not receive training on the use of the data collection and analysis tools. Rapid NGO staff turnover can hinder research partnerships when institutional memory is lost and when staff have limited time to devote to research studies (Olivier et al. 2016). In our case, fewer data collection and analysis sessions took place than planned due to staff turnover. Understandably, staff privileged programmatic work over research.

## CONCLUSIONS

Despite several challenges in doing participatory analysis in transnational, collaborative research settings—such as not scheduling enough time for data collection and analysis sessions and not being able to trace some of the original participants—our findings were still enriched by participants' views, perspectives, and priorities. When we did conduct participatory data analysis sessions, participants' open and honest discussions, increased engagement, and heightened voice led to deep, localized understandings of—and ways to challenge—gender norms and inequalities. Additionally, while there were difficulties stemming from the diverse locations, perspectives, and training needs of our transnational research team, we did engage a large number of team members in data analysis, contribute to the research and programmatic needs of Right to Play, and challenge positivist assumptions about research and data analysis within the organization. Through the projects, research team members increased their understanding, appreciation, and knowledge of participatory data collection and analysis methodologies. Right to Play has also been making positive steps toward establishing intentional, reflexive spaces and processes for staff to discuss their experiences with participatory and feminist research methods.[6]

We have built upon our learnings and reflections to design and implement a new collaborative research project in Mali and Senegal. In an effort to overcome some of the challenges and shortfalls of our previous research, we plan to work with a smaller number of youth and increase the amount of training for in-country research team members and facilitators. We will also tie our research more closely to existing Right to Play programs in both countries to reduce the time and labour burden on in-country research team members. As the existing programs in Mali and Senegal are solidly focused on youth empowerment, we have decided to increase the youths' engagement and role as research partners. Youth participants in Mali and Senegal will be engaged in every step of the research process, from the development of research questions and methodologies, to data collection and analysis, to advocacy and sharing.

While we experienced challenges in realizing a decolonial feminist approach to participatory data analysis, the formation of a collective understanding and appreciation for this approach and Right to Play's "buy-in" for its use in future collaborative projects is a highly positive outcome. Research decisions were driven by team members in Uganda, Lebanon, Rwanda, Mozambique, and Ghana who cultivated strong ties with our youth research participants. In the project in Uganda and Lebanon, we ensured that transnational research team members were able to connect and share ideas and findings throughout the different research phases, including research method and tool design, data collection, analysis, and sharing of findings. We also ensured that our projects' research objectives were linked to the priorities and programs of Right to Play and their program participants, and that participants of all genders were able to participate and exercise their voice and decision making. Overall, when researchers, NGOs, and young people learn and carry out research together, meaning-making is deepened and enriched.

## AUTHOR'S NOTE

I appreciate the dedication and commitment of Right to Play to collaborative research and learning. For our project in Uganda and Lebanon (Human Research Ethics Board protocol number 101026), I gratefully acknowledge funding received from George Washington University's Global Women's Institute (GWI) and the Building GBV Evidence program, and technical support from GWI Research Scientist, Maureen Murphy. For our project in Rwanda, Ghana, and Mozambique (Human Research Ethics Board protocol number 100749), I acknowledge funding from the Social Sciences and Humanities Research Council's Partnership Engage Grant.

I would like to acknowledge the collaborative work of research team members in Uganda and Lebanon: Aamina Adham, Claude Cheta, Rachel Pell, Dr. Victoria Namuggala, Maya Baghdadi, Emmanuel Mbidde, Hope Masika, Ghinwa Monzer, Mohammed Lawah, and junior leaders. I would like to thank Right to Play staff members Yussif Yakubu, Fouzia Alhassan, Harrison Akubor, and Saraswati Arthur in Ghana; Nelson Matsimbe, Amina Issa, and Jose Matavele Jr in Mozambique; Vestine Mukandoli, Robert Umurutasate, and Mary Khozi in Rwanda; and the university students who collected data in these countries. Finally, I would like to thank the youth from Ghana, Rwanda, Mozambique, Uganda, and Lebanon who participated in our research projects.

## NOTES

1.  Intersectionality, a concept originating in critical race theory and Black feminist thought, sharpens the focus on intersecting oppressions that affect historically marginalized groups (Crenshaw 1989; 1990).

2.  I trained the Right to Play staff and local university students in Ghana in person, and those in Mozambique and Rwanda virtually.

3.  Vignettes are short, fictional scenarios or stories developed by researchers to prompt discussions on particular themes. Researchers have used vignettes with adolescents, hoping that fictional stories about sensitive issues would lead to open discussion with less trauma and personal disclosure (Pincock et al. 2023).

4.  Mary-Elizabeth Vaccaro (2023) discusses similar challenges while conducting research with transient populations such as homeless women in Canada.

5.  We chose Dedoose for this project because it allows for multiple users to code the same data for little cost and it is relatively easy to use. However, it requires that users have access to the internet, which sometimes posed problems for research team members in Uganda. Research team members in both countries were pleased with the ability of the software to store and organize data (both written and visual), and to elicit key themes and key quotations that could be used to write evaluation reports, proposals, and advocacy and communication plans.

6.  For more on this, see Alina Potts et al. (2022). Right to Play has a global community of practice for its monitoring and evaluation staff. They are considering including program staff, including gender specialists and junior leaders in this community of practice, and they are organizing more discussions and learning opportunities for their staff on participatory and feminist methodologies.

## REFERENCES

Akerstrom, Jeanette, and Elinor Brunnberg. 2012. "Young People as Partners in Research: Experiences from an Interactive Research Circle with Adolescent Girls." *Qualitative Research* 13 (5): 528–545.

Akesson, Bree, Miranda D'Amico, Myriam Denov, Fatima Khan, Warren Linds, and Claudia Mitchell. 2014. "'Stepping Back' as Researchers: Addressing Ethics in Arts-Based Approaches to Working with War-Affected Children in School and Community Settings." *Educational Research for Social Change* 3 (1): 75–89.

Aniekwe, Chika C., Rachel Hayman, Anna Mdee, Job Akuni, Priya Lall, and Daniel Stevens. 2012. *Academic-NGO Collaboration in International Development Research: A Reflection on the Issues.* Development Studies Association of the UK and Ireland.

Banati, Prerna, Lauren Rumble, Nicola Jones, and Sarah Hendriks. 2021. "Agency and Empowerment for Adolescent Girls: An Intentional Approach to Policy and Programming." *Journal of Youth Development* 16 (2/3): 239–254.

Bhatia, Amiya, Amber Peterman, and Alessandra Guedes. 2020. "Remote Data Collection on Violence against Children during COVID-19: A Conversation with Experts on Research Priorities, Measurement and Ethics." https://www.unicef-irc.org/article/2004-collecting-remote-data-on-violence-against-children-during-covid-19-a-conversation.html.

Bill and Melinda Gates Foundation. n.d. "What Gets Measured Matters: A Methods Note for Measuring Women and Girls' Empowerment Gender Equality Toolbox." https://www.gatesgenderequalitytoolbox.org/wp-content/uploads/BMGF_Methods-Note-Measuring-Empowerment-1.pdf.

Blaisdell, Caralyn, Lorna Arnott, Kate Wall, and Carol Robinson. 2019. "Look Who's Talking: Using Creative, Playful Arts-Based Methods in Research with Young Children." *Journal of Early Childhood Research* 17: 14–31.

Bradbury-Jones, Caroline, and Julie Taylor. 2015. "Engaging with Children as Co-Researchers: Challenges, Counter-Challenges, and Solutions." *International Journal of Social Research Methodology* 18 (2): 161–173.

Campo, Raffaele, Fabrizio Baldassarre, and Rosalind Lee. 2019. "A Play-Based Methodology for Studying Children: Playification." *Systemic Practice and Action Research* 32 (1): 113–123.

Coad, Jane, and Ruth Evans. 2008. "Reflections on Practical Approaches to Involving Children and Young People in the Data Analysis Process." *Children and Society* 22 (1): 41–52.

Collins, Patricia H. 1991. *Black Feminist Thought: Knowledge, Consciousness, and the Politics of Empowerment*. Routledge.

Cottrell, Barbara, and Jane L. Parpart. 2006. "Academic-Community Collaboration, Gender Research, and Development: Pitfalls and Possibilities." *Development in Practice* 16 (1): 15–26.

Crenshaw, Kimberlé. 1989. "Demarginalizing the Intersection of Race and Sex: A Black Feminist Critique of Antidiscrimination Doctrine, Feminist Theory and Antiracist Politics." *University of Chicago Legal Forum* 1 (8): 139–167.

Crenshaw, Kimberlé. 1990. "Mapping the Margins: Intersectionality, Identity Politics, and Violence against Women of Colour." *Stanford Law Review* 43 (6): 1241–1299.

Duncan, Pauline. 2021. "Using Drawing as a Playful Research Encounter with Young Children." In *Research through Play: Participatory Methods in Early Childhood*, edited by Lorna Arnott and Kate Wall. SAGE.

Emmison, Michael. 2021. "Visual Research: Issues and Developments." In *Qualitative Research, 5th Edition*, edited by David Silverman. SAGE.

Falcon, Sylvanna M. 2016. "Transnational Feminism as a Paradigm for Decolonizing the Practice of Research: Identifying Feminist Principles and Methodology Criteria for US-Based Scholars." *Frontiers: A Journal of Women Studies* 37 (1): 174–194.

Gervais, Myriam, Sandra Weber, and Caroline Caron. 2018. *Guide to Participatory Feminist Research*. Institute for Gender, Sexuality, and Feminist Studies, McGill University.

Global Affairs Canada. 2017. "Canada's Feminist International Assistance Policy." https://www.international.gc.ca/world-monde/assets/pdfs/iap2-eng.pdf?_ga=2.166407866.520540043.1672155547-1692220289.1671992538.

Global Affairs Canada. n.d.a. "Policy on Gender Equality." https://www.international.gc.ca/world-monde/funding-financement/policy-politique.aspx?lang=eng.

Global Affairs Canada. n.d.b. "Gender Equality and Empowering Measurement Tool." https://www.international.gc.ca/world-monde/funding-financement/introduction_gender_emt-outil_renforcement_epf.aspx?lang=eng.

Global Women's Institute. 2017. *Gender-Based Violence Research, Monitoring, and Evaluation with Refugee and Conflict-Affected Populations: A Manual and Toolkit for Researchers and Practitioners*. George Washington University.

Guy, Batsheva, and Brittany Arthur. 2021. "Feminism and Participatory Research: Exploring Intersectionality, Relationships, and Voice in Participatory Research from a Feminist Perspective." In *The SAGE Handbook of Participatory Research and Inquiry*, edited by Danny Burns, Jo Howard, and Sonia M. Ospina. SAGE.

Iyer, Pushpa. 2020. "Do Not Colonize Decolonization." *The Peace Chronicle: The Magazine of the Peace and Justice Studies Association* 12 (2): 36–38.

Johnson, Vicky, and Andy West. 2021. "Approaches and Creative Research Methods with Children and Youth." In *The SAGE Handbook of Participatory Research and Inquiry*, edited by Danny Burns, Jo Howard, and Sonia M. Ospina. SAGE.

Jones, Nicola, Elizabeth Presler-Marshall, Agnieszka Malachowska et al. 2019. *Qualitative Research Toolkit: GAGE's Approach to Researching with Adolescents*. Gender and Adolescence Global Evidence.

Joyappa, Vinitha, and Donna J. Martin. 1996. "Exploring Alternative Research Epistemologies for Adult Education: Participatory Research, Feminist Research and Feminist Participatory Research." *Adult Education Quarterly* 47 (1): 1–14.

Khuwaja, Hussain M.A., Rozina Karmaliani, Judith McFarlane, and Rachel Jewkes. 2019. "Use of Activity-Oriented Questions in Qualitative Focus Group Discussions to Explore Youth Violence in Sindh, Pakistan." *Nursing Practice Today* 6 (4): 162–166.

Kimotho, Njeri, Catherine Odenyo-Ndekera, and Janna Visser. 2023. "Reimagining Development from Local Voices and Positions—Southern Feminist Movements in the Lead." In *Reimagining Civil Society Collaborations in Development: Starting from The South*, edited by Margit van Wessel, Tiina Kontinen, and Justice N. Bawole. Routledge.

Kincheloe, Joe L., and Peter McLaren. 2005. "Rethinking Critical Theory and Qualitative Research." In *The SAGE Handbook of Qualitative Research*, edited by Norman Denzin and Yvonna Lincoln. SAGE.

Lather, Patti. 1991. *Getting Smart: Feminist Research and Pedagogy with/in the Postmodern*. Routledge.

Lenette, Caroline. 2022. *Participatory Action Research: Ethics and Decolonization*. Oxford University Press.

MacEntee, Katie, and Claudia Mitchell. 2011. "Lost and Found in Translation: Participatory Analysis and Working with Collections of Drawings." In *Picturing Research: Drawing as Visual Methodologies*, edited by Linda Theron, Claudia Mitchell, Ann Smith, and Jean Stuart. Sense Publishers.

McCleary-Sills, Jennifer, Zayid Douglas, Richard Mabala, and Ellen Weiss. 2011. *Meet Them Where They Are: Participatory Action Research with Adolescent Girls*. International Center for Research on Women.

McLean, Lindsay, and Anny T. Modi. 2016. "'Empowerment' of Adolescent Girls and Young Women in Kinshasa: Research about Girls, by Girls." *Gender and Development* 24 (3): 475–491.

Mitchell, Claudia, Kattie Lussier, and Fatoumata Keita. 2022. "Youth Agency in Times of Crisis: Exploring Education and Conflict in Mali through Participatory Visual Approaches with Youth." *Frontiers in Education* 7: 1–15.

Mitchell, Claudia, and Marni Sommer. 2016. "Participatory Visual Methodologies in Global Public Health." *Global Public Health* 11 (5/6): 521–527.

Mitchell, Claudia, Linda Theron, Jean Stuart, Ann Smith, and Zachariah Campbell. 2011. "Drawings as Research Method." In *Picturing Research: Drawing as Visual Methodology*, edited by Linda Theron, Claudia Mitchell, Ann Smith, and Jean Stuart. Sense Publishers.

Olivier, Catherine, Matthew R. Hunt, and Valéry Ridde. 2016. "NGO–Researcher Partnerships in Global Health Research: Benefits, Challenges, and Approaches That Promote Success." *Development in Practice* 26 (4): 444–455.

Parpart, Jane L., and Swati Parashar. 2019. "Rethinking the Power of Silence in Insecure and Gendered Sites." In *Rethinking Silence, Voice and Agency in Contested Gendered Terrains*, edited by Jane L. Partpart and Swati Parashar. Routledge.

Pederson, Ann, Lorraine Greaves, and Nancy Poole. 2015. "Gender-Transformative Health Promotion for Women: A Framework for Action." *Health Promotion International* 30 (1): 140–150.

Percy-Smith, Barry. 2021. "Creating Spaces for Participatory Social Learning and Change with Young People." In *The SAGE Handbook of Qualitative Research*, edited by Norman Denzin and Yvonna Lincoln. SAGE.

Pincock, Kate, Dianne Verhoeven, Nicola Jones, and Roberte Isimbi. 2023. "'They Say It Was Her Fault...This Is Not True!' Using Vignettes with Adolescent Girls to Collectively Address Norms about Sexual Violence." *International Journal of Qualitative Methods* 22: 1–11.

Plan International UK. 2019. "Girl-Led Monitoring and Evaluation: An Approach to Empowering Girls." https://girlseducationchallenge.org/media/w54dmo5j/gate-gec_girl-led_report_vf.pdf.

Porter, Gina. 2016. "Reflections on Co-Investigation through Peer Research with Young People and Older People in Sub-Saharan Africa." *Qualitative Research* 16 (3): 293–304.

Potts, Alina, Harriet Kolli, and Loujine Fattal. 2022. "Whose Voices Matter? Using Participatory, Feminist and Anthropological Approaches to Centre Power and Positionality in Research on Gender-Based Violence in Emergencies." *Global Public Health* 17 (10): 2530–2546.

Rathgeber, Eva M. 2009. "Research Partnerships in International Health: Capitalizing on Opportunity." Paper presented at the stakeholders meeting on Strengthening Research Partnerships for Neglected Diseases of Poverty, Berlin, March 16–18.

Right to Play. 2021a. Notes from Global MEL Meeting, July 15.

Right to Play. 2021b. RTP Baseline Survey with MEL Staff, GWI Project, September 28.

Right to Play. 2023. Right to Play Manual: "Play-Based Tools and Approaches for Collecting and Analyzing Evidence amongst Adolescents in Humanitarian Settings in Uganda and Lebanon."

Roper, Laura. 2002. "Achieving Successful Academic-Practitioner Research Collaborations." *Development in Practice* 12 (3/4): 338–345.

Save the Children Norway. 2008. "A Compilation of Tolls Used during a Thematic Evaluation and Documentation on Children's Participation in Armed Conflict, Post Conflict and Peace Building, 2006–2008." https://resourcecentre.savethechildren.net/document/kit-tools-participatory-research-and-evaluation-children-young-people-and-adults-compilation/.

Theron, Linda, Jean Stuart, and Claudia Mitchell. 2011. "A Positive, African Ethical Approach to Collecting and Interpreting Drawings: Some Considerations." In *Picturing Research: Drawing as Visual Methodology*, edited by Linda Theron, Claudia Mitchell, Ann Smith, and Jean Stuart. Sense Publishers.

Vaccaro, Mary-Elizabeth. 2023. "Reflections on 'Doing' Participatory Data Analysis with Women Experiencing Long-Term Homelessness." *Action Research* 21 (3): 332–350.

Vanner, Catherine. 2015. "Positionality at the Center: Constructing an Epistemological and Methodological Approach for a Western Feminist Doctoral Candidate Conducting Research in the Postcolonial." *International Journal of Qualitative Methods* 14 (4): 1–12.

SARAH FLICKER, NADHA HASSEN,
JESSICA FIELDS, AND THE
4THERECORD TEAM

# 4THERECORD

An Intersectional Feminist Approach
to Collaborative Data Analysis

## INTRODUCTION

> I literally did not know research can look like this, and it
> does, and it works so well. And now I'm like, why doesn't it
> always do this?—*undergraduate research assistant*

4THERECORD is an interdisciplinary research project that focuses on
understanding whether and how COVID-19 has changed the ways that
queer and racialized women and non-binary young people in Canada,
Australia, and the United States think about risk. Our commitment to
documenting these changed understandings "for the record" emerged
in the early days of the pandemic. Experts and policymakers implored
many of us to stay home while asking others to put their bodies on the
line. Racialized young women in particular were called upon to subject

themselves to higher risks of COVID exposure in their capacities as caregivers and front-line workers, jobs in which women of colour are demographically overrepresented. Those performing these gendered pandemic roles were at once performatively celebrated for their bravery and shunned because of the risks they posed to others. As rates of COVID skyrocketed among poor and racialized communities, these same young people experienced heightened rates of surveillance and social control that made pursuing relationships especially taboo. Ideas and norms about risk seemed to be changing daily. Quotidian routines became dangerous. Our very breath became a potential contagion. Online romances and sexting seemed safer. Decisions people made about their bodies and their movement through the world became burdened by the responsibility of caring for entire communities.

Researchers routinely approach such contexts of vulnerability with a normative understanding of young people as "at risk" and therefore in need of protection from a range of social, emotional, cultural, and physical risks, including sexual violence, unplanned pregnancies, sexually transmitted infections, sexism, and stunted ambitions (Leahy 2014). An intersectional lens (Lokot and Avakyan 2020; Bowleg 2012; Crenshaw 2002) complicates this story: racialized and LGBTQ2S+ young women and gender-expansive youth are regularly cast as sites of (hypersexualized) risk to themselves and others and therefore as in need of extra containment (Fields 2008). Our fields—including public health, sociology, social work, and education—have been so concerned with mitigating the risks of sexual activity for youth that researchers have failed to consider the risks of avoiding risk (Fields and Garcia 2018; Gilbert 2014). Under certain circumstances and for some young women and gender-expansive youth, sexual experimentation is a critical building block of one's sexual self-concept and relationship skills (Fortenberry 2014; Shulman and Connolly 2013). 4theRecord insists that adults need not pretend that youth are not subject to a host of violations (Bay-Cheng and Fava 2014; Flicker et al. 2013; Bay-Cheng 2019); our team reverses the idea that youth are risky to ask how systemic violence and injustice put youth at risk. Sexuality is not the source of danger; instead, the actions young people take that are framed as "risky" by education,

**FIGURE 6.1** | Group photograph of most leads at a knowledge mobilization event.
(Photograph by Madeleine North, used with permission.)

social work, and public health sectors may be meaningful and strategic responses to social, cultural, material, and historical conditions (Fields et al. 2015; Gilbert 2007).

A team of senior and mid-career feminist scholars (hereafter referred to as "leads") who were interested in how the social conditions wrought by COVID were shaping and limiting the possibilities for risk (and reward) came together to design and launch this project. Compelled by disability studies' claim that all people should be afforded the "dignity of risk" (Perske 1972; Gill 2015), the leads approached youth sexual expression and experimentation as developmental rights that adults are ethically bound to support by ensuring young people's entitlement and access—no matter their personal attributes or social locations–to complete information and services (Flicker et al. 2009; Bay-Cheng 2013). Leads wanted to unpack how these "unprecedented" times, on the one hand, reinscribed raced, gendered, and homophobic discourses of risk and, on the other, created space for new possibilities.

The leads committed to using feminist participatory methods to examine these issues and built a team that included university students who were members of queer and/or racialized communities.

To better reflect the demographic that 4theRecord imagined engaging and to explicitly welcome those who commonly experience marginalization, project leads prioritized the hiring, training, and supporting of young people who identify as racialized and/or queer as undergraduate research assistants (uRAs) or graduate research assistants (gRAs). Over the course of two years, this intergenerational and interdisciplinary team involved twelve uRAs, seven gRAs, a project coordinator, and six project leads from five universities across three countries and two time zones. Student participation continues as leads co-author 4theRecord publications with uRAs and gRAs. Leads also now supervise graduate students working with the data in coursework and in conference presentations, theses, and dissertations; most of these students have not worked previously as 4theRecord gRAs.

Between February and June 2022, 4theRecord recruited racialized and/or LGBTQ2S+ young women and non-binary youth (ages sixteen to twenty-one) in Toronto, New York City, and Melbourne to engage in three stages of data collection.

1.  An online survey gathered demographic details and measures of participants' attitudes toward and experiences with risk and risk-taking (n=703).
2.  An interactive timeline invited a subset of participants to record risk experiences (across various life domains) over the preceding three years through a mobile-friendly online portal. The timeline included open- and close-ended prompts and encouraged participants to record feelings and to upload mixed media (n=321).
3.  A subset of the timeline participants also completed in-depth synchronous online interviews that lasted approximately forty-five to seventy minutes (n=102), conducted mostly by trained uRAs to further explore timeline events and other experiences/perceptions of risk.

The resulting cumulative dataset is diverse, complex, rich, and large. Of the participants interviewed, 84 percent identified as something other than straight, 46 percent identified as non-binary, gender fluid, or trans, and 78 percent identified as racialized. Analysis is ongoing, having begun during the design phase and now continuing to unfold as the team makes sense of the data collected.

Much of feminist participatory research outlined in the literature is characterized by intentional, small, and local projects (Reid et al. 2006). Indeed, many of our team members have a long practice of working in this way (see, for example, Switzer and Flicker 2021; Fields et al. 2021), but the scope of 4theRecord was larger than anything any team member had previously attempted. In this chapter, we provide a detailed account of how 4theRecord trained a large and diverse group of uRAs and gRAs to conduct feminist participatory analysis. We describe how we collectively developed and applied a coding framework to our dataset and began the process of making meaning together. Based on these reflections, we identify five lessons learned and conclude by putting our lessons in conversation with the literature on participatory feminist analysis.

## AN EXPLICITLY INTERSECTIONAL FEMINIST PARTICIPATORY APPROACH

> It's opened so many doors for me in terms of like research and understanding, like the bigger concepts of like sexuality, and like identity, intersectionality, it's like you learn about it in class, but then actually applying it to like real life. It's a whole different world and like this is like a big girl job. —*uRA*

4theRecord rests on an intersectional feminist commitment to challenging gendered and other intersecting systems of oppression, emphasizing social change, and creating "new relationships, better laws and improved institutions" (Reinharz and Davidman 1992, 175). Feminist theories provide "intellectual tools for examining injustices we confront, framing arguments to support demands for change, and developing place-appropriate change strategies" (Frisby et al. 2009, 17). They offer 4theRecord a foundation from which to illuminate normative injustices that often go unnoticed.

Drawing on Michelle Fine et al.'s (2021) concept of "participatory contact zones," team members intentionally created "spaces where research teams of very differently positioned people bring distinct levels of power, lines of analysis, experience, and forms of expertise, and together...analyze qualitative and quantitative materials, always centring the perspectives of those most impacted by injustice" (345). By seeking out and hiring a group of graduate and undergraduate students who represented the diversity of the queer and racialized young women and non-binary community members under study, project leads intentionally built diversity into the participatory analytic frames. Leads did so in a staged fashion, by first hiring a core group of gRAs who then recruited and on-boarded uRAs. In this way, 4theRecord fostered multiple layers of mentorship and intergenerational collaboration.

## GETTING READY FOR PARTICIPATORY FEMINIST ANALYSIS

### Gathering In Real Life (IRL)

Throughout data collection, our team met and collaborated online. In June 2022, with the easing of pandemic restrictions and a shift towards data analysis, the leads organized a three-day in-person retreat. Team members travelled to Toronto from Australia, the United States, and the suburbs outside Toronto. The project budget covered travel expenses, including per diems. The retreat aimed to 1) foster team building and networking; 2) provide analysis training; and 3) collaboratively develop a coding framework.

**FIGURE 6.2** | Group photograph of uRAs and gRAs after the scavenger hunt.
(Photograph by author.)

Despite collaborating for nearly a year, the coding retreat was the first time many team members had met in person. The project leads knew one another, and they had spent time in person with students they had previously supervised. These ties were few, however, and they needed to expand if the team was going to cohere more broadly. Our time together began with a fun scavenger hunt to introduce visitors and the RAs to Toronto and one another.

## Developing a Preliminary Coding Framework

To prepare for the retreat, the project leads asked all team members to 1) review a minimum of five timelines and related interviews in which they were neither the interviewer nor the transcriber and 2) examine these alongside interviews (and the related timelines) they *did* facilitate or transcribe. The goal was for each person to identify and compile a

**FIGURE 6.3** | Collaboratively developing our coding framework.
(Photograph by author.)

list of ten themes, ideas, and patterns they observed in at least three different interviews. This list would serve as a basis for discussion during the retreat.

During the initial work session, Sarah introduced the concept of coding as a method for organizing data to compare different participants' experiences. She used the analogy of a #hashtag to explain the importance of using labels to categorize and find information. Each person wrote their pre-prepared themes on sticky notes and grouped them together on a wall. The team collaboratively named these groups based on the #hashtag concept, quickly identifying the most common and meaningful themes.

Next, Sarah demonstrated the mechanics of coding using Taguette, a free online application that allows multiple users to code and share simple datasets. She invited everyone to take a turn, and then illustrated how a theme gets taken up across multiple interviews. This hands-on demonstration reinforced the power of computer-assisted coding in qualitative research. Next, leads divided the team into small groups, ensuring a mix of gRAs, uRAs, and project leads in each group. Each was tasked with providing a clear definition for a series of codes. Small groups presented their initial work to the larger group for feedback and discussion.

While coming to a consensus on some codes was not difficult, others proved much more challenging. For instance, the team had a lengthy and important debate about whether instances of rape, incest, and sexual assault should be included under the code "Sex, Dating, and Romance." One gRA with extensive experience in assault counselling argued these experiences should be coded as violence—not as sex. While there was general support for this assertion, things got more complicated when the team tried to apply this rule to specific examples from the study. Would it be based on how *coders* read the interactions or how *participants* understood their experience? For instance, in one reported case of incest, the participant did not characterize the experience as violence. In another example, a participant recounted a story of unwanted sex that a uRA read as rape, but the participant had never explicitly used that language. The group considered: whose reading mattered more, the researchers' or the participants'?

Ultimately, leads decided to take an expansive approach in this first round of coding: the team would define codes to allow a multiplicity of viewpoints and the application of multiple codes to a single segment of data. Consequently, these instances would be included in *both* the "sex" and "violence" codes. Having these discussions helped us clarify the purpose and value of this first round of coding and decide as a group what was "in" and what was "out" for each code. These discussions also highlighted for us who made the decisions to code, when to code, and how to code. The leads paid close attention to research transcripts, listened carefully to their gRA and uRA colleagues, and recognized gaps across the team's understandings of sex and violence; the team's later work with the data would be stronger because of this discussion during the early coding session. We have no doubt that the gRAs and uRAs shaped the coding and in the remaining months of our work together informed our approach to the data and one another. We also recognize that, at least formally, whether and how the gRAs and uRAs shaped the project remained the decision of the leads.

These discussions were rich, intellectually stimulating, and uncomfortable. The team had similar debates around how to code for queerness and disability and ultimately also adopted expansive and collapsed codes for this first round. It was a moment in our project where lived experience of the phenomenon under study sometimes clashed with the professional data analysis expertise of investigators. These conversations and decisions haunted many of us for months to come— not necessarily because the project leads felt the team had come to the wrong decisions, but because, in the process of making those decisions, the power hierarchies 4theRecord sought to disrupt became apparent and yet, in the end, they remained intact.

## Refining the Framework

While preliminary drafts of the codebook were developed at the retreat, the small groups that worked on the initial definitions were subsequently tasked with refining their work after they had time to assimilate feedback. Groups met over Zoom to reflect, refine, and collate our work. The team used the collaborative writing functions associated with SharePoint's Word applications to ensure that 4theRecord had a centrally accessible repository. Once all drafts were uploaded, co-Principal Investigators (PIs) Jessica and Sarah met to review and refine them. In some cases, Jessica and Sarah amalgamated similar codes; in others, they and other leads added new ones.

After the in-person retreat, Jessica and Sarah explored several qualitative data management software options, including NVIVO, Dedoose, and Taguette. NVIVO was favoured by some project leads due to their familiarity with it, but it had significant drawbacks: it was expensive, had compatibility issues between Mac and PC users, and lacked adequate collaborative functions. Taguette, although free and user-friendly, lacked the necessary functionality for mixed-methods analyses. Ultimately, our team selected Dedoose for its balanced features, cost-effectiveness, and cloud-based model, which facilitated collaboration across devices and allowed multiple coders to work simultaneously from different locations—a crucial aspect for our large, transnational team.

Sarah and Jessica scheduled a series of Dedoose trainings for gRAs and uRAs over Zoom, supported by Cheery Attia, a gRA. These sessions covered both technical elements (which buttons to push when) as well as conceptual elements (how to decide how many codes to apply to any given excerpt and how much contextual information to include in each excerpt). Weekly meetings focused on refining the coding framework, troubleshooting software challenges, supporting one another, and confirming the quality of the completed coding.

To prepare for some of these meetings, uRAs coded the same document and then compared their approaches. The goal was to inculcate a spirit of collaboration, curiosity, and growth. As one gRA offered, it was "not about calling people out, not saying it was wrong, but really like we're here to learn. And that framing was so key, because that trickled down into our smaller group meetings, and also with the interviews." Being asked in a supportive environment to defend their decision to assign (or not assign) a code encouraged accountability, transparency, and deeper engagement with the data and with colleagues.

## Solidifying the Framework

After applying the framework to the first dozen interviews, the team came together to update and refine existing definitions, consolidate and collapse a few codes, and add new codes. Leads wanted to find a balance between, on the one hand, creating a process that was iterative and responsive to emerging themes and, on the other, ensuring a sturdy enough framework for application by diverse coders. Because so many people were involved in interviewing, reviewing transcripts, and asynchronous coding, clear and robust instructions were crucial. Large teams need to be extra careful about ensuring clarity; ambiguity can lead to divergent applications of a single code, and any change to the codebook likely means that previously coded interviews will have to be reviewed. Ultimately, the team decided on fourteen thematic codes.

Each question in the interview guide also became a code. Ironically, these codes proved to be the most challenging for coders to apply because so many of the interviews were semi-structured, and the lines of a conversation were, at times, tricky to follow. Lengthy discussions about how to code answers when people responded to different questions proved necessary: for example, do you code for the question asked, or the one answered, or both, or neither? In the end, many of the codes overlapped and answers were assigned multiple codes.

## Coding the Data and Taking Care of Each Other

Our project coordinator, Amanda, utilized the online project management tool Asana to assign tasks and track workflow. In collaboration with Jessica and Sarah, Amanda formed working groups consisting of small teams of uRAs supervised by gRAs. Throughout the summer of 2022, these teams met regularly until all 102 interviews were coded. The teams contended with tremendous variation in the quality of the audio recordings of interviews (related to internet bandwidth, microphone quality, background noise, speech patterns, and accents); the style of interviewers and participants (for example, how closely interviewers followed interview guides); the quality of the Otter.ai auto-generated transcripts; and team members' transcript "cleaning" styles (for example, thoroughness or attention to gestures and facial expressions). The presence of some conditions resulted in those transcripts requiring more attention and time from coders. The interviews were often quite long (almost two hours), and many covered emotionally difficult content including assaults, trauma, and death.

Meanwhile, uRAs continued to clean, organize, and manage the data. Seventy, a gRA, worked on the survey data and became our de facto SPSS (statistical package for the social sciences) software expert. When the survey data was ready, Cheery uploaded and integrated that quantitative demographic data with the qualitative data already available through Dedoose. She trained herself and then the rest of the team on how to use the mixed-methods functionality in Dedoose to query the data.

Undergraduate and graduate research assistants brought their challenges to small team meetings to solve together, although project leads were also available to debrief. Finally, given the sensitivity of the interview content, our project benefitted from a feminist researcher with training as a psychotherapist who offered her services at no cost to the team. Attending to the emotional labour of carrying stories was an important intersectional feminist practice. Nearly everyone on the team was drawn to this work because of their personal connections to the issues under study. These experiences bear the marks of interlocking systems of oppression related to gender, race, immigration, histories of violence, and age, among others. Sarah and Jessica encouraged team members to step back and ask for support when needed (Flicker et al., 2023). An ethic of care grew amongst the team, even as team members worked across tremendous distance and difference.

## From Coding to Making Meaning

The summer culminated in a second in-person gathering to which all continuing team members were invited. Almost everyone from North America returned in August 2022 to celebrate our work and to find patterns in the organized data. Budgetary and time constraints did not allow the Australian colleagues to join the retreat.

The second retreat included a workshop on how best to navigate Dedoose. While team members had gained some experience with Dedoose through earlier coding efforts, few understood the powerful tools that the software could bring to analysis. The workshop thus began with team members searching the data for specified information (for example, what did a Black lesbian from Melbourne say about wearing face masks? or, how do South Asian youth in Toronto feel about online school?). This allowed participants to become familiar with Dedoose as a platform. Following this exercise, small groups reviewed the same chunk of coded data. While every group had the same full set of quotes, each group's reading was organized by a different category of difference (race, age, or city). Each group was tasked with reviewing their package and then answering several analytical questions drawn from Sarah Flicker and Stephanie Nixon's (2015, 618) DEPICT model:

1. Where is there agreement? Where is there disagreement?
2. What patterns do you see in your data? Are there silences worth noting?
3. To what extent is the race, age, or city of the participant relevant? What other demographics seem salient?
4. What structural factors may help us to understand why people chose to tell us the stories they shared (e.g., homophobia, neoliberalism)?
5. What does it all mean? What questions do we still have?

The team then explored the importance of first being able to accurately *describe* what the data tell us before moving to *analysis* regarding what it all means. This exercise crystalized the purpose and value of having spent all summer coding, and team members witnessed the full potential of the possibilities afforded by their hard work.

Ongoing analysis of 4theRecord data has leaned into practices that were honed during training. In winter 2023, some uRAs were engaged in another round of coding. Others were developing summary code data tables that compare similar groups of data across multiple dimensions of difference. Looking at the same quotes in different orders has helped deepen our intersectional analysis and locate new and emerging patterns. As new graduate students work with the survey, timelines, and interviews, introduce new codes, and pursue analyses we never anticipated, we learn from a new cohort of emerging scholars about the limits of our thinking and the importance of meeting those limits with an intergenerational and diverse community of researchers. As we increasingly relinquish control of coding, we feel the pleasure of having 1) gathered a powerful collection of stories of young queer, non-binary, and racialized lives during the pandemic; 2) created a methodologically sound dataset that reflects intergenerational, intersectional, and feminist thinking; and 3) ensured that this dataset is a resource for emerging and early scholars who will now take the work in untold directions.

## Preparing this Chapter

> I feel like I learned so much, and really grew through the project.—*uRA*

Throughout the project, the entire research team periodically assessed our collective progress and processes. During regular meetings, facilitators (usually leads or gRAs) allowed time for check-ins and feedback. Team members also had the chance to participate in formal process evaluations via surveys and interviews, which were recorded and transcribed. Sarah carefully reviewed these transcripts alongside her fieldnotes, project emails, Slack channels, and documentation to draft this paper. At times, feedback was offered anonymously. Any non-anonymous comments in this paper have been directly attributed (with permission).

Sarah and Nadha met on several occasions to review preliminary ideas and brainstorm possibilities. Sarah wrote the first draft and circulated it to Nadha and Jessica, and then to the rest of the 4theRecord team for feedback. Everyone was encouraged to consider how they were represented and (re-)write themselves in or out. We also held several Zoom calls to work through more challenging conversations and consider reviewer and team feedback. A final draft was re-circulated for sign off before submission to this collection's editors; we shared the final manuscript with the team when writing and editing concluded.

## Importance of Project Management and Technology

As a feminist group, the project leads began the project with an interest in flattening hierarchies and adopting fluid team roles and responsibilities. Sarah and Jessica soon realized that, with such a large team and complicated project, project management assistance would be a priority. When Amanda joined 4theRecord as a project coordinator, the team was stunned by the difference she made in our lives. Amanda was wonderful at organizing information, developing transparent systems and processes, and managing workflow. A personable, empathetic, and mature undergraduate student, Amanda was able to connect as a peer with both uRAs and gRAs. She quickly became a central hub and one-stop-shop for how to find and access project information and resources.

The essential yet often underappreciated administrative tasks of taking and effectively archiving meeting minutes, scheduling and sending calendar invites with Zoom links and reminders, and checking in with team members one-on-one became the glue that kept us together. While such tasks can sometimes be seen as bureaucratic necessities (or taken-for-granted, traditional women's work), within a feminist framework, such labour can and should be reframed as acts of care that build the fabric of community. Project management is skilled labour that is difficult to do and often invisible when done well. When Amanda had to take a brief leave to attend to personal matters, every part of the project stalled. As Nadha articulated, "the desire [for collaboration] is not enough...you need someone to hold that space and make it happen." Amanda held that space, and her project management was pivotal to the project's success.

## Skill Building as an Intentional Practice

In their reflections and debriefs, several uRAs and gRAs expressed pride in their individual and collective accomplishments. They highlighted the skills they cultivated around recruitment, interviewing, coding, and learning Dedoose software. Many talked about being nervous and unsure of their skills and abilities at the start of the project and their feelings of pride and joy as their confidence and competence grew. Caitlin, Cheery, Nadha, and Kethmi all mentioned that at first, they were overwhelmed by the sheer volume of work associated with coding 102 interviews in a limited timeframe. However, all were exceedingly proud when the team met its ambitious goals.

We view intentional skill building as an integral part of intersectional feminist praxis, reflecting our dedication to balancing process and outcome goals, providing ongoing training, and establishing supportive feedback systems. Some of our uRAs, as young, racialized women, have shared their experiences of feeling the need to work harder to prove themselves in academic and professional settings. They expressed feeling that they are not taken as seriously as their White, male, or older counterparts. By actively working to enhance their confidence, skills, and professional expertise, 4theRecord aimed to support their long-term career success. Several uRAs leveraged this experience to secure job opportunities in youth advocacy and mental health care, and some have cited the experience in their applications to graduate programs. Many others updated their CVs to highlight their newly acquired skills and applied experience.

## Value of Meeting, Recognition, and Celebration

Working remotely during the pandemic was a challenge. Feelings of isolation, Zoom fatigue, and burnout were a constant concern. Boundaries between home and work felt fluid during periods where many of us were confined to our domestic spaces. In addition, because 4theRecord included members in Melbourne, New York, and Toronto—two time zones, fourteen hours apart—the team often scheduled meetings outside of "normal" working hours (later in the evening/early in the morning) to avoid middle-of-the-night hours for team members on the other side of the world. While much of the work could be done asynchronously and remotely, synchronous and in-person touch points were invaluable to team building and morale.

**FIGURE 6.4** | gRA night out in Toronto.
(Photograph by taxi driver taken on author's phone.)

While large team meetings were extremely expensive and resource intensive, they were also priceless. After experimenting with fewer meetings, morale lapsed and productivity suffered. Synchronous meetings facilitated enthusiasm for diving into the work ahead, celebrating collective accomplishments, and recognizing team members who had gone above and beyond or who were marking milestones. Even when face-to-face meetings were impossible, the team prioritized time for online check-ins, laughter, and care.

## Disrupting Power Is Complicated

4theRecord played with a model of "participation" in which uRAs stood in and up for their communities. The decision to embrace participatory research was pragmatic—an extremely cost-effective approach to offering a large group of students sustainable employment at rates well above minimum wage standards. The team and project benefitted deeply from the student researchers' situated knowledge, skilled readiness, and training to take on research tasks. The decision to pursue participatory research was also political—an enactment of the project leads' commitment to training a new generation of scholars that "look different" from the academies in which most established researchers were trained.

Nevertheless, the choice also brought with it important tensions around power, relationality, and positionality. uRAs wore many hats—as researchers, employees, trainees, friends, and community representatives. Team members' multiple roles sometimes became complicated and, despite everyone's best efforts, may have inadvertently reinforced hierarchies that the team and project sought to dismantle. As two White middle-aged PIs, Sarah and Jessica were in many ways implicated in these systems of oppression that they and other team members continue to resist. Despite their political commitment to moving differently through the world, as project PIs, Sarah and Jessica were ultimately responsible for project implementation, management, and success. Project decision making was always complicated by the tensions of balancing commitments to equity, care, and process with commitments to outcomes, budgets, and overall project health. It was easy to lean into democratic decision making and consensus models when there was widespread agreement in the room, and it was far more challenging when competing viewpoints and demands were on the table.

## Value of Feminist Participatory Praxis

> The thing that I personally took away from this is like how empowering it is to work on a feminist team.—gRA

For racialized young people who came from communities where research has been wielded as a tool of oppression, this project provided an opening into other possibilities. As Jessica M., a gRA, reflected: "I learned that research, despite being a historically oppressive practice, is something that can provide a lot of meaning and value to marginalized communities. Research teams need not work in a hierarchy, there is a community that can be formed." Several team members positively remarked on the value of working on an explicitly feminist team. For Nadha, a feminist team "includes a commitment to process, discussion, [and] negotiating power dynamics." For many others, this profound shift in culture helped them to see and imagine futures for themselves in the academy where they could bring their "whole self to the table."

Team members provided plenty of examples of how feminist principles came alive for them during the project. Several commented on the ongoing care they felt from their peers and project leads. Many appreciated the space created on the team for people to step away and take health breaks when they needed them, and the ways other project team members were able to step in and pick up the slack. They appreciated the attempts to flatten hierarchies and be responsive to feedback. They talked about feeling seen, heard, and respected for their individual identities and strengths. Some mentioned how special it was to be invited into project leads' homes for celebratory events or the warm welcome offered to children, pets, and other family members who made surprise appearances on Zoom screens. Many commented on how much they appreciated the retreats and especially the time made for social activities and team building.

## CONCLUSION

The liberatory and transformative intentions that undergird feminist and participatory research approaches (Maguire 1996) make them a compelling choice for researchers interested in social change. Collaborative analysis has many benefits including the potential to enhance rigour, support reflexivity, allow for diverse and creative readings of the data, share the burden of a heavy workload, and democratize and demystify the research process (Flicker and Nixon 2015; Lokot and Wake 2021). However, collaborative analysis also requires a significant investment in capacity and team building, excellent coordination, management and facilitation, clear instructions, more rigid structures, and a commitment from team leads to relinquish control and attend to diverse (and sometimes conflicting) viewpoints (Flicker and Nixon 2015; Pushor 2008; Zreik et al. 2022).

Throughout our collaborative analysis process, 4theRecord attended to intersectional feminist principles such as negotiating power dynamics and hierarchies while grappling with the complexity of disrupting power. Thurayya Zreik et al. (2022) have written about the importance of team members coming to the table truly ready to engage and highlight the challenges that arise when some folks "concede" too early just to not "keep disagreeing" (5). We too felt this tension, and we consider it a good sign that people sat with the conflict and repeatedly felt confident to openly voice alternative viewpoints.

Over the course of the pandemic, many of us had to develop new relational practices. Building relationships online between and amongst team members took extra time and effort. Meeting regularly was important for building trust and extending care. Nevertheless, our in-person retreats stood out as especially important learning moments and connection points. Daphne Lordly et al. (2012) have also written about the advantages of "the collaborative retreat" to facilitate collective analysis and inspire creativity. Carving out time to be "totally focused and immersed in the analysis" (95) can help to deepen conversations and engagement. These gatherings provided an opportunity for our team to relax and have fun together; it was the fuel that helped to sustain us during long periods apart. For young queer and racialized people who often feel isolated in the academy, these points of connection were especially important.

Feminist participatory researchers do not always do it right, and often we do it wrong. In most cases, the fruits of this type of labour take years to fully ripen. While not always perfect, the uRAs and gRAs identified positive ways in which feminist principles were embedded throughout the 4theRecord project, in stark contrast to their experiences on other research projects. Drawing from Michelle Lokot and Caitlin Wake (2021), 4theRecord strove to embrace the challenges, messiness, and joy of this work. Consequently, we learned that our feminist participatory approach has the power to enrich not only our research findings but also the lives of people who engage along the way.

Realizing the emancipatory potential that these methods promise takes careful, intentional, and creative work.

## AUTHORS' NOTE

4theRecord was made possible through the Canadian Social Science and Humanities Research Council New Frontiers in Research Fund (NFRFE-2020-01107). The project received additional support from Monash University, University of Buffalo, University of Toronto Scarborough, Wilfrid Laurier University, and York University.

Past and present 4theRecord research team members include: Alanna Goldstein (Post-Doctoral Fellow), Amanda C. Galusha (Project Coordinator), Angela D. Norwood (Collaborator, Gallery), Anjalee Srinivasan (uRA), Bryanna "Ryn" Van Leeuwen (uRA), Caitlin Arizala (uRA), Cheery-Maria Attia (gRA), Ciann L. Wilson (Lead), Deana Leahy (Lead), Emily Sutton (uRA), Helen Yaqing Han (gRA), Janelle Athansius (uRA), Jen Gilbert (Lead), Jessica Mencia (gRA), Joy Kirsten Tolledo (uRA), Jules Ferguson (uRA), Julia Chapman (uRA), Kethmi C. Egodage (uRA), Kezia Arinka (uRA), Laina Y. Bay-Cheng (Lead), Nadia Bevan (gRA), Reece Rabanal (uRA), Seventy F. Hall (gRA), Vaish Puvipalan (uRA), and Zarin Parisa Tasnim (gRA).

## REFERENCES

Bay-Cheng, Laina Y. 2013. "Ethical Parenting of Sexually Active Youth: Ensuring Safety While Enabling Development." *Sex Education* 13 (2): 133–145.

Bay-Cheng, Laina Y. 2019. "Agency Is Everywhere, but Agency Is Not Enough: A Conceptual Analysis of Young Women's Sexual Agency." *The Journal of Sex Research* 56 (4/5): 462–474.

Bay-Cheng, Laina Y., and Nicole M. Fava. 2014. "What Puts 'At-Risk Girls' at Risk? Sexual Vulnerability and Social Inequality in the Lives of Girls in the Child Welfare System." *Sexuality Research and Social Policy* 11 (2): 116–125.

Bowleg, Lisa. 2012. "The Problem with the Phrase Women and Minorities: Intersectionality—An Important Theoretical Framework for Public Health." *American Journal of Public Health* 102 (7): 1267–1273.

Crenshaw, Kimberlé. 2002. "Mapping the Margins: Intersectionality, Identity Politics, and Violence against Women of Color." In *An Introduction to Women's Studies: Gender in a Transnational World*, edited by Inderpal Grewal and Caren Kaplan. McGraw Hill.

Fields, Jessica. 2008. *Risky Lessons: Sex Education and Social Inequality.* Rutgers University Press.

Fields, Jessica, and Lorena Garcia. 2018. "Loving Possibilities in Studies of Sexuality Education and Youth." In *The Cambridge Handbook of Sexuality: Childhood and Adolescence,* edited by Sharon Lamb and Jen Gilbert. Cambridge University Press.

Fields, Jessica, Jen Gilbert, and Michelle Miller. 2015. "Sexuality and Education: Toward the Promise of Ambiguity." In *Handbook of the Sociology of Sexualities*, edited by John Delamater and Rebecca F. Plante. Springer.

Fields, Jessica, Stephanie Johnson, Bex Macfife, Patricia Roach, and Era Steinfeld. 2021. "Embodied Engagements: Body Mapping in a Sociology of Sexuality Classroom." *Teaching Sociology* 49 (3): 256–266.

Fine, Michelle, María Elena Torre, Austin Gerhard Oswald, and Shéar Avory. 2021. "Critical Participatory Action Research: Methods and Praxis for Intersectional Knowledge Production." *Journal of Counseling Psychology* 68 (3): 344–356.

Flicker, Sarah, Jessica Danforth, Erin Konsmo et al. 2013. "'Because We Are Natives and We Stand Strong to Our Pride': Decolonizing HIV Prevention with Aboriginal Youth in Canada Using the Arts." *Canadian Journal of Aboriginal Community-Based HIV/AIDS Research* 5 (1): 3–23.

Flicker, Sarah, Susan Flynn, June Larkin, Robb Travers, Adrian Guta, Jason Pole, and Crystal Layne. 2009. *Sexpress: The Toronto Teen Survey Report.* Planned Parenthood Toronto.

Flicker, Sarah, Nadha Hassen, Jessica Fields et al. 2023. "Engendering a Feminist Ethic of Care to Training a New Generation of Public Health Researchers: Reflecting on 4theRecord." In *Critical Perspectives in Public Health Feminisms*, edited by Renée Monchalin. Canadian Scholars.

Flicker, Sarah, and Stephanie A. Nixon. 2015. "The DEPICT Model for Participatory Qualitative Health Promotion Research Analysis Piloted in Canada, Zambia and South Africa." *Health Promotion International* 30 (3): 616–624.

Fortenberry, J. Dennis. 2014. "Sexual Learning, Sexual Experience, and Healthy Adolescent Sex." In *Positive and Negative Outcomes of Sexual Behaviors: New Directions for Child and Adolescent Development,* edited by Eva S. Lefkowitz and Sara A. Vasilenko. Wiley.

Frisby, Wendy, Patricia Maguire, and Colleen Reid. 2009. "The 'F' Word Has Everything to Do with It: How Feminist Theories Inform Action Research." *Action Research* 7 (1): 13–29.

Gilbert, Jen. 2007. "Risking a Relation: Sex Education and Adolescent Development." *Sex Education* 7 (1): 47–61.

Gilbert, Jen. 2014. *Sexuality in School: The Limits of Education.* University of Minnesota Press.

Gill, Michael. 2015. *Already Doing It: Intellectual Disability and Sexual Agency.* University of Minnesota Press.

Leahy, Deana. 2014. "Assembling a Health[y] Subject: Risky and Shameful Pedagogies in Health Education." *Critical Public Health* 24 (2): 171–181.

Lokot, Michelle, and Yeva Avakyan. 2020. "Intersectionality as a Lens to the COVID-19 Pandemic: Implications for Sexual and Reproductive Health in Development and Humanitarian Contexts." *Sexual and Reproductive Health Matters* 28 (1): 40–43.

Lokot, Michelle, and Caitlin Wake. 2021. *The Co-Production of Research between Academics, NGOs and Communities in Humanitarian Response: A Practice Guide.* London School of Hygiene and Tropical Medicine.

Lordly, Daphne, Debbie Maclellan, Jacqui Gingras, and Jennifer Brady. 2012. "A Team-Based Approach to Qualitative Inquiry: The Collaborative Retreat." *Canadian Journal of Dietetic Practice and Research* 73 (2): 91–97.

Maguire, Patricia. 1996. "Considering More Feminist Participatory Research: What's Congruency Got to Do with It?" *Qualitative Inquiry* 2 (1): 106–118.

Perske, Robert. 1972. "The Dignity of Risk and the Mentally Retarded." *Mental Retardation* 10 (1): 24–27.

Reid, Colleen, Allison Tom, and Wendy Frisby. 2006. "Finding the 'Action' in Feminist Participatory Action Research." *Action Research* 4 (3): 315–332.

Reinharz, Shulamit, and Lynn Davidman. 1992. *Feminist Methods in Social Research.* Oxford University Press.

Shulman, Shmuel, and Jennifer Connolly. 2013. "The Challenge of Romantic Relationships in Emerging Adulthood: Reconceptualization of the Field." *Emerging Adulthood* 1 (1): 27–39.

Switzer, Sarah, and Sarah Flicker. 2021. "Visualizing DEPICT: A Multistep Model for Participatory Analysis in Photovoice Research for Social Change." *Health Promotion Practice* 22 (2): 50S–65S.

Zreik, Thurayya, Rozane El Masri, Sandy Chaar et al. 2022. "Collaborative Coding in Multi-National Teams: Benefits, Challenges and Experiences Promoting Equitable Research." *International Journal of Qualitative Methods* 21: 1–8.

7

CATHERINE VANNER, ANGELINA WEENIE,
CLAUDIA MITCHELL, MEEGWUN LOGAN,
JILLIAN GRACE GOYEAU, AND
KATHRYN KENDAL RYAN

# COLLECTIVE DATA ANALYSIS
# AS FEMINIST METHODOLOGY

Reflecting through Research Memos on
Education about MMIWG2S in Canada

THIS CHAPTER DESCRIBES how our research team adopted an
approach to analyzing data on teaching about Missing and Murdered
Indigenous Women, Girls, and 2SLGBTQQIA people (MMIWG2S).
After conducting research on teaching about gender-based violence,
Catherine was left with a data subset focused on teaching about
MMIWG2S. Following the National Inquiry on Missing and Murdered
Indigenous Women and Girls' (2019) call for "all elementary, secondary,
and post-secondary institutions and education authorities to educate
and provide awareness to the public about missing and murdered
Indigenous women, girls, and 2SLGBTQQIA people" (79), this felt
important to analyze directly. Yet, as a non-Indigenous researcher recognizing the history of damaging research about Indigenous peoples,
she was hesitant to tackle it. Catherine decided to undertake a team
approach involving Indigenous and non-Indigenous researchers to

ensure the centrality of Indigenous self-determination, empowerment, and capacity-building to the analysis. Claudia, Catherine's former post-doctoral supervisor, invited Angelina, and Catherine recruited three undergraduate research assistants: Jill, Kendal, and Meegwun. Only once a team was formed that involved both an established Indigenous scholar (Angelina) and emerging Indigenous scholars who could be supported within a team environment (Jill and Meegwun) did it feel appropriate to move forward. Together, we embarked upon a process of collaborative data analysis that drew on our various perspectives, social locations, and relationships to the data. We situate our approach as feminist by emphasizing how researcher subjectivity influences data analysis and by positioning data analysis as relational: involving mentorship, friendship, and a process that matters as much as the outcome.

Writing about Indigenous communities and issues that affect them from the perspective of a non-Indigenous person is wrought with a history of damage in which researchers have exploited, manipulated, and misrepresented Indigenous communities and their knowledge (Tuck 2009; Snow 2018). This chapter describes a collaborative research project examining experiences of teaching and learning about the subject of MMIWG2S in Canada—a devastating phenomenon in which centuries of colonial violence and systemic discrimination have led to Indigenous women in Canada being murdered or going missing twelve times more frequently than non-Indigenous women (National Inquiry 2019; Weenie 2019). The participants in our study included those of diverse ethnicities and heritages including many non-Indigenous students and teachers, but because the subject is so traumatic for many Indigenous people, it felt inappropriate to research and write about it from a non-Indigenous, or settler Canadian, perspective. However, when a three-year research project on teaching about gender-based violence in Canadian schools led to a subset of data that spoke specifically to the practice of teaching about MMIWG2S, it also felt inappropriate to ignore it.

Catherine, Claudia, and Angelina gathered virtually from three provinces and agreed to analyze the collected data. We recruited a group of research assistants from the University of Windsor, bringing Jill, Meegwun, and Kendal on board to form our team. Data collection included individual open-ended interviews with Grade 8 to 12 teachers in which we asked them to tell a story about a time they had taught about gender-based violence in their classroom; three participatory workshops with youth groups that used multiple qualitative and participatory visual methods to respond to the prompt, "What do you want your teachers to know when teaching about gender-based violence?"; and a teacher workshop where participants analyzed data from their interviews and the student workshops. We separated the data collected on participants' experiences teaching and learning about MMIWG2S from the broader data on teaching and learning about gender-based violence more generally. This enabled us to respond to the research question: "How can teachers enhance the critical consciousness of young people in Canada about MMIWG2S?" The response to the research question was informed by data collected from both student and teacher perspectives.

In May 2022, our team began a process of collaborative data analysis that drew upon our various perspectives, social locations, and relationships to the data. The dataset specific to teaching about MMIWG2S included eight open-ended interviews with teachers, along with data from a workshop with eleven Indigenous girls aged eleven to seventeen that included eight carousel papers (Vanner et al. 2021),[1] five cellphilms (MacEntee et al. 2016),[2] and a focus group with four of the participants (seven opted not to join the focus group). Following Kathy Charmaz's (2014) guide to constructing grounded theory, Catherine trained Jill, Kendal, and Meegwun on initial and focused coding, leading to the creation of an emergent theory. We met monthly with Angelina and Claudia to get their input on our analysis. Each step was collaborative, involving Jill, Kendal, and Meegwun in all levels of coding, developing, and presenting the emergent analysis, preparing an annotated bibliography, connecting the literature and conceptual framework to the results via the preparation of a final paper (Vanner et al. 2024), and creating two presentations to showcase the study's findings. Here, we reflect on our process of feminist collaborative data analysis with a decolonizing intent. The process was imperfect; we remained constrained by time, technology, professional obligations, scheduling conflicts, and unforeseen life challenges. However, in applying a team process that valued, made space for, and supported the development of all perspectives across an intergenerational team of Indigenous and non-Indigenous women, we applied a process characterized by listening to and learning from each other and speaking what was true for ourselves.

## TEAM

Acknowledging one's background and how it informs one's perspective on and relationship to the research is an important component of Indigenous and feminist research methodologies (Kovach 2009; Linabary et al. 2021; Olukotun et al. 2021). It is additionally important here to underscore the diverse experiences we brought to our research collaboration. The following paragraphs are written in the first-person voice by each team member and identify their positionality and relationship to this work.

### Catherine Vanner

I identify as a white settler woman of British ancestry. I began researching teaching about MMIWG2S while starting my Postdoctoral Fellowship at McGill University on the unceded Indigenous land of the Kanien'keha:ka Nation. After reframing the project to focus on teaching about gender-based violence more broadly, I was honoured to return three years later to the initial subject matter with a team of incredible women. I now work and live in Windsor, Ontario on the Traditional Territory of the Three Fires Confederacy of First Nations, including the Ojibwa, the Odawa, and the Potawotami.

### Angelina Weenie

I am a nēhiyaw iskwēw, Plains Cree woman, from Sweetgrass First Nation which is in Treaty Six Territory. I am an Associate Professor at the First Nations University of Canada. My lived experience with domestic violence draws me to this research. As a teacher I often encounter stories from my students about their experiences with domestic violence. I now know that my life path was intended to help others in their own journeys.

## Claudia Mitchell

I identify as a white settler of British ancestry. My background with this project comes out of my engagement with arts-based methodologies in working with rural Black youth in South Africa and Indigenous youth in Canada, particularly in the context of gender-based violence and health inequities. Central to this work has been the idea of developing and adapting methods such as cellphilming that engage participants in the co-production of knowledge. Working with both Indigenous girls and young women in Canada in the context of colonial violence surrounding MMIWG2S and the ongoing incidence of sexual violence in South Africa has been important to educating myself about colonialism and the need for methodologies and pedagogies that frame deep engagement.

## Meegwun Logan

Boozhoo, Nimiiki-Kwe ndi zhinikaaz, Bkejwanong ndoonjibaa, mishiikenh ndoodem, Boodawaadami-Odawa-Lenni Lenape Kwe ndaw. Hello, I have introduced myself in my language to tell you I am "Thunder woman." I am a Potawatomi/Lenape woman, my clan is Turtle, and my nation is Three Fires Confederacy. In addition, I am a second-generation Residential School Survivor. I am completing the requirements for my Bachelor of Arts program in International Relations with a minor in Philosophy at the University of Windsor. I come from a long line of resilient people, although they have faced many hardships in life such as abuse, poverty, and colonialism. I am only the second generation to attend post-secondary education and the first in my father's family.

## Jillian Goyeau

I joined Catherine as a research assistant while I was partway through my undergrad in Sociology and working with the University of Windsor's Belonging, Inclusion, Diversity & Equity team. I grew up in Windsor, Ontario on the Traditional Territory of the Three Fires Confederacy of First Nations, including the Ojibwa, the Odawa, and the Potawotami. My positionality is informed by my intersecting identities as a Métis woman from a working-class family that also has a French settler history. I come to this research from somewhat of a place of privilege as a cisgender, able-bodied woman with various forms of social support. I am also a musician, artist, and freelance writer.

## Kendal Ryan

I began as a research assistant with this project during my final summer of undergraduate education at the University of Windsor. I identify as coming from a position of significant socio-economic privilege as a white, heterosexual, educated woman who was raised and currently lives in Windsor, Ontario, on the Traditional Territory of the Three Fires Confederacy of First Nations, including the Ojibwa, the Odawa, and the Potawotami.

## DECOLONIZING FEMINIST RESEARCH

Recognizing relationality is an essential step in studies that attempt to overcome the damaging legacy of colonial research about subjects that disproportionately affect Indigenous people. Gina Snooks et al. (2021) reflect on why and how they chose to study human trafficking prevention and response in Northern Ontario through an Indigenous/settler research partnership. They sought to draw on the strengths and commonalities of feminist, decolonial, and Indigenous approaches, as well as participatory action research methodologies, noting the importance for non-Indigenous researchers to learn from Indigenous worldviews. Margaret Kovach (2009) speaks to the necessity of nurturing relationality between the researcher, research participants, and their community; in a collaborative research partnership, relationality should also be an emphasis among team members. In asking how researchers, particularly settlers, can establish trust and mutual benefit, Elaine Swan (2017) speaks to the value of Tanja Dreher's (2009) concept of "political listening," which aims to produce social change through consciousness-raising as a valuable form of decolonial praxis. Swan (2017) observes that white settler researchers need to lean more deeply into listening practices that involve patience, humility, openness, and flexibility, but notes that they often skip over these practices in their urgency to act and produce.

Snooks et al. (2021) note the role of critical self-reflection in decolonizing research, particularly on the part of settler researchers. Dolores Calderon (2016) also emphasizes this theme in her recognition of the ways that researchers inadvertently reproduce norms of settler colonialism by, for example, allowing pathologizing narratives to define the story that researchers tell about a community. Kathy Snow (2018) observes that working within an Indigenous research paradigm involves shifting one's ontology and practice to focus on contextually derived knowledge rather than published literature, and crafting a shared story that is collectively negotiated and mutually beneficial to all contributors. We do not classify our methodology as inherently Indigenous or decolonizing, but we tried to embody principles of reciprocity, relationality, and reflexivity that are emphasized in Indigenous methodologies as we work toward decolonizing research objectives. Snooks et al. (2021) identify decolonizing research as revolving around Indigenous self-determination, empowerment, and capacity-building; Kovach (2009) indicates that it must lead toward healing and transformation. We build on these principles to foster our approach to collective data analysis as influenced by both feminist and Indigenous methodologies and epistemologies.

Gwendolyn Beetham and Justina Demetriades (2007) observe that "there is not one specific method or combination of methods that necessarily makes research 'feminist,' but rather that the research comes from an approach that is considerate of the multifaceted

nature of gender" (199). While some, for example Bagele Chilisa and
Gabo Ntseane (2010), have criticized feminist research for reproducing colonial norms and representations, similarities across feminist,
Indigenous, and decolonizing methodologies include an emphasis on
critical reflexivity in relation to positionality (Olukotun et al. 2021),
ethical communication and representation (McCormick 2012), power
dynamics (Presser 2005), and relationality (Philip and Bell 2017).
Feminist research is additionally characterized by embracing emotion
(Gazso and Bischoping 2018) and by an activist orientation (Archibald
and Crnikovich 2019). Mary Holmes (2010) argues that reflexivity—
often characterized by fear, comparison, or guilt when identifying
how one's actions are incongruent with one's values—is an inherently
emotional process. One way of mediating these complex emotions is
by channelling them into action, yet this can be counter-productive
when the actions are identified primarily by researchers instead of
by participants and affected communities. Jasmine Linabary et al.
(2021) observe that most scholarship on feminist reflexivity focuses on
individual researcher reflexivity; they advance "collaborative feminist
reflexivity" as both a methodological approach and a set of practices for
feminist research teams. Their use of reflective journaling prompted
them to identify the ways that collaborative feminist reflexivity led to
the co-production of situated knowledge that confronted epistemological differences among team members, negotiated (and exposed) power
dynamics, and fostered caring relationships across statuses, roles,
responsibilities, and identities.

In bringing together feminist and Indigenous methodologies,
Chilisa and Ntseane (2010) insist that researchers "have to be activists
[and] use their research experiences to make a difference in the lives of
those researched" (630), but caution that doing so should derive directly
from the recommendations of participants, who are most aware of
what is culturally appropriate in their context. This call aligns with Eve
Tuck's (2009) concept of "desire-centered research" that is embedded
in "the hope, the visions, the wisdom of lived lives and communities"
(417). We thus sought a process that required transparent communication, capacity-building, and mutual benefit for all team members. We

maintained a practical orientation with the goal of influencing more teachers to respectfully teach about MMIWG2S, in alignment with the Calls for Justice in the final report of the Indigenous-led National Inquiry on Missing and Murdered Indigenous Women and Girls (National Inquiry 2019). We situated our analysis in not only our own perspectives and those of our participants, but also in the recommendations of the *Their Voices Will Guide Us* teaching and learning guide (Bearhead 2020) produced in conjunction with the National Inquiry. Simultaneously, we tried to stay flexible and responsive to our six team members' needs during our fleeting time together.

## ANALYTICAL PROCESS

We began our analytic process by familiarizing ourselves with the data. Teacher participants had been recruited within professional networks and on social media while Catherine partnered with Jennifer Altenberg, a community scholar and co-founder of the Young Indigenous Women's Utopia (YIWU), a community group that supports Indigenous girls to challenge colonial and gender-based violence by drawing on traditional Indigenous knowledge systems. Together, they developed a workshop that illuminated student experiences of learning about gender-based violence while providing an empowering experience for the Indigenous girl participants in Treaty Six Territory, Traditional Homeland of the Métis People. After reading through the transcripts independently, each team member selected three quotes that particularly resonated with them to reflect on. We began our collective data analysis process by reading these quotes aloud to each other and reflecting on why they stood out to us as significant. We then held a screening of five cellphilms created by the YIWU workshop participants, responding to the question, "What do you want your teachers to know when teaching about gender-based violence?" Our initial sharing of quotes and reflections from each team member shaped our thinking before Catherine, Meegwun, Jill, and Kendal began more formal data analysis. During this meeting, Angelina also shared some of her own teachings in relation to MMIWG2S.

Meegwun, Jill, and Kendal are undergraduate students who, prior to this project, had never been involved in qualitative research; as such, we began with a training process on initial coding and memoing following a constructivist grounded theory approach. Memos are short free-written notes documenting observations arising from analysis. Charmaz (2015) refers to memos as "private conversations grounded theorists have with themselves as they take their codes apart and analyze what they might mean" (1617). After reading several chapters of Charmaz's (2014) book *Constructing Grounded Theory*, Catherine and the research assistants met to practice coding by individually coding the same interview and then trading papers and reflecting on the similarities and differences between the codes we had each identified. We then divided the data among the team members to undertake initial coding of the interviews, focus group, cellphilm transcripts, and carousel papers. We met partway through to discuss our emerging analysis and began memoing about patterns we were seeing arise within the data, following Charmaz's guidelines for moving back and forth between data sources and initial analysis. We discussed the process of focused coding, which refers to the generation of overarching codes that serve as analytic categories (Charmaz 2015). We each independently reviewed our codes to identify our own lists of potential focused codes and met again to agree upon a list of focused codes. We then divided the data again to be recoded to fit within the focused codes. We met again to consider the relationship between the focused codes and the theory that this generated about our findings before presenting our analysis to Claudia and Angelina. These findings showed that participants were driven by a desire to make change, which they believed could be accomplished through education that expanded the curriculum to centre on Indigenous lived experiences and the creation of safe spaces for all voices. In the final steps of our analysis, we compared the emergent analysis against the literature within an annotated bibliography that the research assistants had built, which concentrated on the themes of decolonizing education, Indigenous feminist theory and intersectionality, teaching about residential schools, and Indigenous-settler research collaborations. Each research assistant reviewed the findings and identified connections with the sections of the annotated bibliography they had worked on, which Catherine then used to draft an article that was shared with Claudia and Angelina for input.

## Reflective Memos

At the culmination of the project, each team member wrote a one-page memo, the content of which are the focus of the following reflection. Our memo-making process was adapted from Charmaz's (2014) protocol, in which she advises drafting memos that use free writing to quickly record initial observations and reflections, constituting an initial analysis that can be re-analyzed as data. Memos are an essential element of constructivist grounded theory that initiate deeper engagement with the research process and findings (Birks et al. 2008). Charmaz (2006) observes that there is no required formulation for memos and encourages researchers to "do what works for you" (80). Anselm Strauss and Juliet Corbin (1998) encourage researchers to classify their memos as operational, coding, or theoretical. While we used memos for all three of these purposes, the memos we focus on here could be categorized as operational since they map the various stages of conducting research (Birks et al. 2008). At the same time, we extended Strauss and Corbin's categories by creating "reflective" memos that *look back* on the research process. Reflective memos not only document choices that took place during data collection, but also capture how those choices influenced the subsequent research outcomes. Christine Mayor (2022) observes the power of memos to initiate self-reflection for the researcher; our memos demonstrate reflexivity both in relation to ourselves as individual researchers and our relationships to each other as a collective. Our reflections align with Linabary et al.'s (2021) use of journaling at various stages of the research process for documentation, analysis, and reflection, including a final stage in which they wrote journal entries *reflecting on their reflections* of the process.

At the end of our project, each team member wrote a memo responding to the prompt, "How did you experience the process of feminist collective data analysis within this project?" The memos varied greatly, some focusing on the process and skills learned, others on personal experience, one situating the process in comparison to prior research experiences, and another describing the application of the experience to other aspects of their work. Catherine analyzed the memos using a process similar to the multi-stage coding used to analyze the data itself, focusing on common themes and significant variations. Unfortunately, as the team's work together had concluded, we were unable to use the same collective data analysis approach to analyze the memos, but all team members had the opportunity to validate the analysis drafted by Catherine and ultimately presented here.

## EMERGENT REFLECTIONS

Across the memos, reflections spoke to each person's unique experience and perspective relating to the project. Descriptions of each member's motivations and experiences are recounted here in relation to the following themes: attending to identity and perspective, blending the personal and professional, and contributing to something larger than ourselves. Ultimately, the memos reflect the conviction that a collective research approach enabled us to create work that was more valuable because of the many perspectives that had contributed to it, using a process that was as generative and rewarding as the work we produced.

### Attending to Identity and Perspective

As our analysis dealt with the sensitivities of teaching about MMIWG2S, drawing on both Indigenous and non-Indigenous participants and aiming to encourage broader K–12 teaching about the subject, particularly by non-Indigenous teachers, identity was a central part of our work together and a motivating factor for the team approach. As referenced above, Catherine had begun this project independently but recognized that her settler identity was an impediment that could undermine the legitimacy of the analysis. She wrote, "I strongly desired a collective, a group to work within. I knew or felt it was inappropriate for me to conduct this analysis by myself, as a settler Canadian." Everyone recognized the ability of our team to valuably contribute from our different perspectives, with Claudia describing our collection of Indigenous and non-Indigenous team members working in tandem as "such a special feature of our group." Jill observed, "Everyone on our team has brought unique ideas contributing to the puzzle that only together are we able to solve." Jill further noted that our ability to maintain a team approach throughout the analysis was a key strength: "As we continued through different stages of our work that is now on its legs, our team-based approach has remained consistent, enabling us to cover more ground while we analyze with different lived experiences and world views." At each stage, all team members were able to provide input and shape the process as it evolved.

Our diverse identities connected us to the data and analysis in very different ways. Catherine reflected on how her identity and insecurity around handling the data from a settler perspective enabled her to connect to the fears and insecurities that characterized much of the data emerging from the non-Indigenous teacher participants. She wrote, "I felt the whole research and analysis process was tinged by insecurity and uncertainty but sensed that this was actually in alignment with how many teachers feel when trying to teach about MMIWG2S or other topics affecting groups that they are not them-selves a member of." Angelina connected her Indigenous identity to other applications of the work outside of our project, speaking to how her perspective was intertwined with her application of the analysis to her work with Indigenous teacher candidates as well as her work with language more broadly:

> As a Cree-speaking person, I have sought ways to name [the concept of intersectionality] in our language. This term can be described within a framework of how we see things. The words, where the rivers of humanity cross, seems to be the best way to describe the many ways which Indigenous people are affected. Sometimes the water is

murky, and it is hard to discern the way forward and at times we can see our way through knowing there may be more obstacles on the horizon.

Meegwun also reflected on how her Indigenous identity shaped her contributions to the data analysis, writing, "I feel that I've contributed to this project with my identity and offering a perspective that was achieved through my family history." She explained, however, that the project also influenced her understanding of her identity. She described transformational realizations that occurred through working on the annotated bibliography, in which she was summarizing readings on decolonizing education. She specifically reflects on Marie Battiste's (2013) work on decolonizing education:

> In these readings, a particular passage stuck out to me that was written by Battiste and stated that Indigenous students tend to avoid speaking out too much and prefer to fly under the radar for fear of sounding stupid. Upon realizing the restrictions I'd previously placed on myself, I am much more confident in overcoming these barriers knowing that it is not a single experience that only affects me. Not only that, but I'd realized that intergenerational trauma has affected me in more ways than just surface level barriers I'd seen in my father growing up...Within the last year, especially with this project, I've come to self-analyze a lot more gently and open mindedly.

Meegwun's reflection shows how the process of relating to the data is highly personal and multi-directional; not only do we shape the project and analysis, but it shapes us and teaches us about ourselves in turn.

## Blending the Personal and the Professional

Multiple team members referenced how the team approach enabled them to feel more confident about the tasks they were undertaking, both within the project and outside of it. Kendal wrote:

> Starting the position with minimal coding and technical experience in data collection, the responsibility of thoroughly examining our teacher interview data was quite daunting initially. Fortunately, Catherine not only tackled the task of training us for this specific task, but she also set us up for success by equipping our toolbox with valuable research skills to apply in the future.

For Kendal, the training that Catherine provided helped break down nebulous, complex work into achievable tasks that both she and others planned to use in future. While Kendal describes Catherine's support as helpful in building her confidence, Catherine's memo in turn spoke to the support she received from Claudia and Angelina as instrumental: "I felt more confident knowing we had Claudia and Angelina steering us and providing input...they both have such wisdom and experience and are always so thoughtful and respectful of their students and participants that I knew we would not go astray." The intergenerational nature of our team meant that each of the younger generations was able to gain strength from the experience and support of the more experienced team members.

Each team member spoke about how the project's influence transcended its stated goals and impacted them either personally or professionally in a way that they had not anticipated. Angelina explained how the project influenced her teaching practice:

> I recently had an opportunity to do a guest lecture for a group of undergraduate Indigenous students. I chose to use the guide, Their Voices Will Guide Us [referenced in this chapter]. The class focuses on social justice issues,

and I felt that this was a great opportunity to share the resource...Given the sensitivity of the topic and that many in the Indigenous communities are impacted, I started the class with a smudging ceremony, a prayer, and a talk by our resident Elder. It is understood that the spiritual will guide us.

Meegwun described gaining confidence, but in ways that extended far beyond the research: "Working with this team on this project has given me a level of confidence I never thought that I would achieve. I feel that in both school, personal, and work, my work will benefit for the rest of my life." Catherine also identified how the relationships of the project transcended professional work:

My favourite part was seeing the team support each other...seeing one research assistant offer to lend another a hand with something when she was through her task more quickly. I was very touched when [Kendal, Meegwun, and Jill] stepped in to support me with a gift after my mother-in-law passed away suddenly and they knew I was struggling...It felt like we had achieved a form of friendship, support, excitement, and admiration for each other.

Although we only worked together for four months, the collective nature of our approach, combined with the intimacy and sensitivity of the topic, quickly bled into other aspects of our lives, blurring professional boundaries during what can otherwise be a fairly dry phase of research.

## Contributing to Something Larger Than Ourselves

Moving together as a team of women provided a sense of community and belonging that elevated our work beyond being simply productive to something that felt more significant. Jill wrote, "I felt very connected to our project and team...I was highly inspired by the warm feeling of contributing to something larger than all of us as a women/non-binary led team." Multiple team members brought up two team meetings as particularly significant: the meeting where we each read specific quotes from the data that stood out to us, and the one where our University of Windsor team presented our initial analysis to Claudia and Angelina. Both Claudia and Kendal wrote about how reading the quotes from the data aloud deepened their understanding of and connection to the data. Claudia reflected:

> Somehow the experience moved away from reading data to becoming one of reading real narratives of real people. As we took turns reading/performing, there was something magical happening, a type of intimacy that is not always easy to create in an online setting...as we listened to each other, we started gathering a greater appreciation for what the teachers in the interviews had been saying, but we also had a greater appreciation for each other. That appreciation for each other—listening to each other—is fundamental in feminist collective analysis.

Kendal reflected on the same process: "With our discussion that followed, the team was able to identify and examine the various elements and quotes that stood out to us. I particularly enjoyed this reading and found the data to be captivating, as it was an organic human conversation put into text and showed a raw level of information communication on such a serious and often filtered topic." These reflections both observe that the process of reading the selected quotes aloud to each other deepened their understanding of the data and caused them to see it in new ways. Kendal's reflection highlights the perspective of someone encountering qualitative data analysis for the first time, while Claudia's reflection is built on the experiences of working with collective data analysis in many previous projects that she came to see in a new light.

Almost all team members mentioned the gravity of our work together and that immersing ourselves in the data and analysis caused us to see its urgency. These sentiments are perhaps best expressed by Angelina, who wrote:

> Teachers need to find the inner resources and move forward with a full and unremitting approach. Gender-based violence cannot be ignored, and we must work as a collective to empower each other...The violence against women and girls is not ending and it seems to go unnoticed in educational circles. We need to teach about this issue within the various contexts which present themselves with a mindset that a safe space is essential.

We used a process imbued with relationality, excitement, learning, and even fun, yet we did not lose sight of the reasons why we were doing this work; we remained committed to the mandate of raising attention within educational spaces about the devastating loss of life experienced at dramatically disproportionate rates by Indigenous women, girls, and 2SLGBTQQIA people.

## DISCUSSION

Our memos demonstrate that relationships were firmly embedded in our process, both in the many ways we supported each other, and in the vast respect for our study's participants. It was critically import-ant to us that each team member gained methodological skills and experience from the project that would support them in achieving their own professional aspirations outside of it. Several team members talked about their intent to use the skills they developed through the project in future, Angelina demonstrated her application of the work in her teaching, and Meegwun described how her experience in the project shifted the way she understood her identity. These outcomes reflect the objectives of decolonizing research, described by Snooks et al. (2021) as centring on Indigenous self-determination, empower-ment, and capacity-building, and by Kovach (2009) as contributing to healing and transformation. We aspired to achieve those objectives through our knowledge production and dissemination, but these reflections demonstrate that the process resulted in similar, personal outcomes for members of our team. The memos also demonstrate that the collective approach to data analysis, particularly in the process of selecting and reading aloud the quotes that resonated with each of us, provoked genuine and political listening (Swan 2017), both in relation to each other and to our participants. In responding to the calls for action-oriented research that is situated within contextually derived knowledge (Snow 2018), we responded directly to the recommendations made by Indigenous girls from the YIWU workshop in our analysis and incorporated recommendations from Charlene Bearhead's (2020) *Their Voices Will Guide Us* teaching and learning guide. Emphasizing these voices was our attempt to embed our work in recommendations from Indigenous girls and Indigenous educators with strong ties to the National Inquiry and the extensive work done in consultation with family members of Indigenous women, girls, and 2SLGBTQQIA people who had been killed or remain missing.

## CONCLUSION

We are proud of our process and outcomes, but there are significant opportunities for deepening the benefits, particularly through more intentional and explicit reflexivity in relation to the power dynamics that characterized our process and by applying the collective approach earlier in the project. While positionality was a pivotal factor for our team, we did not directly interrogate how our identities as Indigenous and non-Indigenous team members or our various ages, experience levels, and positions within academia shaped power dynamics within our team. If we had used reflective memoing throughout the entire analysis process, rather than only at the end, we could have explored this theme more directly and perhaps further enhanced our relationality with each other and the benefits that different team members derived from the process. Similarly, for all the benefits of having a diverse team, these could have been amplified had we used a collective approach earlier on to inform research design and data collection. This would reflect Kovach's (2009) call for method, methodology, and epistemology to form an "interdependent relational research framework" (122) rather than treating them as disconnected steps in the process.

Bringing Indigenous and non-Indigenous researchers together can result in a deeper analysis as we each come from different worldviews. Our process and our reflections demonstrate that we are all invested in this work and that our positioning did not deter us from a common goal of bringing light and awareness to this issue. The steps we used reflect our desire to honour the data that was collected and the significance that we perceived in it. Future research could use a collective reflective memoing approach throughout each step of the research process, continuously returning to explicit discussions of power and relationality to provide ever-richer opportunities and experiences in relation to decolonizing feminist research.

## AUTHORS' NOTE

This work was possible because of the study participants and community leaders who generously shared their time, reflections, and experiences with us. The project was supported by a Social Sciences and Humanities Research Council of Canada Postdoctoral Fellowship [756-2018-0576] and an Insight Development Grant [430-2019-0223].

## NOTES

1. Carousel papers are a form of interactive visual data collection in which participants rotate between papers and respond to prompts on the different papers—in this case, "How have you learned about gender-based violence in and out of school?" and "What do you think your teachers should know when teaching about gender-based violence?" (from an intellectual/spiritual/physical/emotional perspective)—building on the ideas of the other participants as they go.

2.   Cellphilms are one-to-two-minute videos produced using basic digital technology such as a tablet or cellphone. Participants were asked to develop cellphilms responding to the prompt, "What do you think your teachers should know when teaching about gender-based violence?"

## REFERENCES

Archibald, Linda, and Mary Crnikovich. 2019. "Intimate Outsiders: Feminist Research in a Cross-Cultural Environment." In *Changing Methods: Feminists Transforming Practice,* edited by Sandra Burt and Lorraine Code. University of Toronto Press.

Bearhead, Charlene. 2020. *Their Voices Will Guide Us: Student and Youth Engagement Guide.* National Inquiry into Missing and Murdered Indigenous Women and Girls. https://www.mmiwg-ffada.ca/wp-content/uploads/2018/11/NIMMIWG-THEIR-VOICES-WILL-GUIDE-US.pdf.

Beetham, Gwendolyn, and Justina Demetriades. 2007. "Feminist Research Methodologies and Development: Overview and Practical Application." *Gender & Development* 15 (2): 199–216.

Birks, Melanie, Ysanne Chapman, and Karen Francis. 2008. "Memoing in Qualitative Research: Probing Data and Processes." *Journal of Research in Nursing* 13 (1): 68–75.

Calderon, Dolores. 2016. "Moving from Damage-Centered Research through Unsettling Reflexivity." *Anthropology & Education Quarterly* 47 (1): 5–24.

Charmaz, Kathy. 2006. *Constructing Grounded Theory.* SAGE.

Charmaz, Kathy. 2014. *Constructing Grounded Theory, 2nd Edition.* SAGE.

Charmaz, Kathy. 2015. "Teaching Theory Construction with Initial Grounded Theory Tools: A Reflection on Lessons and Learning." *Qualitative Health Research* 25 (12): 1610–1622.

Chilisa, Bagele, and Gabo Ntseane. 2010. "Resisting Dominant Discourses: Implications of Indigenous, African Feminist Theory and Methods for Gender and Education Research." *Gender and Education* 22 (6): 617–632.

Dreher, Tanja. 2009. "Eavesdropping with Permission: The Politics of Listening for Safer Speaking Spaces." *Borderlands E-Journal* 8 (1): 1–21.

Gazso, Amber, and Katherine Bischoping. 2018. "Feminist Reflections on the Relation of Emotions to Ethics: A Case Study of Two Awkward Interviewing Moments." *Forum Qualitative Sozialforschung/Forum Qualitative Social Research* 19 (3): 1–19.

Holmes, Mary. 2010. "The Emotionalization of Reflexivity." *Sociology* 44 (1): 139–154.

Kovach, Margaret. 2009. *Indigenous Methodologies: Characteristics, Conversations, and Contexts.* University of Toronto Press.

Linabary, Jasmine R., Danielle J. Corple, and Cheryl Cooky. 2021. "Of Wine and Whiteboards: Enacting Feminist Reflexivity in Collaborative Research." *Qualitative Research* 21 (5): 719–735.

MacEntee, Katie, Casey Burkholder, and Joshua Schwab-Cartas. 2016. "What's a Cellphilm? An Introduction." In *What's a Cellphilm? Integrating Mobile Phone Technology into Participatory Visual Research and Activism,* edited by Katie MacEntee, Casey Burkholder, and Joshua Schwab-Cartas. Sense Publishers.

Mayor, Christine. 2022. "Anti-Racist Research Praxis: Feminist Relational Accountability and Arts-Based Reflexive Memoing for Qualitative Data Collection in Social Work Research." *Affilia* 37 (4): 624–644.

McCormick, Melinda. 2012. "Feminist Research Ethics, Informed Consent, and Potential Harms." *The Hilltop Review* 6 (1): 23–33.

Olukotun, Oluwatoyin, Elizabeth Mkandawire, Jeri Antilla et al. 2021. "An Analysis of Reflections on Researcher Positionality." *The Qualitative Report* 26 (5): 1411–1426.

Philip, Georgia, and Linda Bell. 2017. "Thinking Critically about Rapport and Collusion in Feminist Research: Relationships, Contexts and Ethical Practice." *Women's Studies International Forum* 61: 71–74.

Presser, Lois. 2005. "Negotiating Power and Narrative in Research: Implications for Feminist Methodology." *Signs: Journal of Women in Culture and Society* 30 (4): 2067–2090.

Snooks, Rosemary Nagy, Rebecca Timms, Donna Debassige, Kathleen Jodouin, Brenda Quenneville, and Lanyan Chen. 2021. "Blending Feminist, Indigenous, and Participatory Action Research Methodologies: Critical Reflections from the Northeastern Ontario Research Alliance on Human Trafficking." *Feminist Formations* 33 (2): 160–184.

Snow, Kathy. 2018. "What Does Being a Settler Ally in Research Mean? A Graduate Students Experience Learning from and Working within Indigenous Research Paradigms." *International Journal of Qualitative Methods* 17 (1): 1–11.

Strauss, Anselm, and Juliet Corbin. 1998. *Basics of Qualitative Research: Techniques and Procedures for Developing Grounded Theory, 2nd Edition.* SAGE.

Swan, Elaine. 2017. "What Are White People to Do? Listening, Challenging Ignorance, Generous Encounters and the 'Not Yet' as Diversity Research Praxis." *Gender, Work & Organization* 24 (5): 547–563.

Tuck, Eve. 2009. "Suspending Damage: A Letter to Communities." *Harvard Educational Review* 79 (3): 409–428.

Vanner, Catherine. 2015. "Positionality at the Center: Constructing an Epistemological and Methodological Approach for a Western Feminist Doctoral Candidate Conducting Research in the Postcolonial." *International Journal of Qualitative Methods* 14 (4): 1–12.

Vanner, Catherine, Jillian Goyeau, Meegwun Logan, Kendal Ryan, Angelina Weenie, and Claudia Mitchell. 2024. "Teaching about Missing and Murdered Indigenous Women, Girls, and 2SLGBTQQIA People: Implications for Canadian Educators." *Canadian Journal of Education* 47 (1): 1–26.

Vanner, Catherine, Yasmeen Shahzadeh, Allison Holloway, Claudia Mitchell, and Jennifer Altenberg. 2021. "Round and Round the Carousel Papers: Facilitating a Visual Interactive Dialogue with Young People." In *Facilitating Community Research for Social Change*, edited by Casey Burkholder, Funké Aladejebi, and Joshua Schwab-Cartas. Routledge.

Weenie, Kendra. 2019. *Surviving Domestic Violence. My Journey of Self-Care and Healing.* Independently published.

MITCHELL MCLARNON, DAWN WISEMAN,
CATHERINE MALBOEUF-HURTUBISE,
L. REBECA ESQUIVEL, TERRA LÉGER-
GOODES, AND EMMA C. COGNET

# WHAT DO TEACHERS NEED IN THE CONTEXT OF CLIMATE CHANGE?

Reflecting on Feminist, Interdisciplinary, and
Collaborative Survey Design and Analysis Processes

THIS CHAPTER DISCUSSES the premise, collaborative creation, and
data analysis of a bilingual (French and English) and mixed-methods
(qualitative, quantitative, and arts-based) needs assessment survey that
focused on teaching for and about climate change and eco-anxiety in
the context of climate emergency. A needs assessment is a diagnostic
process through which a population can articulate their needs to move
from its current condition to a desired one (Sleezer et al. 2014). In our
case, we wanted to learn more about what educators (and, by extension, learners) need, both educationally and emotionally, to better
understand and react to the climate crisis. Beyond the physical health
concerns of flooding, heatwaves, hurricanes, forest fires, and other
events that have been increasing in frequency and worsening in terms
of their impacts on communities, the climate crisis can lead to significant emotional and mental health concerns such as post-traumatic

stress disorder, anxiety, and depression (Pihkala 2022). In this historical moment of climate emergency, as researchers and educators we are concerned about how ecological anxiety, grief, and paralysis can act as barriers to teaching and learning.

While "ecological grief" refers to the sadness and sense of loss that occurs when people experience or learn about environmental degradation (Cunsulo and Ellis 2018), and "ecological paralysis" is conceptualized as an emotional shock or cognitive dilemma of feeling unable to act and react to the climate crisis (Albrecht 2011), "ecological anxiety" is more slippery in its terminology. Anne-Sophie Gousse-Lessard and Félix Lebrun-Paré (2022) describe eco-anxiety as psychological (and physical) discomfort related to future environmental uncertainty and connected to climate change. It is in this context of climate emergency that our interdisciplinary research team brings together researchers from the fields of education and psychology to explore the question, "How do we (as a research team and society) prepare for teaching and learning in the context of human-driven climate change?"

Before creating the needs assessment survey, we collectively mapped out the project's feminist and participatory ethos and ethics. We shared our experiential knowledge as educators and researchers and listened to each other's complex concerns about teaching and learning for climate change mitigation, communication, and education. Through non-hierarchal and participatory processes, we came to cultivate a better understanding of our collective aims, each other, and our individual research roles. In this chapter, there are multiple voices. We have attempted to transparently convey some of the complexities and methodological tensions that emerged during research design, activities, and ongoing analysis. Therefore, throughout this chapter, there are sections where we (as authors and a research team) employ the communal "we." Here, our intention is to highlight a shared analysis or sentiment. In other sections, individual team members are acknowledged by name to highlight their contributions to the project and to this chapter. In this sense, we subscribe to feminist sociologist Dorothy Smith's (2005) expansive conceptualization of work to mean any action that takes time, effort, and intent, and that aims to make "labour visible" (D'Ignazio and Klein 2020, 3). We employ feminist practices such as storytelling (Haraway 2016) and dialogue (hooks 1993) to disrupt conventional academic rhetoric, and to reflect on moments that influenced the survey design and analysis. Given that we are an interdisciplinary research team, feminist epistemologies such as ecofeminism (Mies and Shiva 2014), feminist historical materialism (Smith 1987; Bannerji 2020), and intersectional feminism (Crenshaw 1989; hooks 1993, 2003; D'Ignazio and Klein 2020) provided not only participatory frameworks for working with one another, but they also gave us a common language and discourse to communicate across research paradigms.

In the sections which follow, we expand on the survey development, how we worked with the data in a participatory way, and our reflexive findings related to a) the project background in relation to past research as well as our research team development; and b) the participatory design processes we used to create and analyze the survey. These processes included the team discussing Catherine D'Ignazio and Lauren Klein's (2020) seven intersectional feminist principles (on which we expand below) for working with data in the context of COVID-19. We conclude this chapter by outlining some of the benefits and challenges we encountered when working in a participatory way. We highlight what insights we can offer in relation to participatory research based on our thorough and communal documentation of each step of the research process.

## SITUATING OUR RESEARCH AND FORMING THE RESEARCH TEAM

The research collaboration that we describe in this chapter began in late 2019/early 2020 when Dawn brought together Catherine and Mitchell to think through preparing an interdisciplinary research proposal related to teaching and learning in the context of human-driven climate change. After a series of discussions outlining our methodological and theoretical differences, similarities, tensions, and approaches, we submitted the initial funding application, an internal team research grant at Bishop's University. Weeks later, the World Health Organization declared COVID-19 a global pandemic. When the funding was approved months into the pandemic, our research considerations expanded from teaching and learning in the context of climate change to teaching and learning in the context of both crises.

While COVID-19 added numerous tasks for teachers beyond simply preparing educational content, teaching about and in the context of human-driven climate change is also challenging and complex in perhaps less straightforward ways. Typically, climate change education involves engaging explicitly with environmental degradation, yet does not necessarily find ways to manage emotions associated with climate change, such as fear, anxiety, and grief (Doherty and Clayton 2011; Gifford and Chen 2017). These feelings can often be barriers to both teaching and learning (Cunsolo and Ellis 2018). Interestingly, there are growing calls for education to better address the difficulty of teaching for a more hopeful approach to climate change (UNESCO n.d.). For example, Italy, Finland, Scotland, and other countries are mandating interdisciplinary approaches to climate change education in K–12 settings with a particular focus on wellness so that teachers and students feel they can bring about change (United Nations 2021). However, moving from the current condition (where climate change education is often and possibly inadvertently connected with fear and anxiety) to the changes being proposed (where teachers and learners can see themselves as agents of change and mobilize their emotions to action) requires much work.

Two recent surveys about Canadian curricula and educators (Field et al. 2019; Wynes and Nicholas 2019) indicate that while most teachers are willing to teach about climate change and consider it integral, they encounter several constraints. For example, these same surveys found that only one-third of responding educators teach about climate change explicitly. When teachers are engaging in climate change education and content, it is limited to one to ten hours per academic year and occurs in science-related courses. Moreover, this content is taught with an almost exclusive focus on human-driven warming (Wynes and Nicholas 2019), which might add to feelings of grief and anxiety, leading to eco-paralysis and limiting feelings of making meaningful change. Aside from time constraints and potential curricular restrictions, other reasons that prevent climate change education include: lack of professional development and resources for teaching, particularly beyond the sciences (Field et al. 2019; Wynes and Nicholas 2019); persistent, strongly held beliefs among teachers and other educators that difficult knowledge about issues such as climate change is inappropriate for students before grade four (Sobel 2018); and teachers' own emotions and anxieties related to climate change (Hufnagel 2015). While past research provides a clear illustration of what challenges teachers are currently encountering, it does not clearly identify what is needed by teachers to overcome these barriers. In response, our needs assessment was designed for teachers to articulate their needs based on their experiential knowledge of the problem as it occurs in their teaching and learning contexts.

As educators and researchers, we discussed how the scope of our existing individual work might collectively address limitations in current climate change education research. We attempted to address these limitations by examining how we might combine and rework our collective research into a coherent process for supporting teaching and learning about/within the context of climate change. However, we also knew that to achieve this ambitious objective of supporting educators and designing research to address the messiness and complexity of teaching and learning, we would require even more diverse perspectives. Inspired by other feminist research collaborations like Max Liboiron et al. (2017) and Jasmine Linabary et al. (2021), we recruited people inside and outside of our personal research, teaching, and community networks, resulting in a team of six researchers (Dawn, Catherine, Rebeca, Terra, Emma, and Mitchell) who brought with them hope, humility, a sense of accountability, and a multiplicity of perspectives on feminist approaches to teaching, learning, and researching within the climate crisis.

## RESEARCHING HOPE

Given our interdisciplinary research team, it is important to note that not all team members subscribe to the same feminist theorizing. What has been important in our research activities (and keeping feminist practices in mind) is our prerogative to not separate data from lived experiences, nor to use theory (feminist or otherwise) to abstract or objectify the lives of research participants (Smith 1987). Having a team with different intellectual interests and diverging life experiences is an ongoing reminder not to overtheorize. By transcribing, counting, and compiling, researchers run the risk of smoothing out the complexities of human existence in favour of oversimplified representations and digestible findings. Following Donna Haraway (1998, 2016), data is representative of experience; it is not the experience itself. Based on our experiences, we argue that there is an urgent need to better understand and address these barriers for the well-being of people and our planet.

As bell hooks (2003) reminds us, teaching for optimism and hope is typically most effective when individuals and communities begin from a place of positivity, focusing on what works. Teaching for optimism was our intention when developing the needs assessment survey. Even though the survey gathered information from educators about teaching and learning for climate change, we are acutely aware that educators in all contexts are finding creative ways to teach for and about climate change. In our meetings, we agreed on the importance of not wanting respondents to enter a space of eco-paralysis where individuals and communities are unable to move from frustrations to collective action and inter-individual accountability. Our orientation toward optimism has allowed us to understand that there are more climate change teaching and learning successes than failures, and even in dire circumstances, it is better to try something that may not work than to give up and ensure failure. As noted above, there is a growing body of educational research addressing climate change; however, much of the research reports on the effectiveness of educational programming (Lavey 2019), educators' engagement with teaching about climate change (Anderson 2012), or students' perceptions of climate change programs (Brownlee et al. 2013). Little work considers the lived experiences of educators. Furthermore, no research that we have encountered asks educators to consider the broad systemic changes required for educational systems to effectively implement climate change education or the impact of the climate crisis on teachers' and learners' psychological ability to engage with the subject matter.

The climate crisis requires new and creative ways of thinking and being and a depth of imagination that breaks down neoliberal, capitalist, Eurocentric, patriarchal, and settler-colonial logics to allow for transformative engagements with research through teaching and learning (Liboiron et al. 2017). For us, the way we engage in research as a hopeful collective is as important as the research itself. Our overlapping and diverging research interests provide us with multiple entry points and embodied understandings that influence how we might individually and collectively engage with the research problematic of better understanding what teachers need to teach for climate awareness within the climate emergency.

## METHODS OF INQUIRY: DEVELOPING THE NEEDS ASSESSMENT

Before we collectively designed the survey, we assembled to determine what exact information we were seeking from educators and what kinds of educators we wanted answers from. At this step in our process, we each read a short essay by feminist data scientists D'Ignazio and Klein (2020) that framed our early meetings and influenced the design of our survey. In their paper, D'Ignazio and Klein (2020) propose seven intersectional feminist research considerations (or principles) for data collection, analysis, and mobilization. Their seven principles are "examine power; challenge power; elevate emotion and embodiment; rethink binaries and hierarchies; embrace pluralism; consider context; [and] make labor visible" (3–4). As implied by these principles, their view of feminism is not exclusively concerned with women and gender. As intersectional feminists they are interested in disrupting power relations and power imbalances for social change in the context of COVID-19. Having a text that we could refer to individually and collectively allowed the team to convey their own interpretations in relation to the needs assessment, which led to additional interconnections across methodologies and analyses.

As a research team working across two languages (English and French), different disciplines, and diverse research paradigms, we did not conform to one methodological approach and intentionally sought to gather quantitative, qualitative, and arts-based data. Specifically, we employed a questionnaire that incorporated quantitative methods and modes of questioning from psychology (Neumann et al. 2010), qualitative methods influenced by institutional ethnography (Smith 1987, 2006), and arts-based participatory methods from education and sociology (Barone and Eisner 2012; Fine and Torre 2021). The needs assessment survey was co-developed and tested by the research team over the course of two months to generate our own insights on the kinds of questions being asked, the potential emotional impact of the questions, the overall flow of the questions, and the timing of the questions (how long on average it would take to respond). This process allowed the team to reflect on redesigning and rewriting questions that privilege and/or "elevate people's emotions and embodiment" (D'Ignazio and Klein 2020, 3) while increasing potential participation.

As the survey grew in length, we also considered how to best maintain respondents' interest when filling it out. We devoted a substantial amount of time to language use and translation. The survey was initially written in English and then translated into French. Because translation is neither neutral nor benign (Battiste and Henderson 2000), for some questions, the literal translation was insufficient to convey meaning and to avoid confusion on the part of the respondents. For instance, in the write-up of the survey, we specified that we were all teaching (and living) in the context of climate change and COVID-19 whether it is explicitly acknowledged or not, and we needed to be sure that survey respondents understood the original emphasis we placed on our current context in both French and English. It was important for us to have this emphasis on the intersection of the climate emergency and the pandemic to underscore how much additional labour educators were taking on during the everchanging COVID health protocols along with working during ice storms, heatwaves, intense rain, wildfires, and other environmental consequences of climate change.

The needs assessment survey itself was not participatory. Survey respondents did not directly help inform the research questions or take part in the analysis. However, as a research team, we relied on participatory and non-hierarchal processes to ensure that our questions emerged from the embodied standpoints of team members working closely with young people and educators to better understand eco-anxiety. For example, since we wanted to gather insights from K–12 educators, the teachers on the research team were adamant that the survey first be made available at the conclusion of the school year in Canada and the United States so as not to overburden educators already stressed by changing protocols for teaching during the pandemic. When the survey sections and questions were finalized, everything was entered into LimeSurvey, an open-source survey software, and housed on a university server that ensured participant confidentiality. The survey was presented to respondents in three sections: demographic data and teaching environment(s); teaching about and in the context of climate change; and wellness and impacts. Rather than simply expanding on each section and subsection below, we describe the collaborative development of the survey and how we collectively implemented D'Ignazio and Klein's (2020) seven research considerations.

## COLLABORATING ON CONTEXT AND ADDRESSING POWER IMBALANCES

As noted, the opening section of the survey focused on respondents' demographic data and general teaching contexts. To carefully consider the multiple social, environmental, and geographical circumstances of respondents (D'Ignazio and Klein 2020), we asked nineteen questions that ranged from language (and language of instruction), gender, racial identity/background, geographical location, teaching context, subjects taught, and curricular supports. In developing these important contextual questions, we made some very specific decisions that sought to address power imbalances. For instance, instead of asking respondents to identify sex and gender explicitly, we asked them to identify their preferred pronouns (or at least the pronouns by which they would like to be referred to within the research context). In attempts to "embrace pluralism," "rethink binaries and hierarchies" (D'Ignazio and Klein 2020, 3), and challenge the built-in linear structural assumptions of LimeSurvey software, we made deliberate efforts to problematize technological assumptions. Therefore, in the preferred pronouns section, we chose to begin with non-binary options and in nearly all questions, and we provided options for participants who preferred not to answer or to provide their own wording. This obviously added time to the overall experience, but we deemed it an important consideration that aligned with our ethos.

The overall research objective in this section was to better understand the interplay between who teachers are as educators (what subjects they taught, where they work, and what barriers they encounter teaching about climate change, in the context of climate change, and at the height of COVID-19) and their educational contexts. The closing question of this section was qualitative in nature and provided respondents with an opportunity to express themselves beyond the boundaries of check boxes and close-ended Likert scale questions. One point we kept in mind throughout the opening section of the survey pertained to how climate change is often taken up primarily within science curricula. This is perhaps because many educators situate climate change within ecological/biological processes that are collectively and discursively understood as climate change science. With science occupying a privileged position in relation to other subjects across the curricula, we felt compelled to examine and challenge that privilege and the power associated with it (D'Ignazio and Klein 2020). To challenge science's implied hierarchies, and the presumed superiority of positivist research traditions (which was one of the core impetuses for early feminist research), we listed subjects alphabetically:

What subject area(s) do you teach? (Check as many as apply)

a. Creative arts (art, drama, dance, music)
b. Ethics and personal development
c. Language arts
d. Mathematics
e. Physical education
f. Science (science; science and technology; environmental science, chemistry, physics, biology etc.)
g. Social studies (geography, history, citizenship)
h. Other (please specify)

As a team, we discussed how a seemingly small detail calls attention to the myriad of ways educators are teaching about climate change across the curriculum. Since many team members are educators who teach about climate change in non-science courses, we wanted to acknowledge these efforts and be inclusive to subjects that are perhaps not considered as having a role in teaching about climate change, despite growing calls for them to do so (Ghosh 2016).

## MAKING LABOUR VISIBLE AND ELEVATING EMBODIMENT

In the second section of the survey, we asked teachers to think about when, where, and how they teach for and about climate change as well as the structures and resources that enable or constrain them. This section was more qualitative insofar as there were many exploratory and open-ended questions, and we provided space for participants to respond creatively and/or artistically to certain prompts. In developing this section, we were attempting to "make labor visible" and "value multiple forms of knowledge, including the knowledge that comes from people as living, feeling bodies in the world" (D'Ignazio and Klein 2020, 3–4). As such, beyond the prescribed options provided to respondents, there was space within this section for participants to write about their dreams for teaching about climate change. We purposefully recognized the connection between dreaming and emotions, and how feelings are sometimes challenging to express in words and are perhaps unquantifiable. To elevate emotion and embodiment and to elicit different kinds of responses from educators, we encouraged participants to respond to the prompts in whatever manner worked for them—through poetry, photos, drawings, spoken word, etc.—and we provided the means for them to upload files as well.

First, we asked the educators to describe how they approached teaching for climate change—for example, through specific teaching resources or introductions to social movements (like #FridaysforFuture)—and their reasons for adopting these approaches. We also wanted to know if educators were teaching climate change content themselves, or if they invited guest speakers, or both. Next, we inquired about where teachers would ideally like to be with their teaching about climate change, asking them to think outside of the scope of curricular, financial, structural, and time constraints. Finally, we asked teachers what they required to move from where they were currently to where they would like to be. Implicitly and explicitly, we focused on the concepts of time and labour. Not only did we want to underscore the immense time, effort, and intent it takes for educators to teach within and outside of the curricula-as-prescribed, but we also aimed to ask these kinds of questions from a place of hope/optimism. While the intention in this section (and the survey more broadly) was to better understand teachers' needs when teaching for/about climate change, we also co-crafted questions to identify what would make teaching for climate change more satisfying. These questions emerged from our own embodied observations and experiential knowledge as educators and related to issues that had been raised most frequently in research team discussions, including time, organizational support, resources, and curricula and professional development.

## ELEVATING EMOTIONS

The third section of the survey focused on "elevating emotions" (D'Ignazio and Klein 2020, 3) related to teaching and learning about climate change and asked questions about how eco-anxiety influences (or not) the ways that educators teach and go about their daily lives. Because eco-anxiety is a contested term (Kurth and Pihkala 2022) that is ever-present in media accounts and popular culture (and making its way into education discourse), we asked teachers if they had heard of the concept and to define their understanding of it in their own words. We also asked educators to describe how often they had experienced eco-anxiety to give us an idea of its overall frequency and impacts. Based on our meetings and conversations where we discussed our own emotional reactions to climate change, we asked participants to think about their affective responses to climate change—feeling over-whelmed, feeling powerlessness to meaningfully respond to the climate crisis, or feeling that they lack the competency to teach about climate change and within the context of climate change—and the ways that they deal with these eco-anxieties. As some of these questions may produce discomfort, at the conclusion of the survey, we provided a list of resources where educators could find psychological support.

## TEAM DATA ANALYSIS

Despite the survey being active for over six months with concentrated recruitment efforts aimed at increasing participation, only nine people completed the survey in its entirety. In some ways, the final number of respondents was disappointing, given the careful planning, collaboration, excitement, and effort that went into the survey's creation, development, translation, and dissemination. However, the respondents that did complete the survey were generous with their responses and provided us with a lot of data to analyze. Since Terra was the team member responsible for entering the questions into LimeSurvey, she was most familiar with the software, and as such, also closest to the data. In our first data analysis meeting, Terra led the discussion where she outlined her initial impressions from each section of the survey, highlighting key points, commonalities, and other noteworthy findings. The dataset was first discussed and analyzed in larger team meetings, and then smaller teams analyzed specific sections more deeply. For example, Catherine, Terra, and Emma looked closely at section three of the survey (wellness and impacts), while Dawn, Rebeca, and Mitchell explored section two (teaching about and in the context of climate change). Furthermore, individual researchers had their own data analysis processes and then shared those processes and findings with the larger team during weekly meetings. For example, in one team meeting, we devoted ninety minutes to discussing one participant's response to one question. Through these collective processes, we analyzed the data multiple times at different levels and through various lenses.

As we analyzed the data individually, collectively, in sections, in subsections, and as an entire dataset, we reminded ourselves and each other that data are merely representative. Data are two-dimensional placeholders for complex and complicated human experiences and not a replacement for that experience. As we made sense of the data together, we raised our thoughts in meetings with the rest of the team to deepen our reflections and gain insight from each other's unique perspectives. Through this process, each team member had the opportunity to point out what was salient to them from the data and how they wanted to work with it. Some team members wanted to dwell with the data to digest what respondents had stated, while others were interested in moving onto another stage of data collection. In supporting each other in our different research interests and directions, we learned to find hope in our processes and in other educators working to raise awareness and make a difference within their own sphere of influence.

## SURVEYING TENSIONS

In this section, we reflect on the ways in which team members reacted to moments that were theoretically and methodologically challenging and how these tensions manifested while developing the survey and analyzing its data. By responding to these questions individually and as part of a larger team, we aim to offer hopeful directions to other researchers and research teams looking to work across disciplines and learn from each other.

**Catherine:** The most challenging aspect of this research for me is the impression that I get from time to time that I come from a different planet than Dawn, Rebeca, and Mitch. I sometimes get the feeling of being an alien setting foot on Earth for the first time, trying to decipher a new language or a new way of either conceiving research or designing it. I come from a very quantitative background and have experience in implementing randomized controlled trials, so qualitative research is new to me. Certain terms pertaining to qualitative and participatory research are also new and I realize that we sometimes use different terms in psychology to express the same idea. Taken together, I don't think it has complicated the survey development, as I'm comfortable enough to express openly when I feel out of my depth. At the end of the day, I feel like I got insight into educational research, which I wouldn't have had I done this research solely with psychologists.

**Dawn:** In my dissertation (Wiseman 2018), I wrote at length about my tensions with theory and methodology. While I understand the need to limit and frame research so that it is manageable, I am more interested in active, transformational research that brings about change than intellectual frameworks primarily rooted in the thinking of Western traditions largely laid out by men. While raging against the machine can bring about transformation, sometimes it can get in the way of getting things done because I think, "Who am I to limit someone else's lived experience by the questions I ask?" In many ways, this is exactly why I am interested in bringing together the various methodologies team members bring to the table. They offer the possibility of seeing multiple perspectives on the same problem. On the other hand, with respect to the survey, we perhaps went too far—too many questions, too many possibilities. It was daunting for participants. Perhaps it would be better as more than one survey. At the same time, the survey development was a playful learning experience. The time we took to listen to what we were each interested in and how we would go about searching for answers, was like some of my best graduate courses—generative, joyful, and surprising.

Terra: I entered this research team as an undergraduate student, and I never would have thought that research could bring me to such introspection about my values and beliefs. We took the time to discuss our perceptions of the project. I had a voice and was listened to while being exposed to a variety of perspectives to learn from. This experience, although enriching, was also confronting, because things were not familiar nor similar to my past research/project experiences. I had to let go of the need to get to the next step as quickly as possible and embrace the journey. In the end, this method of creating a project brought much more meaning to the research itself and its impacts.

**Emma:** Like Terra, I entered this research team as an undergraduate student. Coming from a psychology background, I was challenged by some of the terms used or discussions we had pertaining to the educational system and methods of research. As part of this research team, I was exposed to many different perspectives to learn from which allowed me to develop better critical thinking skills while broadening my own perspectives. This journey, while challenging, is also very enriching and generative for me as I always learn new things from this process.

**Rebeca:** Because of the interdisciplinarity of the research team, we brought together the underlying frameworks and the unconscious biases that underpin our different fields of research. These frameworks were sometimes expressed overtly, and sometimes were "baked into" individual researchers' contributions to the research process. This manifested in the process of development for the survey. We divided the survey development into sections that addressed questions around pedagogy and questions around the emotional experience of learners. This process was complimented by team members consequently reviewing and commenting on the sections of the survey they did not develop, resulting in an overall collaborative process.

**Mitchell:** For something so inevitable in everyday life, tension often infers a negative connotation or conflict. Like self-proclaimed "Bad Feminist" Roxane Gay (2014), I'm a mass of contradictions, and as such often feel conflicted. However, to the extent that's possible, I try to understand my internal conflicts to better understand who I am. I contend that tensions between and amongst theories, methodologies, and even people (friends, family members, research teams, and so on) can provide an opening for a deep understanding and a closeness that wouldn't have been possible without the tension. Perhaps the survey reflected a tension. Perhaps not. I think it's likely that the length of the survey reflected how long it took us to discuss and create it. Importantly, the time we took allowed everyone's ideas and lived experiences to be considered and appreciated.

Despite the disciplinary and methodological tensions that we describe above, we learned to work together and with data in slow and meaningful ways. As a result, on occasion, tensions that emerged in our work remained (and remain) unresolved. This is perhaps because our research itself is unresolved and ongoing. Some of us learned to ask more direct questions and appreciate patterns made evident in quantitative research, while others learned to consider the power of story and the ways that ongoing colonial practices inform the wider context of the questions we explored. What emerged collectively is a focus on values as opposed to objectivity in research, the importance of embodying ourselves as whole people in our inquiry processes, and how such engagement allows for imagining hopeful futures in the face of multiple crises. While at times, *dwelling with* data and working in dialogue (instead of acting, reacting, or quickly moving to the next phase of the research) feels daunting, it has in fact allowed us to develop a more coherent and deliberate process where both research and practice inform each other.

## REFLECTING, REVISITING, REFRAMING

Because our research project aligned with the beginning of the pandemic, it has not advanced quite as much or in the exact manner that we imagined. This presented several challenges. However, the time we were forced to take was remarkably generative. At key moments in our research activities, we were forced to slow down and rethink research. In doing so, we relied on feminist principles and epistemologies to work with one another in collaborative and participatory ways. We benefitted from deep conversations about what we wanted collectively for and from the research. We learned about the experience and expertise of all team members and found ways for them to contribute to and be sustained by what we did. We talked at length about the challenges of bringing different disciplinary foci and research paradigms together and D'Ignazio and Klein's (2020) intersectional feminist principles provided a discursive model to interconnect disciplines. Importantly, these discussions gave us hope. As a collaborative research team "our capacity to generate excitement is deeply affected by our interest in one another, in hearing one another's voices, in recognizing one another's presence" (hooks 1993, 8).

Writing this chapter provided us with an opportunity to pause and reflect on what we have learned from our research activities and on where we might go next with our inquiry. Because we relied on our experience and the experiences of others to inform our study, our work is deeply personal and political. By starting with the personal and linking to the political, we invoke feminist scholarship to show other educators and researchers "what they are up against (politically) and where they might want to apply pressure" (DeVault 2006, 295). As we move forward with a better understanding of ourselves, each other, our research processes, the tensions and challenges in which we collectively engage, and teachers' needs for facing that engagement in their own practices for and about climate change, we gained deeper insight into the work we are attempting to do.

## AUTHORS' NOTE

This research was supported by Employment and Social Development Canada and a Bishop's University Senate Research Committee Interdisciplinary Team Grant.

# REFERENCES

Albrecht, Glenn. 2011. "Chronic Environmental Change: Emerging 'Psychoterratic' Syndromes." In *Climate Change and Human Well-Being: Global Challenges and Opportunities*, edited by Inka Weissbecker. Springer.

Anderson, Allison. 2012. "Climate Change Education for Mitigation and Adaptation." *Journal of Education for Sustainable Development* 6 (2): 191–206.

Bannerji, Himani. 1995. *Thinking Through: Essays on Feminism, Marxism and Anti-Racism*. Women's Press.

Barone, Tom, and Elliot W. Eisner. 2012. *Arts Based Research*. SAGE.

Battiste, Marie Ann, and James Y. Henderson. 2000. *Protecting Indigenous Knowledge and Heritage: A Global Challenge*. Purich Publishing.

Brownlee, Matthew T.J., Robert B. Powell, and Jeffery C. Hallo. 2013. "A Review of the Foundational Processes That Influence Beliefs in Climate Change: Opportunities for Environmental Education Research." *Environmental Education Research* 19 (1): 1–20.

Crenshaw, Kimberlé. 1989. "Demarginalizing the Intersection of Race and Sex: A Black Feminist Critique of Antidiscrimination Doctrine, Feminist Theory and Antiracist Politics." *University of Chicago Legal Forum* 1 (8): 139–167.

Cunsolo, Ashlee, and Neville R. Ellis. 2018. "Ecological Grief as a Mental Health Response to Climate Change-Related Loss." *Nature Climate Change* 8 (4): 275–281.

DeVault, Marjorie. 2006. "What Is Institutional Ethnography?" In *Institutional Ethnography as Practice*, edited by Dorothy E. Smith. Rowman & Littlefield.

D'Ignazio, Catherine, and Lauren F. Klein. 2020. "Seven Intersectional Feminist Principles for Equitable and Actionable COVID-19 Data." *Big Data & Society* 7 (2): 1–6.

Doherty, Thomas J., and Susan Clayton. 2011. "The Psychological Impacts of Global Climate Change." *American Psychologist* 66 (4): 265–276.

Field, Ellen, Pamela Schwartzberg, and Paul Berger. 2019. "Canada, Climate Change and Education: Opportunities for Public and Formal Education." http://lsf-lst.ca/media/National_Report/National_Climate_Change_Education_FINAL.pdf.

Fine, Michelle, and María Elena Torre. 2021. *Essentials of Critical Participatory Action Research*. American Psychological Association.

Gay, Roxane. 2014. *Bad Feminist: Essays*. Harper Perennial.

Ghosh, Amitav. 2016. *The Great Derangement: Climate Change and the Unthinkable: The Randy L. and Melvin R. Berlin Family Lectures*. University of Chicago Press.

Gifford, Robert D., and Angel K.S. Chen. 2016. "Why Aren't We Taking Action? Psychological Barriers to Climate-Positive Food Choices." *Climatic Change* 140 (2): 165–178.

Gousse-Lessard, Anne-Sophie, and Félix Lebrun-Paré. 2022. "Regards Croisés Sur Le Phénomène 'D'écoanxiété': Perspectives Psychologique, Sociale et Éducationnelle." *Éducation Relative à l'Environnement: Regards–Recherches–Réflexions* 17 (1): 1–18.

Haraway, Donna. 1988. "Situated Knowledges: The Science Question in Feminism and the Privilege of Partial Perspective." *Feminist Studies* 14 (3): 575–599.

Haraway, Donna. 2016. *Staying with the Trouble: Making Kin in the Chthulucene*. Duke University Press.

hooks, bell. 1994. *Teaching to Transgress: Education as the Practice of Freedom.* Routledge.

hooks, bell. 2003. *Teaching Community: A Pedagogy of Hope.* Routledge.

Hufnagel, Elizabeth. 2015. "Preservice Elementary Teachers' Emotional Connections and Disconnections to Climate Change in a Science Course." *Journal of Research in Science Teaching* 52 (9): 1296–1324.

Kurth, Charlie, and Panu Pihkala. 2022. "Eco-Anxiety: What It Is and Why It Matters." *Frontiers in Psychology* 13: 1–13.

Lavey, Warren G. 2019. "Teaching the Health Impacts of Climate Change in Many American Higher Education Programs." *International Journal of Sustainability in Higher Education* 20 (1): 39–56.

Liboiron, Max, Justine Ammendolia, Katharine Winsor et al. 2017. "Equity in Author Order: A Feminist Laboratory's Approach." *Catalyst: Feminism, Theory, Technoscience* 3 (2): 1–17.

Linabary, Jasmine R., Danielle J. Corple, and Cheryl Cooky. 2021. "Of Wine and Whiteboards: Enacting Feminist Reflexivity in Collaborative Research." *Qualitative Research* 21 (5): 719–735.

Mies, Maria, and Vandana Shiva. 2014. *Ecofeminism.* Zed Books.

Neumann, Anna, Pol A.C. van Lier, Kim L. Gratz, and Hans M. Koot. 2010. "Multidimensional Assessment of Emotion Regulation Difficulties in Adolescents Using the Difficulties in Emotion Regulation Scale." *Assessment* 17 (1): 138–149.

Pihkala, Panu. 2022. "The Process of Eco-Anxiety and Ecological Grief: A Narrative Review and a New Proposal." *Sustainability* 14 (24): 1–53.

Sleezer, Catherine, Darlene F. Russ-Eft, and Kavita Gupta. 2014. *A Practical Guide to Needs Assessment, 3rd Edition.* Wiley.

Smith, Dorothy E. 1987. *The Everyday World as Problematic: A Feminist Sociology.* Northeastern University Press.

Smith, Dorothy E. 2005. *Institutional Ethnography: A Sociology for People.* AltaMira Press.

Sobel, David. 2019. *Beyond Ecophobia: Reclaiming the Heart in Nature Education.* Orion Magazine.

UNESCO. "Only Half of the National Curricula in the World Have a Reference to Climate Change, UNESCO Warns." https://www.unesco.org/en/articles/only-half-national-curricula-world-have-reference-climate-change-unesco-warns.

United Nations. 2021. "Education Is Key to Addressing Climate Change." https://www.un.org/en/climatechange/climate-solutions/education-key-addressing-climate-change.

Wiseman, Dawn. 2018. "Finding a Place at Home: The TRC as a Means of (R)Evolution in Pre-Service (Science) Teacher Education." *McGill Journal of Education* 53 (2): 331–349.

Wynes, Seth, and Kimberly A. Nicholas. 2019. "Climate Science Curricula in Canadian Secondary Schools Focus on Human Warming, Not Scientific Consensus, Impacts or Solutions." *PLOS ONE* 14 (7): 1–21.

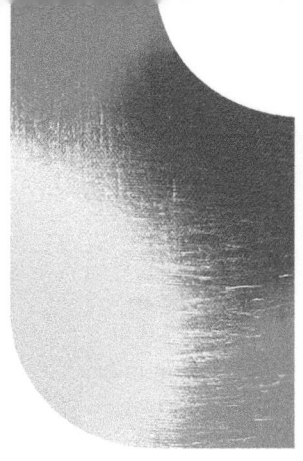

CLAUDIA MITCHELL,
REBEKAH HUTTEN, AND
KAYLAN C. SCHWARZ

# FEMINIST ENDINGS

Designing a Seat around the Table

COMING TO THE LAST CHAPTER of what, for us, has felt like such a beautiful journey of co-inquiry and collaboration about participatory data analysis feels like anything but an ending. Our ongoing engagement with the chapter contributors, their ongoing engagement with study participants, and our own engagement with each other as co-editors have opened a seat around the table for all of us. Charlotte L. Clarke et al.'s (2018) titular use of "a seat around the table" to describe participatory data analysis and the "multiple voicing" it seeks to engender is a particularly apt image to encapsulate our thinking about collaborative methods in feminist research (1421). We are also reminded of Judy Chicago's (2007) iconic art installation, *The Dinner Party* (1974-1979), made up of thirty-nine place settings at a massive triangular table, evoking a dialogue between historically significant women. Chicago's (2007) demand for each of them to have a "seat around the table" remains a powerful metaphor to guide participatory data analysis, as are contemporary critiques of the project, which invite feminist scholars to consider whose voices and contributions were excluded from *The Dinner Party* (namely, women of colour) and "what it might mean to fill in those voids" (Ceisel 2024, 153).

Our collection maps a broad spectrum of ways to approach the intersection between participatory data analysis and feminist research. Some chapters demonstrate how researchers involve participants in participatory data analysis processes, including "informal and formal, unstructured and structured, trained and untrained, explicit and implicit approaches" (Nind 2011, 349). Other chapters demonstrate how collaborative research teams work with data, including how "divisions of labour vary across research teams depending on the nature of the research, size of the project, structure and organization of the team, and researchers involved" (Mauthner and Doucet 2008, 974). Taken together, the chapters are meant to deepen and expand readers' thinking about the co-production of knowledge.

The chapters represent a wide range of research contexts, showing the fluid boundaries of what constitutes participatory data analysis and, at the same time, the tensions and negotiations that may arise. Our collection is meant to encompass the myriad ways that participants can engage with the data they have generated, whether visual productions, interview transcripts, or survey data, but also the ways that research teams can engage ethically and meaningfully in collaborative analysis. Bringing these two angles together, we posit, signals an ongoing feminist project of collectivity in socially engaged research.

In the end, we have endeavoured to introduce participatory data analysis as falling along what Nicole Brown (2022) refers to as a "continuum between fully egalitarian work with participants as co-researchers and the limited involvement of participants as supporters or advisors" (202). We have also emphasized that feminist research is a spectrum, acknowledging that its contours and configurations "are generally a source of contention, given the existence of multiple and varied feminisms" (Linabary and Hamel 2017, 98). We embraced this breadth of meaning from the outset and encouraged authors to be explicit and specific about their engagements with both research traditions, opening up rather than closing down the possibilities for others to work within them.

## BRINGING THE COLLECTION TOGETHER

In the introductory chapter, we endeavoured to review a wealth of participatory and feminist research, such that the development of the reference list is itself a meaningful scholarly exercise and contribution. While we attempted to cite emerging and established scholars writing from a variety of social locations, like Carrie Mott and Daniel Cockayne (2017) we recognize that "our citational milieu is also a reflection of our respective positionalities as white academics trained in Anglo-[Canadian] educational and geographical contexts" (957). We also sought to be in touch with feminist histories so that we acknowledge the roots of current feminist research practices—what Claudia refers to elsewhere as feminist "charting" (Mitchell 2016).

While we circulated the call for papers through broader academic networks, many of those who responded were Claudia's current or former graduate students and postdoctoral fellows working in connection with the Participatory Cultures Lab at McGill University (Nesa Bandarchian Rashti, Mitchell McLarnon, Milka Nyariro, Grace Skahan, and Catherine Vanner), as well as established scholars such as Sarah Flicker and Angelina Weenie who are closely attached to the Participatory Cultures Lab. In hindsight, this is unsurprising because the Participatory Cultures Lab (2020) is topically "organized around the study and use of visual and other participatory approaches to research and social action," but also because it is pedagogically organized around community building, mentorship, and a feminist ethic of care. Two of the chapters (Bandarchian Rashti and Nyariro) are presented within a girlhood studies framework, something that is further supported by the network of girlhood scholars working with the Participatory Cultures Lab, its flagship journal *Girlhood Studies: An Interdisciplinary Journal* (Mitchell and Smith 2024), and the book series

*Transnational Girlhoods.* While many of the chapter contributors share this training and connection, "they each write as feminists from specific genealogies, embodied contexts and experiences" (Dupuis et al. 2022, 3), and their chapters demonstrate breadth in terms of research topics, study contexts, and methodologies.

While we position this collection at the intersection of participatory data analysis and feminist research, we observe another strong overlap between participatory data analysis and *visual* research (see also Ellingson and Sotirin 2020; Seppälä et al. 2021). Given the power of feminist visual culture and its place in participatory research (Carson and Pajaczkowska 2001; Mitchell 2015), it is not surprising that so many of the chapters draw on photovoice or related arts-based methods such as clay-elicitation. Indeed, the richness of visual methods is not just at the level of production, but in how these approaches invite opportunities for participatory data analysis at the post-production stage.

Participatory data analysis also lends itself to large teams of researchers, something we saw in the final three chapters of the book, with two teams made up of six members (McLarnon et al. this volume; Vanner et al. this volume) and one international team comprising more than two dozen members (Flicker et al. this volume). This is an important point in support of the ways in which social science labs, centres, institutes, and other academic structures can facilitate collaborative co-inquiry and a recognition of the type of training and feminist mentorship that can occur in such configurations (see also Bang-Jensen et al. 2023; Caretta and Faria 2020; Liboiron et al. 2017).

Finally, chapter contributors' openness to interrogating unforeseen challenges and limitations underscores the egalitarian goals of participatory data analysis, starting with the basic tenet that not everyone wants to or is in the position to participate. For example, Grace Skahan (this volume) and Milka Nyariro (this volume) speak to the predicament of participant attrition between the data collection and data analysis phases due to scheduling conflicts or transient circumstances (see also Vaccaro 2023), while Geetanjali Gill (this volume) speaks to the tensions she encountered while navigating the different paradigms and priorities held by academic researchers and NGO partners. Chapter contributors' vulnerability in exploring these dilemmas reveals their reflexive adaptability to participants' shifting capacities—a feminist praxis rooted in non-exploitative, non-extractive values.

## REFLECTIONS ON FEMINIST EDITING PRACTICES

Following the collaborative writing practices of Margot Ely et al. (1991) and others, we would be remiss as feminist scholars if we did not comment on the process of putting this book together. We view edited collections as a form of feminist production that goes beyond publishing the "text itself" to generate social and intellectual communities based on a labour of care. Kate Eichhorn and Heather Milne (2016), for instance, explain that "editorial labour creates proximities across space and time, including relationships across generations. It is frequently the catalyst for establishing new social networks, new communities, and sometimes simply what makes existing social networks and communities visible to people working beyond their borders" (193). In some fields, researchers are discouraged from publishing in edited collections and encouraged to instead publish their work as monographs or single-authored articles in high-impact journals noted for their high rejection rates (Webb 2023). However, edited collections offer avenues for different kinds of knowledge production and can generate capacious spaces for diverse perspectives and methodologies. Furthermore, assembling coherently related but uniquely different chapters in one place "may also enhance the likelihood of [the] work being read" since edited collections "can be more creative and diverse in their ideas, approaches, and coverage" (Leal 2013, 381).

We also see edited collections as a feminist praxis wherein the editors show care and offer labour to support other scholars' work in ways that are often more detailed than a blind peer review process. It is an opportunity to provide "critical academic friendship," a practice that "aligns with feminist care ethics and slow, meaningful work in academia" (Sotiropoulou and Cranston 2023, 1106; see also Ackerly et al.

2021). Commitments to offering time and care are crucial "for building those relationships of trust, respect, and conviviality so essential for rigorous research" and for resisting "mounting neoliberal competitive pressures" within the academy (Caretta and Faria 2020, 173; see also Mountz et al. 2015).

Editors of collections practice collaboration with one another and with chapter contributors in various ways. For example, in one of Claudia's previous edited collections (Pithouse et al. 2009), contributors commented on each other's chapters, reflected on the process of completing these reviews, and considered how doing so may lead to social action. In our case, we recognized that having three editors meant that we could offer three perspectives on each chapter. We took turns adding comments to draft chapters, we responded to one another within these comments, and we left these comments in so that chapter contributors could see our dialogue. However, we tried to ensure that none of our feedback was directly contradictory, which would put authors in the uncertain position of deciding whose advice to follow or reject. For us, our divergent academic backgrounds, editing approaches, and positions within the academy have led not to conflict but to a generative space of collaboration and cross-generational friendship.

Because we were building on and responding to each other's comments, in our first round of reviews we produced a significant amount of feedback for each chapter, both in terms of content suggestions and line edits. Reflecting on her tenure as editor of the *Journal of Children and Media*, and the feminist editing principles she adopted, Dafna Lemish (2021) similarly notes that "drafting very detailed and respectful constructive reviewer letters that are educative, thoughtful, conscientious, and ethical was a beacon of the editorial process" (22). However, in a few cases, chapter contributors were startled by the sheer volume of feedback we offered, and our suggestions were sometimes read as heavy-handed. Through this process, we realized that what we regarded as our "generous" editing approach, though informed by a practice of feminist care, did not always feel like care. In these instances, we appreciated that chapter contributors felt they could push back at us—to incorporate the suggestions they felt would improve their arguments and to disregard the suggestions they felt detracted from the point or created unnecessary revision labour. Despite our intentions, we acknowledge that we did not always get this right and regard our own learning as feminist praxis.

It was important for us as collaborators to share authorship across this text in a way that signals "collective responsibility and shared ownership" (Houston et al. 2010, 67). We have purposely rotated our three names across the book cover, introduction chapter, and conclusion chapter. This, too, is meant to be a feminist practice, in part to highlight joint efforts, investments, and insights. Like Max Liboiron et al. (2017), we adopt "a situated and context dependent process that assumes decisions about author order will be different for every paper" (5). Though the author order varies, we have each contributed meaningfully to the book and have taken turns writing, rewriting, editing, and re-editing.

## EMERGING ISSUES, PRODUCTIVE TENSIONS, AND FUTURE DIRECTIONS

As much as feminist research is about learning, it is also about unlearning. In Karijn van den Berg et al.'s (2022) conclusion to an edited collection exploring feminist methodologies, the authors reflect that "a practice of unlearning, of not knowing, requires the sort of openness that is central to a feminist ethics and practice of care," and by extension, their book "may leave the reader with new openings and questions rather than necessarily new empirical knowledge" (286). Similarly, we see this collection as a "work in progress"—our methodological reflections are ongoing and iterative. And so, in this final section, we ask how our contribution to feminist, participatory, and collaborative data analysis processes could be expanded.

Immediately evident across the text are the creative, material, and sensory approaches to engaging participants in data analysis. Some chapter contributors included images of these processes to give the reader a sense of the interactive, tactile, and embodied aspects of this work—showing participants moving around the room, working with sticky notes and posterboards, and getting "up close" to the printouts of transcripts or photographs (see also Peterson 2022). While we might take these practices simply as representations of participation, they also evoke what Gill W. Miller (2021) refers to as "somatic praxis" in feminist research. Claudia recalls that in a participatory data analysis activity with environmental studies and agriculture practitioners from Ethiopia, Botswana, and Kenya (see Starr and Mitchell 2018), participants enacted Carl Bagley and Mary Beth Cancienne's (2002) notion of "dancing the data," as they physically interacted with and literally crawled across large printouts of the photographs they had produced.

Many of the chapter contributors are visual scholars, and almost all are working as social scientists. While particular methodological approaches tend to circulate in some disciplines more than others, often passed down from supervisors and adopted by students, examples of participatory data analysis are emerging in diverse fields, spanning ethnomusicology (Cambria et al. 2016), economics (Palka 2024), medical education (Foreshew and Al-Jawad 2022), archival studies (Moore et al. 2023), and sustainability studies (McRuer and Zethelius 2017), among others.

Although most of the chapters in this collection highlight the experience of facilitating participatory data analysis with youth and adults, a promising avenue for future study comes out of a rights-based framework that advocates for the meaningful and ethical inclusion of young children in socially engaged research. For example, Joshua Schwab-Cartas et al. (2022) consider how young children could participate in, help to categorize, and reflect on cellphilm screenings. Other emerging scholarship within critical disability studies is centred on designing participant-friendly protocols, recognizing that "participatory research that relies upon the traditional grammars and processes of research cannot maximise its participatory nature" (Rix et al. 2022, 151). Charlotte L. Clarke et al.'s (2018) and Bing Y. Li and Rainbow T.H. Ho's (2019) work with people living with dementia and Xuan T. Nguyen et al.'s (2022) work with girls and women with disabilities offer hopeful routes for adapting participatory research tools and practices.

Ethics are paramount to feminist research processes, and these considerations can be particularly heightened with participatory data analysis because, when conducted in focus group settings or through visual mediums, the identities of fellow participants and the content of their datasets may become visible to one another. Here, we must consider the implications of exploring participants' perspectives as both the *producers* and the *audience* of their own data. Furthermore, many feminist scholars address sensitive research topics, as exemplified in Claudia's work with girls and young women in South Africa, wherein participants revisited the experience of screening cellphilms they had created about sexual and reproductive rights (Mitchell et al. 2023). Through the participatory data analysis process, participants discussed who *they* wanted to invite to the screening event. In the end, they decided to show their cellphilms to their parents (all of whom, the girls reported, were so proud of them), but chose not to show their cellphilms to the local priest (for fear of reprisals). This represents another angle on Gillian Rose's (2023) notion of "audiencing" and underscores the importance of engaging reflexively with affective research data (see also Mitchell et al. 2018).

On the theme of "audiencing," we note that, especially when research is positioned as community-engaged or community-based, other stakeholders besides the original research participants might be involved in participatory data analysis. For example, Nadha Hassen and Sarah Flicker (this volume) worked with a community advisory committee who supported the authors with event planning and report writing, while Nyariro (this volume) invited representatives from local organizations to walk through and respond to the exhibition participants had curated. Here, study findings are interconnected with a relational ethic that values meaningful exchange, grounded in "multiple perspectives, adequate representation and ongoing discussions" (Maiter et al. 2008, 321).

As highlighted in the introductory chapter and by Hassen and Flicker (this volume), participatory data analysis and feminist collaboration can be challenging (and frustrating!) to undertake within academic structures that valorize hyper-productivity. We believe participatory research methods matter and should be robustly supported by universities and grant agencies—echoing Will Mason's (2023) argument that "it is ethically imperative that these institutions accommodate and (re)value the investments necessary to carry out such work" (721). As one corrective measure, May Lin (2023) recommends creating recruitment, tenure, and promotion policies that account for elongated study timelines and that acknowledge "relationship development with organizations as significant 'outcomes' of research" (19). Lin's (2023) argument is entirely in line with wider calls for social change in most Canadian institutions, particularly in relation to Equity, Diversity, and Inclusion (EDI) and other widening participation initiatives.

Several chapters draw attention to the *pleasures* of participatory research, a point that Claudia has illustrated in previous writings on feminist collaboration and co-authorship (see Weber and Mitchell 2003). This is something we could have asked contributors to say more about in their chapters, but even without prompting, most included a reference to some aspect of pleasure, despite the very serious nature of their project themes. Some contributors intentionally utilized data collection techniques that participants might find enjoyable—like Gill's (this volume) adoption of "playful" research methods—while others pointed out "the unplanned and spontaneous emergence of fun in the research process and its effects" (Wright et al. 2021, 2). For example, Flicker et al. (this volume) recalled that gathering together and co-developing analytical skills during team-based retreats sparked feelings of pride and joy, while also enhancing their collective understanding of young, queer, and racialized lives during the pandemic. At a time when sites of social connection have become so crucial, we think even more about the relational pleasure of participatory data analysis and the affective significance of collaborative work.

Throughout this collection and in our original call for papers, we have favoured the term participatory data analysis to refer to the various ways of involving participants in the organization, coding, or interpretation of their own datasets. As we sifted through the literature, we noted the use of other terms, including participatory thematic analysis (Liebenberg et al. 2020), participatory visual analysis (Switzer and

Flicker 2021), collaborative qualitative analysis (Flicker and Nixon 2015), collective analytical practices (Nic Giolla Easpaig 2017), and data parties (Franz 2013), to name a few. What all have in common is the recognition that those most affected by the research ought to have a say in how it is analyzed and what happens to it. Ultimately, we advocate for engaging participants, colleagues, and communities in the processes of data analysis as a standard—albeit flexible and context-specific—component of feminist research.

## REFERENCES

Ackerly, Brooke A., Elisabeth J. Friedman, Krishna Menon, and Marysia Zalewski. 2021. "Feminist Editing in an Unfeminist World." *International Feminist Journal of Politics* 23 (2): 189–191.

Bagley, Carl, and Mary Beth Cancienne. 2002. *Dancing the Data.* Peter Lange.

Bang-Jensen, Bree, Bernadette Bresee, Sarah K. Dreier et al. 2023. "The Lab as a Classroom: Advancing Faculty Research through Undergraduate Experiential Education." *PS: Political Science & Politics* 56 (4): 455–462.

Brown, Nicole. 2022. "Scope and Continuum of Participatory Research." *International Journal of Research & Method in Education* 45 (2): 200–211.

Cambria, Vincenzo, Edilberto Fonseca, and Laíze Guazina. 2016. "'With the People': Reflections on Collaboration and Participatory Research Perspectives in Brazilian Ethnomusicology." *The World of Music* 5 (1): 55–80.

Caretta, Martina A., and Caroline V. Faria. 2020. "Time and Care in the 'Lab' and the 'Field': Slow Mentoring and Feminist Research in Geography." *Geographical Review* 110 (1/2): 172–182.

Carson, Fiona, and Claire Pajaczkowska, eds. 2001. *Feminist Visual Culture.* Routledge.

Ceisel, Christina M. 2024. "The Dinner Party: Feminist Transdisciplinary Research and Critical Cultural Food Studies." In *The Routledge International Handbook of Transdisciplinary Feminist Research and Methodological Praxis*, edited by Jasmine B. Ulmer, Christina Hughes, Michelle Salazar Pérez, and Carol A. Taylor. Routledge.

Chicago, Judy. 2007. *The Dinner Party: From Creation to Preservation.* Merrell.

Clarke, Charlotte L., Heather Wilkinson, Julie Watson, Jane Wilcockson, Lindsay Kinnaird, and Toby Williamson. 2018. "A Seat around the Table: Participatory Data Analysis with People Living with Dementia." *Qualitative Health Research* 28 (9): 1421–1433.

Dupuis, Constance, Wendy Harcourt, Jacqueline Gaybor, and Karijn van den Berg. 2022. "Introduction: Feminism as Method–Navigating Theory and Practice." In *Feminist Methodologies: Experiments, Collaborations and Reflections*, edited by Wendy Harcourt, Karijn van den Berg, Constance Dupuis, and Jacqueline Gaybor. Palgrave Macmillan.

Eichhorn, Kate, and Heather Milne. 2016. "Labours of Love and Cutting Remarks: The Affective Economies of Editing." In *Editing as Cultural Practice in Canada*, edited by Dean Irvine and Smaro Kamboureli. Wilfrid Laurier University Press.

Ellingson, Laura L., and Patty Sotirin. 2020. *Making Data in Qualitative Research: Engagements, Ethics, and Entanglements*. Routledge.

Ely, Margot, Margaret Anzul, Teri Friedman, Diane Garner, and Ann McCormack-Steinmetz. 1991. *Doing Qualitative Research: Circles within Circles*. Routledge Falmer.

Flicker, Sarah, and Stephanie A. Nixon. 2015. "The DEPICT Model for Participatory Qualitative Health Promotion Research Analysis Piloted in Canada, Zambia and South Africa." *Health Promotion International* 30 (3): 616–624.

Foreshew, Abi, and Muna Al-Jawad. 2022. "An Intersectional Participatory Action Research Approach to Explore and Address Class Elitism in Medical Education." *Medical Education* 56 (11): 1076–1085.

Franz, Nancy K. 2013. "The Data Party: Involving Stakeholders in Meaningful Data Analysis." *The Journal of Extension* 51 (1): 1–3.

Houston, Serin D., D. James McLean, Jennifer Hyndman, and Arif Jamal. 2010. "Still Methodologically Becoming: Collaboration, Feminist Politics and 'Team Ismaili.'" *Gender, Place & Culture* 17 (1): 61–79.

Leal, David L. 2013. "Chapters, Volumes, Editors! Oh My! Reassessing the Role of Edited Volumes in the Social Sciences." *PS: Political Science & Politics* 46 (2): 380–382.

Lemish, Dafna. 2021. "Feminist Editing of a Mainstream Journal: Reckoning with Process and Content Related Challenges." In *Reflections on Feminist Communication and Media Scholarship: Theory, Method, Impact*, edited by Stine Eckert and Ingrid Bachmann. Routledge.

Li, Bing Y., and Rainbow T.H. Ho. 2019. "Unveiling the Unspeakable: Integrating Video Elicitation Focus Group Interviews and Participatory Video in an Action Research Project on Dementia Care Development." *International Journal of Qualitative Methods* 18: 1–10.

Liboiron, Max, Justine Ammendolia, Katharine Winsor et al. 2017. "Equity in Author Order: A Feminist Laboratory's Approach." *Catalyst: Feminism, Theory, Technoscience* 3 (2): 1–17.

Liebenberg, Linda, Aliya Jamal, and Janice Ikeda. 2020. "Extending Youth Voices in a Participatory Thematic Analysis Approach." *International Journal of Qualitative Methods* 19: 1–13.

Lin, May. 2023. "'Actually Changing Our Way of Being': Transformative Organizing and Implications for Critical Community-Engaged Scholarship." *Social Sciences* 12 (10): 1–24.

Linabary, Jasmine R., and Stephanie A. Hamel. 2017. "Feminist Online Interviewing: Engaging Issues of Power, Resistance and Reflexivity in Practice." *Feminist Review* 115 (1): 97–113.

Maiter, Sarah, Laura Simich, Nora Jacobson, and Julie Wise. 2008. "Reciprocity: An Ethic for Community-Based Participatory Action Research." *Action Research* 6 (3): 305–325.

Mason, Will. 2023. "On Staying: Extended Temporalities, Relationships and Practices in Community Engaged Scholarship." *Qualitative Research* 23 (3): 706–726.

Mauthner, Natasha S., and Andrea Doucet. 2008. "'Knowledge Once Divided Can Be Hard to Put Together Again': An Epistemological Critique of Collaborative and Team-Based Research Practices." *Sociology* 42 (5): 971–985.

McRuer, Jennifer, and Margarita Zethelius. 2017. "The Difference Biocultural 'Place' Makes to Community Efforts towards Sustainable Development: Youth Participatory Action Research in a Marine Protected Area of Colombia." *International Review of Education* 63 (6): 847–870.

Miller, Gill W. 2021. "Feminism and Somatic Praxis." In *Companion to Feminist Studies*, edited by Nancy A. Naples. John Wiley & Sons.

Mitchell, Claudia. 2015. "Girls' Texts, Visual Culture, and Shifting the Boundaries of Knowledge in Social Justice Research: The Politics of Making the Invisible Visible." In *Girls, Texts, Cultures*, edited by Clare Bradford and Mavis Reimer. Wilfrid Laurier University Press.

Mitchell, Claudia. 2016. "Charting Girlhood Studies." In *Girlhood and the Politics of Place*, edited by Claudia Mitchell and Carrie Rentschler. Berghahn Books.

Mitchell, Claudia, Pamela Lamb, and Haleh Raissadat. 2018. "Exploring the Impact of Youth-Produced Images on Family, Community, and Policy." *International Journal of Qualitative Methods* 17: 1–10.

Mitchell, Claudia, and Ann Smith. 2024. "Girlhood Studies: The First 15 Years." In *The Routledge Companion to Girls' Studies*, edited by Sharon R. Mazzarella. Routledge.

Mitchell, Claudia, Ntomboxolo Yamile, Miranda D'Amico, Warren Linds, and Myriam Denov. 2023. "On the Ethics of Getting the Word Out: Rural Girls Reflect on Ownership in Participatory Visual Research in Rural South Africa." *YOUNG* 31 (3): 250–267.

Moore, Niamh, Rachel Thomson, and Ester McGeeney. 2023. "Putting Place Back into the Patriarchy through Rematriating Feminist Research: The WRAP Project, Feminist Webs and Reanimating Data." In *Temporality, Space and Place in Education and Youth Research*, edited by Julie McLeod, Kate O'Connor, Nicole Davis, and Amy McKernan. Routledge.

Mott, Carrie, and Daniel Cockayne. 2017. "Citation Matters: Mobilizing the Politics of Citation toward a Practice of 'Conscientious Engagement.'" *Gender, Place & Culture* 24 (7): 954–973.

Mountz, Alison, Anne Bonds, Becky Mansfield et al. 2015. "For Slow Scholarship: A Feminist Politics of Resistance through Collective Action in the Neoliberal University." *ACME: An International Journal for Critical Geographies* 14 (4): 1235–1259.

Nguyen, Xuan T., Claudia Mitchell, and Tammy Bernasky. 2022. "Qualitative Visual Methods in Research with Girls and Women with Disabilities in the Global South." In *Handbook of Disability: Critical Thought and Social Change in a Globalizing World*, edited by Marcia H. Rioux, Alexis Buettgen, Ezra Zubrow, and José Viera. Springer.

Nic Giolla Easpaig, Bróna. 2017. "Capturing Collective Processes of Analysis in Participatory Research: An Example from a Memory Work Investigation into How Gender and Sexual Identities Are Experienced." *International Journal of Social Research Methodology* 20 (1): 49–61.

Nind, Melanie. 2011. "Participatory Data Analysis: A Step too Far?" *Qualitative Research* 11 (4): 349–363.

Palka, Jessica. 2024. "The Potential of Participatory Social Economics: A Framework and Feminist Perspective." *Forum for Social Economics* 53 (2): 141–169.

Participatory Cultures Lab. 2020. "The PCL." https://participatorycultureslab.com/the-pcl/.

Peterson, Melike. 2022. "Objects in Focus Groups: Materiality and Shaping Multicultural Research Encounters." *Qualitative Research* 22 (1): 24–39.

Pithouse, Kathleen, Claudia Mitchell, and Relebohile Moletsane. 2009. "Going Public with Scholarly Collaboration: Reflections on a Collaborative Self-Study Book Process." In *Making Connections: Self-Study & Social Action,* edited by Kathleen Pithouse, Claudia Mitchell, and Relebohile Moletsane. Peter Lang.

Rix, Jonathan, Helena G. Carrizosa, Kieron Sheehy, Jane Seale, and Simon Hayhoe. 2022. "Taking Risks to Enable Participatory Data Analysis and Dissemination: A Research Note." *Qualitative Research* 22 (1): 143–153.

Rose, Gillian. 2023. *Visual Methodologies: An Introduction to Researching with Visual Materials, 5th Edition.* SAGE.

Schwab-Cartas, Joshua, Prudence Caldairou-Bessette, and Claudia Mitchell. 2022. "Let's Get Cellphilming! Expanding the Use of Participatory Visual Methods with Young Children." In *STEM, Robotics, Mobile Apps in Early Childhood and Primary Education: Technology to Promote Teaching and Learning*, edited by Stamatios Papadakis and Michail Kalogiannakis. Springer.

Seppälä, Tiina, Melanie Sarantou, and Satu Miettinen. 2021. "Introduction: Arts-Based Methods for Decolonising Participatory Research." In *Arts-Based Methods for Decolonising Participatory Research*, edited by Tiina Seppälä, Melanie Sarantou, and Satu Miettinen. Routledge.

Sotiropoulou, Panagiota, and Sophie Cranston. 2023. "Critical Friendship: An Alternative, 'Care-Full' Way to Play the Academic Game." *Gender, Place & Culture* 30 (8): 1104–1125.

Starr, Lisa, and Claudia Mitchell. 2018. "How Can Canada's Feminist International Assistance Policy Support a Feminist Agenda in Africa? Challenges in Addressing Sexual Violence in Four Agricultural Colleges in Ethiopia." *Agenda* 31 (1): 107–118.

Switzer, Sarah, and Sarah Flicker. 2021. "Visualizing DEPICT: A Multistep Model for Participatory Analysis in Photovoice Research for Social Change." *Health Promotion Practice* 22 (2): 50S–65S.

Vaccaro, Mary-Elizabeth. 2023. "Reflections on 'Doing' Participatory Data Analysis with Women Experiencing Long-Term Homelessness." *Action Research* 21 (3): 332–350.

van den Berg, Karijn, Constance Dupuis, Jacqueline Gaybor, and Wendy Harcourt. 2022. "Epilogue: Learning, Unlearning, and Relearning." In *Feminist Methodologies: Experiments, Collaborations and Reflections*, edited by Wendy Harcourt, Karijn van den Berg, Constance Dupuis, and Jacqueline Gaybor. Palgrave Macmillan.

Webb, Patricia. 2023. "A Case for Using Feminist Editorial Practices in Scholarly Journals: An Analysis of Computers and Composition." *Cultural Intertexts* 13: 173–189.

Weber, Sandra, and Claudia Mitchell. 2003. "Collaboration and Co-Authorship: Reflections from the Inside." *Journal of the Canadian Association for Curriculum Studies* 1 (1): 83–91.

Wright, Laura H.V., Kay Tisdall, and Niamh Moore. 2021. "Taking Emotions Seriously: Fun and Pride in Participatory Research." *Emotion, Space and Society* 41: 1–7.

# CONTRIBUTORS

**Nesa Bandarchian Rashti** holds a SSHRC-funded Postdoctoral Fellowship at York University, focusing on the experiences of Afghan refugee girls and young women and their resilience narratives in Canada. She completed her PhD at McGill University, where her passion for working with diverse refugee populations was ignited. Her research interests primarily revolve around girlhood studies and participatory visual methodologies.

**Emma C. Cognet** is completing an individualized, interdisciplinary master's degree at Bishop's University. Her work brings together psychology and program evaluation on community-based quality employment programming for youth. Methodologically, Emma draws on narrative inquiry and storytelling to raise awareness of the ways in which educational policies influence how youth navigate interconnected public-facing institutions.

L. Rebeca Esquivel is a PhD student at Concordia University. She is a climate change educator working with both children and adults. Her work revolves around supporting educators and learners in engaging in meaningful learning experiences by making connections between their own lives and the climate crisis.

Jessica Fields is Professor of Health and Society at the University of Toronto Scarborough and Professor of Sociology in the University of Toronto Department of Sociology. In her ethnographic research, Fields considers school's lessons about gender and sexuality, the discursive power of risk, and emotion as a methodological opportunity to reimagine feeling and understanding.

Sarah Flicker is a full professor in the Faculty of Environmental and Urban Change at York University (Toronto, Canada) where she holds a Research Chair in Community-Based Participatory Research. Her research focuses on health promotion and engages youth and allied actors in environmental, sexual, and reproductive justice scholarship and activism.

Geetanjali Gill is Associate Professor, Chair of the Global Development Studies Program, and Director of the Centre for Justice, Equity, and Sustainable Action at the University of the Fraser Valley. Dr. Gill has a PhD in Development Studies from the University of Sussex, UK, a MSc in Social Policy and Planning in Developing Countries from the London School of Economics and Political Science, UK, and a BA in International Development Studies from the University of Toronto. She uses participatory methodologies to study gender norms and inter-secting inequalities in South Asia and Sub-Saharan Africa. She has also worked as a gender and development practitioner for more than seventeen years.

Jillian Grace Goyeau is a fifth year, self-identified Métis undergraduate student at the University of Windsor studying Sociology. Working with the University of Windsor's Belonging, Inclusion, Diversity, and Equity student-led team, Jillian is happy to be contributing to a celebration of intersectionality from a ground-up approach. As a student, musician, artist, and Windsor community member, Jillian strives to embrace a sociological framework that helps her understand various aspects of her surroundings and society at large.

**Nadha Hassen** is a Postdoctoral Fellow at the Dalla Lana School of Public Health, University of Toronto (Toronto, Canada). Her work explores health equity in different environments, bridges research, policy, and practice, and takes an interdisciplinary, community-engaged approach with a focus on intersectional anti-racism.

**Rebekah Hutten** is a PhD Candidate in Musicology and Women's and Gender Studies in the Schulich School of Music at McGill University, where she researches women's musical labour in rural music scenes. Her work bridges ethnomusicology, visual sociology, feminist philosophy, and participatory research. Rebekah is also Senior Consultant at 21FSP Advisory.

**Terra Léger-Goodes** is a PhD student in clinical psychology at Université du Québec à Montréal. She is particularly interested in the psychological experiences of children in the context of climate change. Through her work, Terra explores connection to nature, philosophy for children, photovoice, and children's literature as tools to address the climate crisis while inviting emotions to the conversation.

**Meegwun Logan** is an Anishinaabe, Potawatomi, and Lenape woman from Walpole Island Unceded Territory in southern Ontario. While completing her BA in International Relations at the University of Windsor, she participated in many protests regarding land rights and MMIWG awareness and travelled to gatherings of the Potawatomi Nation. Being a second-generation university graduate on her mother's side, she was given the confidence to pursue her passions in international relations while also keeping strong ties with her communities. Meegwun aspires to create an international partnership between Canadian/US First

Nations and other Indigenous nations around the world so they may combat issues of equality, poverty, and promote research. She now works as a Research Associate with the City of Toronto.

**Catherine Malboeuf-Hurtubise** is an Associate Professor at Bishop's University and holds a Fonds de recherche du Québec Young Scholar Junior 1 Award. She is a licensed child psychologist and specializes in youth mental health. She is a leading figure in mindfulness and youth research, in art therapy, and in philosophy for children in the province of Québec, Canada. She is a Principal Investigator or co-Principal Investigator on multiple grants that fund projects on children's mental health and well-being in school settings.

**Mitchell McLarnon** is an Assistant Professor in the Department of Education at Concordia University. His research interests include, but are not limited to, institutional ethnography, community-based and participatory research, visual methodologies, land-based/environmental education, community gardening, social and environmental justice, gentrification, food insecurity, and urban political ecology.

**Claudia Mitchell** is a Distinguished James McGill Professor in the Department of Integrated Studies in Education at McGill University and the Director of the Institute for Human Development and Well-being. As the founder of the Participatory Cultures Lab, a Canadian Foundation for Innovation funded unit, she is particularly interested in research and training related to participatory visual methodologies. She is the Editor-in-Chief of the award-winning journal *Girlhood Studies: An Interdisciplinary Journal*.

**Milka Nyariro** holds a PhD in Educational Studies with a major in Gender and Women's Studies from the Department of Integrated Studies in Education at McGill University and a Masters in Anthropology from the University of Nairobi. She completed a McGill Third Century Postdoctoral Research Fellowship in the

Department of Sociology at McGill University. Her research interests span feminist, gender, women's, and sexuality studies; girlhood and Black African girlhood studies; adolescence and youth well-being; teenage pregnancy and young motherhood; and racial, gender violence, and inequality in schools and the African Diaspora. Milka adopts the use of arts-based, participatory, and community-action research approaches.

**Kathryn Kendal Ryan** is a Concurrent Education and History graduate from the University of Windsor. She is particularly drawn to learning about social injustices throughout history as a means of understanding our world today and plans on using her history and education degrees to educate others through a more critical lens. Kendal wishes to continue to utilize her education and experience to explore further research endeavours.

**Kaylan C. Schwarz** is an Assistant Professor in the School of Liberal Education at the University of Lethbridge. Previously, she held a SSHRC Postdoctoral Fellowship in the Department of Integrated Studies in Education at McGill University, working with the Participatory Cultures Lab. She is the Principal Investigator on the SSHRC Insight Development Grant project "Constructing Feminist Identities through Visual and Participatory Methods" and she is the co-editor of *Studies on the Social Construction of Identity and Authenticity*.

**Grace Skahan** is pursuing her PhD in McGill University's Department of Integrated Studies in Education. She holds a Master of Arts in Education from McGill University (2023) and a Bachelor of Arts in Political Science and Women's Studies from Concordia University (2014). Grace is particularly interested in issues related to gender-based violence prevention, masculinities, and participatory and arts-based education and research. She currently works as an instructional designer on topics related to equity, diversity, and inclusion at the Canada School of Public Service.

**Catherine Vanner** is an Assistant Professor of Educational Foundations at the University of Windsor. Her research uses qualitative and participatory methods to study the relationship between gender, violence, education, and activism in diverse contexts. She completed a PhD in Education at the University of Ottawa and an MA in International Affairs at Carleton University. She previously worked as an Education Advisor for Plan International Canada and the Canadian International Development Agency and as a Postdoctoral Fellow at McGill University. She lives with her partner and three children in Windsor, Canada on the Traditional Territory of the Three Fires Confederacy of First Nations including the Odawa, the Ojibwe, and the Potawatomi.

**Angelina Weenie** is a nēhiyaw iskwēw Plains Cree woman from Sweetgrass First Nation which is in Treaty Six Territory. She is the Dean of Indigenous Knowledge, Education, and Applied Research at the University of Prince Edward Island. She holds a PhD in Education from the University of Regina and an MEd, BEd, and BA from the University of Saskatchewan. Her research interests include Indigenous pedagogy, Indigenous research methodologies, cultural knowledge, and language and literacy development. She is a Cree language keeper.

**Dawn Wiseman** is an Associate Professor in the School of Education at Bishop's University in Ktinékétolékouac (Sherbrooke, Québec, Canada). She has engaged in thinking about Science, Technology, Engineering, Arts, and Mathematics (STEAM) with young people and educators for over three decades, most often alongside Indigenous people, peoples, and communities in what is currently Canada. Her research exams how Western and Indigenous ways of knowing, being, and doing might circulate together in STEAM education, student-directed STEAM inquiry, the distinctiveness of Canadian science education research, and the possibilities of teaching and learning within the context of human-driven climate change.

# INDEX